# THE SMALL garden

# THE SMALL
# garden

DAVID SQUIRE

*p*

This is a Parragon Publishing Book
This edition published in 2003

Parragon Publishing
Queen Street House
4 Queen Street
Bath BA1 1HE, UK

Created and produced for Parragon by The Bridgewater Book Company Ltd.

*Creative Director* Stephen Knowlden
*Art Director* Tony Seddon
*Editorial Director* Fiona Biggs
*Senior Editor* Lorraine Turner
*Editor* Richard Rosenfeld
*Editorial Assistant* Tom Kitch
*Photography and Picture Research* Liz Eddison
*Studio Manager* Chris Morris
*Mac artwork* Richard Lloyd
*Designer* Terry Hurst

ISBN: 0–75259–912–7

Printed in China

NOTE
For growing and harvesting, calendar information applies only to the Northern
Hemisphere (US zones 5–9).

# contents

# introduction

Gardening is a lifelong hobby, and you do not need a big space to do it. Even a small garden can be designed and planted in thousands of different ways. Besides the satisfaction of seeing plants grow and flower, there is the added opportunity of creating an oasis of tranquillity and peace that is so necessary in a world of increasing stress.

Many garden features, from arbors to courtyards, are good for creating seclusion and privacy, while some also have a therapeutic quality. Such features include scented plants with their wide range of memorable fragrances, and comforting sounds produced by wind chimes, rustling leaves, and garden birds.

## Inspirational yet practical

This all-color, information-packed book has been created to help novice and experienced gardeners create a beautiful garden in a small area. The aim of the first chapter is to inspire. It makes a visual exploration of the many different styles of gardening that can be featured in a small area, and gives advice on tackling difficult soils, adverse terrain, and severe conditions such as deep shade and intense sunlight.

Chapter 2 is thoroughly practical and leads gardeners through the complexities of a wide, varied spectrum of tasks that range from assessing the acidity or alkalinity of soil to laying paving slabs and constructing a compost pile. Chapter 3 explains how best to use plants in small gardens. This covers borders saturated in a medley of colors, and color-themed beds where flowers of a specific color are grown. These single-color features range from pink and red borders to those with white and silver flowers or foliage. In addition there is advice on creating distinctive displays throughout the year, especially on planning spring, summer, fall, and winter displays. Producing displays in window boxes, hanging baskets, tubs, pots, and sink gardens on a patio or a terrace is also explained, with tips on scented borders, a flower-arranger's garden, and growing roses.

Chapter 4 has information on more than 100 plants, including hardy annuals, herbaceous perennials, shrubs, trees and

▲ *A border can become awash with colorful flowers and attractive leaves. There are plants for all places, sunny and shady.*

> ### HEIGHTS AND SPREADS
>
> The heights and spreads given for shrubs and trees in Chapter 4 relate to 15–20-year-old specimens growing in good conditions. Eventually, these plants may grow even larger.

climbers, including detailed explanations of how best to grow them. In addition, there is information about garden and greenhouse pests and diseases, including their identification and control. The identification and eradication of garden weeds is another key feature. The book ends with a detailed glossary.

With this inspiring and thoroughly practical book at your side, you can enrich a small garden with beautiful plants and attractive garden structures, such as paths, fences, patios, and terraces.

► Achillea *is an ideal herbaceous perennial for growing in a dry, sunny border. Its flowers are ideal for cutting and displaying indoors.*

▼ *Plants with variegated leaves create color all summer long, and evergreens keep their color through the year.*

# design
# inspirations

# soils, contours, shapes, and aspects

Beautiful gardens can be created in all types of soil, and in shade and full sun. Do not be alarmed if your garden has heavy clay soil or well-drained sandy ground, because such extremes are not an insurmountable problem. Solutions range from improving the soil to creating raised beds and growing plants in containers. Even steep slopes can be turned to your advantage using some inspired design tips.

# making the best of your soil

*Soil can be slowly improved by adding well-decayed manure or garden compost, but more instant ways to create a colorful garden are to select plants that survive the conditions in the garden being planted. It is inevitable, however, that gardeners will wish to grow other kinds of plants.*

### Raised beds

Where the ground is continually moist and drainage is difficult, or if the soil is exceptionally chalky or acid, construct a raised bed 12–18in/30–45cm high and fill it with good soil. This enables a wide range of plants to grow. Use cascading plants at the sides to cloak the edges.

### Preparing planting areas

Where the soil is exceptionally dry or of poor quality, small areas can be improved to enable climbers and other plants to be grown. Dig out the soil from an area about 2ft/60cm square and deep, and fill the lower 4in/10cm with rubble. Top up with good topsoil, and firm it. Put in the plant and water the area regularly until it is established. Do not plant climbers less than 1ft/30cm from a wall, because the soil is always fairly dry close to a wall.

### Growing acid-loving plants

Most soils are only slightly acid and can be improved by dusting the surface with hydrated lime or ground limestone each winter (see pages 58–59). It is better to grow acid-loving plants such as callunas and heathers on soils that are strongly acid and formed mainly of peat. There are many varieties of these plants. Some have attractive foliage and others are grown for their flowers. Many varieties flower through cold winter months. Azaleas can be planted in lightly shaded

◀ *When there is a problem with the soil, a raised bed is an ideal solution. It also enables plants to be seen and reached easily.*

areas with slighlty acid soils to create a spectacular spring display.

## Growing chalk-loving plants

It is more difficult to correct chalky soils than acid types. Acidic fertilizers, such as sulfate of ammonia, can be used with additions of peat, but if the underlying soil is alkaline it is better to grow only chalk-loving plants. A raised bed is the best solution for gardeners with acid soil and an irrepressible desire to grow chalk-loving plants.

## Wet and boggy areas

Many soils with a high water level can be drained, enabling a wide range of plants to be grown. However, if the area is naturally wet, difficult to drain, and perhaps close to a stream, it is better to plant moisture-loving plants. They include *Lysichiton americanus* (skunk cabbage) with bright yellow, arum-like flower heads in spring and its near relative *Lysichiton camtschatcensis*, with pure white flowers. Along the sides of streams plant shrubs such as *Cornus stolonifera* 'Flaviramea' and *C. alba* 'Sibirica' for their colored winter stems.

## Hot, dry soils

Gardening successfully on hot, dry soils depends on three factors: mixing in bulky materials such as well-rotted manure and garden compost annually, to aid water retention; regular watering; and adding a mulch each spring. Selecting plants that survive in hot, dry soils is also important (see pages 64–65).

## Pots, tubs, and other containers

Some soils are so inhospitable that plants cannot be grown easily. This problem is best solve by planting a wide range of plants in containers. They range from pots and tubs to window boxes, hanging baskets, troughs, and wall baskets. Buying, planting and looking after plants in containers is more expensive and involves more work than caring for plants in borders and beds. However, it does provide you with the opportunity to change and recreate your garden as often as you wish, which can be a great advantage and very rewarding.

▼ *Cloak the sides of a natural stone wall in plants. They may grow in the wall or be planted at its foot. Planted pots are an alternative.*

▲ *To bring color through the year, plant large pots with dwarf or slow-growing conifers and position them along the edges of a path.*

# gardening on slopes

*Sloping ground offers an opportunity to create an unusual garden, but it will be more expensive to develop than a flat site. A number of paved, terraced areas around a house make an attractive feature when the ground slopes downward from the house.*

▲ *A paved area halfway up a slope creates an exciting yet practical leisure area, especially when it features a pond and a fountain.*

## Terraced gardens

A garden may be terraced in formal or informal style, depending partly on the style of the house. Formal terraces connected by flights of steps usually suit modern houses. Cottages demand an informal style. A slope dotted with fruit trees is an attractive feature.

## Paved areas

When a house stands at the bottom of a facing slope, a flat, paved area can usually be laid at the base of the slope. An alternative is to create a paved area about one-third of the way up the slope to break up the degree of incline. Where possible, position the area so that it is easily visible from the ground floor of the house, so that people do not have to look sharply up to see it.

Where the ground falls away from the house, lay a flat, paved area as near to the house as possible. Meandering paths can be laid to lead downward from it, perhaps criss-crossing the slope to make them appear less steep and easier to use. These paved areas need not be central but off to one side, which particularly suits informal gardens. Where the end of a garden rises, lay a paved area and erect a summerhouse on top. Check that the neighbors will not think it an intrusion on their privacy.

## Retaining walls

These are invariably constructed across slopes to retain banks of soil up to 4ft/1.2m high. Some walls are formal, perhaps built from bricks or blocks, while others are made of natural stone. These are particularly suitable for planting *Aurinia saxatilis* (still better known as *Alyssum saxatile*) and aubretia. By positioning wide paths along the base of informal retaining walls the plants can be admired without being damaged. Formal retaining walls, especially when made of brick, do not need a wide path alongside them. However, if a lawn is positioned close to them, construct a mowing strip at the base to enable a lawn mower to cut as close to the wall as possible.

## Sloping woodland and wild gardens

Old railroad ties are ideal for retaining soil on steep slopes in rustic areas. Secure the ties in position, using strong wooden posts or metal spikes. Beds of heathers and deciduous azaleas create superb displays on slopes. Peat blocks can also be used to restrain soil and to form areas to grow acid-loving plants. Where the peat is likely to become dry and crumbly, use a combination of railroad ties to form the main soil-retention edging, with peat blocks behind them.

## Lawn banks

Traditionally, especially on large country estates, slopes were terraced and grassed, with 45° slopes separating level areas 10–12ft/3–3.6m wide. These dramatic features can easily be replicated on a smaller scale in formal gardens. The key is to keep it all in proportion.

▲ *Flights of steps create visually exciting features in gardens. Insure that they are soundly constructed and have all-weather surfaces.*

◄ *Slopes are ideal places for a series of waterfalls. If these cover a large area, a reservoir tank may be needed at the top.*

# the long and short of gardens

*Few small gardens have a perfect shape. They may be long and narrow, short and wide, or with a tapering outline that makes planning difficult. Fortunately, beautiful gardens can be created on the most improbably shaped piece of land, and there are many excellent ways to disguise a garden's true shape.*

### Shortening gardens

When a plot of land is long and narrow the easiest way to create the impression of a shorter garden is to split it into several smaller units. Either create a long path down the center or one that alternates from one side to the other as it progresses through the garden areas. If a path is constructed down the center of a garden, passing through separate areas, insure that a focal point such as a large urn or a fountain is at the end, and not just a blank fence or wall. Hedges and freestanding trellises play an important role in dividing gardens.

### Broadening gardens

Shortening a garden by bringing the far boundary closer to the house will give the impression of a wider and a shorter garden, but take care not to overdo it; this will only confuse the eye. A free-standing trellis makes an ideal boundary with a central feature such as a sundial or an armillary sphere.

### Narrowing gardens

It is easier to create the impression of narrowness in a large garden than in a small one. Free-standing trellises, pillar roses, narrow conifers, and hedges can be used to section off the central area. Alternatively, position a summerhouse in one corner and perhaps a paved area in the other.

### Informal gardens

An informal area can even be created within the formal outline imposed by a square or rectangular area, by introducing flower beds and lawns with serpentine outlines. An informal pond—made with a flexible liner—can be designed to any shape or size, and integrated into casually shaped borders and lawns. Rustic trellis and arches over paths are useful features because they add height and informality.

▲ *Meandering paths make interesting features in gardens and often enable secluded areas to be created, hidden from immediate view.*

▲ An attractive feature at the end of a short,
square garden makes a focal point, which brings
interest to a small area.

# aspect, light, and shade

*The range of trees, shrubs, herbaceous perennials, annuals, and other garden plants is wide, and there are types for all aspects and intensities of light or shade. Some of these extremes can be lessened by planting or cutting down trees, but it is usually a matter of learning to live with your garden.*

◄ *A shady border can bloom as brightly as a sunny border. Plants with colorful flowers and attractive leaves will grow in all garden areas.*

## The lottery of aspect

A garden's aspect is not usually the first consideration when buying a house. Rather, it is one of the lotteries of gardening. Cold, searing wind is a problem for some plants, while strong, intense sunlight causes difficulties for many. All gardens have possibilities and limitations, and there are plants for even the most inhospitable places. This book explores many ideas that will make growing plants easy. For example, pages 64–65 suggest plants for hot, sunny areas and advise on growing them, and shade-loving plants are on pages 66–67.

## Coastal considerations

Coastal gardens are at risk from several factors. Cold, strong, buffeting winds may deform trees and shrubs, especially in winter, and the salt-laden wind will damage leaves and flowers. It is essential to create windbreaks and hedges to filter the wind and reduce its speed, especially in gardens close to the sea. A range of plants that thrive in coastal areas is given on pages 68–69.

## Winter wonderlands

In some areas, winter weather is so harsh that the likelihood of growing flowers is dramatically reduced. However, several hardy trees flower during winter and they include *Hamamelis mollis* (Chinese witch hazel) and *Cornus mas* (Cornelian cherry). Bear in mind that frost forms attractive patterns on leaves, while a light dusting of snow can be attractive.

In exceptionally cold areas, a layer of snow helps insulate bulbs against low temperatures, but where possible remove snow carefully from the leaves of evergreen shrubs before it weighs them down and disfigures the branches.

▲ *Steps strongly constructed and recessed in a retaining wall are attractive, and give ready access to the border behind.*

▼ *An ornamental pond needs to be positioned in good light and where leaves will not litter the water through the fall.*

# gardening styles

The most exciting part of gardening is deciding which style you want. There is a big choice, from traditional cottage gardens with flowers, fruit trees, rich colors, and scented flowers, to smart formal designs with special bedding schemes for spring and summer, using tulips and all kinds of annuals. You can be as nostalgic or as modern as you want. You can even try Mediterranean gardening with brightly colored pots and drought-tolerant plants, or elegant Japanese gardens with calm stretches of gravel and water.

# English flower gardens

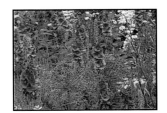

*Few gardening styles are as relaxed and informal as an English country garden. Herbaceous borders are packed with plants that mostly die down to soil level in the fall, and develop fresh shoots and leaves in spring. Mixed borders are a medley of plants, including shrubs and bulbs.*

▲ *The fleshy-rooted border perennial agapanthus creates a mass of large, umbrella-shaped flower heads mainly during mid- and late summer.*

## Herbaceous borders

During the late 1800s the Irish garden writer William Robinson (1838–1935) published *The English Flower Garden*, in which he enthused about herbaceous perennials. He claimed that the English cottage had for many years been a repository for herbaceous plants. His writings came at a time when there was a general hunger for information about plants, and a popularization of gardening books and magazines. However, Gertrude Jekyll (1843–1932) is the best-known advocate of herbaceous plants. Her first book about these plants, *Wood and Garden*, appeared in 1899, followed by others that included ideas about single-color borders. Pages 178–189 explain color-themed borders, including pink and red, blue and mauve, yellow and gold, and white and silver plants.

## Mixed borders

Few small gardens can have more than a corner devoted to a color-themed border, so tend to display a mixture of herbaceous perennials, bulbs, annuals, shrubs, and trees producing a rich array of colors, sizes, and shapes. Such borders create a good opportunity to have all the plants you like.

Hardy and half-hardy annuals are excellent space fillers during the early years of a mixed border. The half-hardy

annuals are planted in gaps in early summer, as soon as all risk of frost has passed, while hardy annuals can be sown earlier. Always sow the seeds of hardy annuals thinly.

Bulbs provide extra color and include lilies that delight in soil shaded and cooled by other plants. Clumps of trumpet-type daffodils are very welcome in early spring and, although they leave a legacy of untidy leaves during early summer, they are rich in color.

## Hardy annual borders

If you have a passion for bright colors which you can change each year, think of planting a border of hardy annuals. A few packets of seeds will produce glorious displays of color. Sowing and looking after hardy annuals is discussed on pages 126–127. Be careful not to sow seeds too early in the year. They will not germinate if the soil is not warm enough, and they may start to decay if conditions are too wet.

In windy areas, select moderately tall hardy annuals, and support them with twiggy sticks. A few annuals have special appeal to children, particularly *Helianthus annuus*, the sunflower, which has large flowers often as wide as 12in/30cm wide. Some grow as high as 10ft/3m, although others are much shorter, and these varieties are ideal for windy sites. Sunflowers are easy to grow in a sunny position and look especially attractive against a white wall that highlights the yellow petals and brown or purple centers.

▲ Use relatively low-growing and lax flowering plants to create bright edges to paths, especially where informality is desired.

◄ Floriferous herbaceous borders, with their relaxed and informal nature, have been a traditional part of English gardens.

### HARDY ANNUALS FOR ROCK GARDENS

Even in a small garden hardy annuals have a useful role, especially in rock gardens where they fill bare areas and add extra color. There are several plants to choose from, including:
*Adonis annua* (pheasant's eye)—10in/25cm high with deep crimson flowers with black centers.
* *Limnanthes douglasii* (Poached-egg plant)—6in/15cm high with bright white flowers with yellow centers.

# informal gardens

*Informal gardens appeal to many gardeners because they have a more restful atmosphere than more regimented gardens with plants in straight lines and borders in geometric shapes. Cottage gardens are the epitome of informality because plants of many types grow together in a relaxed way.*

### Cottage gardens

To many gardeners, the key features of cottage gardens are secluded bowers, rustic trellises with scented climbers and beds patchworked with flowers, fruit, and vegetables. There is even space for topiary birds and animals trained in *Taxus* (yew) and *Ligustrum* (privet). Armillary spheres, with their circular arrangement of rings showing the relative positions of celestial bodies, are less formal than sundials, and add to the relaxed atmosphere.

To insure an authentic cottage garden, you can also grow apple varieties with wonderful flavors. They include 'McIntosh', 'Gold Rush', 'Rome', 'Newtown Pippin', and 'Spartan'. Good pear varieties include 'Comice', 'Harrow Delight', 'Harvest Queen', and 'Stark Honeysweet'. Pole beans (*Phaseolus vulgaris*) on tripods in borders add height and create a background for other plants.

### Wild gardens

Wild gardens are not a contradiction in terms but a way of bringing a hint of the wild landscape into a small, controlled environment. A light, overhead canopy of trees helps to create shade for plants from *Hyacinthoides* (bluebell) to azaleas. If you have inherited a garden with deeper shade you can alleviate the conditions by thinning branches, but in any case stick to shade-loving plants (see pages 66–67). Other features to include are meandering rustic paths linking garden areas, and alpine "meadows" with low-growing bulbous plants in short grass. These are lovely in full sun, especially on a slope.

◄ *Benches and other seats are an essential feature in a garden, since they create places from which it can be admired.*

Wild flowers are also necessary to attract a wide range of insects. Many seed companies sell special mixtures of wild flowers and they are best sown in the spring. Most will reseed themselves during the following year and, although not all gardeners will wish to create such informal areas, they constitute an environmentally friendly way of keeping a healthy garden.

## Soothing sounds

Most gardens have colorful flowers and attractive foliage, but why not add comforting sounds as a new dimension? These can range from the rustling of leaves to the reassuring pitter-patter of water splashing and tumbling from fountains or bubbling along in streams. Some plants are especially known for

their ability to create sound in even the slightest breeze. Grasses and bamboos rustle, as do the leaves of some trees, and a gravel path with bamboos on either side is a joy throughout the year. Encourage birds and birdsong with a bird bath or a feeding area well out of the reach of cats. Continue feeding the birds in winter, but go not leave whole peanuts, hard fat, or too much bread in early spring when there may be young in the nests.

### WIND CHIMES

Wind chimes suspended from trees close to a house add a gentle and comforting sound to the garden. However, do not put them where they may cause irritation through being repeatedly knocked.

▲ *A stream meandering through a wild flower garden is a captivating feature. A bench is a resting point from which plants may be admired.*

▼ *Wild flower gardens are easily created and mixtures of wild flower seeds are available from seed companies. Always sow the seeds thinly.*

# formal gardens

*Formally designed gardens appeal to many gardeners. They provide a neat appearance and a better opportunity than informal types to change arrangements of plants from spring to summer, as well as from one year to another. Small front gardens often have a formal design.*

## Carpet bedding

During the mid-1800s many low-growing, subtropical plants were introduced into gardens, and by the 1870s they were grown to form carpets of color in borders. Most were planted in geometric patterns, but some formed monograms, especially in large estates.

The art of carpet bedding spread to botanical and municipal gardens, and

*▲ Formal gardens have a clinical nature that suits many small areas. Ponds, either round or square, create attractive features.*

towns competed to create the most original and attractive display. Some designs of carpet bedding were even used as advertisements, as commemorative notices, and to depict the names of towns. Carpet bedding is still widely practiced in formal parks, the centers of large cities, and in popular coastal resorts.

Home gardeners pursue this type of gardening by growing half-hardy annuals in summer, and bulbs and biennials in spring and the fall.

## Summer displays

Plant summer bedding displays in late spring or early summer, as soon as all risk of damage from frost has passed. The plants are raised from seeds sown in late winter or early spring in gentle warmth in greenhouses, and are later acclimatized to outdoor conditions. As well as half-hardy annuals, plants with attractive foliage are also used and they range from *Bassia scoparia trichophylla* better known as *Kochia trichophylla* (burning bush, summer cypress) and *Euphorbia marginata* 'Snow on the mountain' to *Abutilon pictum*

'Thompsonii'. They are often used as "dot" plants to create height in an otherwise low display.

Plants traditionally used in formal bedding displays include *Lobularia maritima,* still known as *Alyssum maritimum* (sweet alyssum), bushy forms of *Lobelia erinus* in colors including blue, white, and red, and the many forms of *Tagetes* (marigold).

## Spring displays

Early bedding displays usually contain a medley of biennials and spring-flowering bulbs, especially tulips. Biennials are sown in nursery beds in late spring or early summer, and are planted in borders in late summer or early fall. Bulbs such as tulips are planted at the same time.

Spring displays can be a rich mix of colors, shapes, and heights and include biennials such as *Bellis perennis* (English daisy), wallflowers, *Dianthus barbatus* (sweet william) and *Myosotis sylvatica* (forget-me-not). In late spring or early summer, after their display has finished, the plants are pulled up. The soil is then forked over, lightly firmed by shuffling over it, and planted with summer-flowering displays.

## Knot gardens

The knot garden was once an expression of the unchanging, endless nature of life. By the mid-1600s "knot garden" had become a term to describe a flower garden surrounded by and interwoven with paths. Today, it is associated with miniature hedges of *Buxus sempervirens* 'Suffruticosa' (edging boxwood) surrounding small flower beds. These intricate shapes are ideal in small gardens.

## Formal ponds

Round ponds are simple but distinctive, especially when they feature a fountain. They need a formal setting, perhaps in a wide lawn surrounded, at a distance, by a formal hedge of *Taxus baccata* (English yew). Alternatively, lay wide paths around the pond and divide the surrounding space into four separate garden areas planted with summer-flowering bedding plants. Use dot plants to create height.

### FORMAL TOPIARY

Unlike topiary animals and birds, which are traditional in cottage gardens, topiary cones, pyramids, and squares may be more suited to formal areas. These can be grouped, perhaps toward the end of a formal lawn, or dotted around a garden.

▶ *Miniature hedges grown from edging boxwood are ideal for encircling a border. They create formality without dominating the garden.*

# Mediterranean gardens

*Clear blue skies, warm breezes, and little rain epitomize the Mediterranean, especially to visitors who know the region and its multicolored gardens only through summer visits. Yet the gardens change through the year, reflecting a dramatic swing from hot, dry summers to cooler, wetter winters.*

### Mediterranean plants

Spring-flowering bulbs and tuberous-rooted plants soon burst into flower as the cool of winter is replaced by spring warmth, while annuals burgeon into growth ready for later flowering. Native plants include rosemary, myrtle, *Cistus* (rock rose), laurel, olives, figs and dwarf palms. Best known is *Cupressus sempervirens* (Italian or Mediterranean cypress), particularly the narrow forms. They are often seen in small clusters in Mediterranean gardens.

Silver-leaved plants are better able to survive hot, dry conditions than plants with green leaves. They include shrubby and herbaceous *Artemisias*. Plants with hairy leaves are also equipped for hot regions and perhaps one of the best known is *Stachys byzantina* (lamb's ears). It has oval leaves densely covered with white, silvery hairs. *Cistus* (rock rose) has leaves that emit resinous scents and it also thrives in warm areas.

◄ *Bright surfaces, colored tiles, and plants with variegated, daggerlike leaves, such as Agave americana 'Marginata', create a vibrant setting.*

## Warm terraces

Wide terraces with ornate stone balustrades are ideal areas for enjoying outdoor life. These areas are also perfect for plants in a wide range of containers. Where possible, position them in partial shade, which helps prevent the compost becoming too hot, and reduces the amount and frequency of watering.

Shade is as important for people as plants, and a tall tree with a climber such as *Clematis montana* 'Elizabeth'—or another mountain clematis—clambering through its branches makes a spectacular feature when flowering in late spring and early summer. It also gives shade in summer and so is splendid for creating a cool outdoor living area. If it becomes too large, cut it back as soon as the flowers fade. Other climbers create shade, and where there is a large pergola, a wisteria can be planted to clamber over it, although it needs more pruning than the clematis, and it will not create such a dense canopy of shade.

## Brightening steps

Wide flights of steps that link terraces with lower levels need not be solely functional. Position clusters of plants in containers at the top and bottom, especially if the lower area is wider. Narrow steps, perhaps positioned to one side of a terrace and connecting to a lower garden, can have their sides clothed in trailing plants. If the sides have a dry stone wall, plant the yellow-flowered *Aurinia saxatilis* (still better known as *Alyssum saxatile*) and the contrasting *Aubrieta deltoidea* (aubretia) for a wealth of purple to rose-lilac flowers in late spring and early summer.

### TEMPERATE PALM

A few palms are sufficiently hardy to survive temperate areas and they include the Chinese *Trachycarpus fortunei*. Plant it in well-drained but moisture-retentive soil in a warm, sunny, sheltered position. Placed near a terrace it will provide shade. It takes about 15 years to grow to 10ft/3m high and has large, pleated leaves up to 3ft/90cm wide, and a trunk covered decoratively in wiry black fiber.

▲ *Even the smallest paved area can have Mediterranean plantings. Color-washed walls and metal-framed furniture complete the design.*

◄ *Colorful pots with low-growing and slightly bushy plants are ideal for positioning along the edges of steps. Insure that they are secure.*

# Japanese gardens

*The traditional gardens of Japan exude serenity and peace. They are simple, uncluttered, and well-defined, engendering an atmosphere of tranquillity and contemplation. The design of early Japanese gardens was influenced in the seventh century by a Japanese ambassador returning from China.*

### Gravel gardening

Few features in Japanese gardens are as restful to the eye as a gravel garden, perhaps composed of a large, level area of gravel and well-spaced groupings of two, three or five large rocks that assume the appearance of small islands. The gravel is raked to create the impression of shallow waves. Large areas of gravel can be given extra interest by laying a stepping stone path across them, but avoid splitting up the area and producing two seas of gravel. If laying a second path, use smaller stone to make the feature less dominant.

### Paths and rivers

In slightly less formal areas—and where there is a gentle slope—use pebbles instead of gravel and create two or three paths and rivers. Using large, irregular-shaped stepping stones and surrounding them with colored shale will create the impression of a stream. Where the area is moderately steep, stones and shale may be used to form a narrow stream; in flatter areas this may be made wider to give a more natural, harmonious outline.

### Water and bridges

Moving water is an essential element in some Japanese gardens. Tumbling and splashing water can be achieved with a small pump and this creates an exciting feature throughout the year. Japanese wooden bridges are distinctive and often have a misleading appearance of frailty. Where just a simple bridge is needed

◀ *Japanese gardens have a serenity unmatched by any other style of gardening. Large rocks, gravel, and bamboos are the main features of many gardens.*

over a narrow stream, thick planks of wood or long slabs of stone are attractive and easy to use. Where the stream is wide and the current is slow, several pieces of stone or wood can be linked. Large stepping stones also look attractive and may occasionally be located down the center of a stream.

## TEA GARDENS

Tea gardens are the traditional, tranquil setting for the tea ceremony. Those taking part first assemble in the garden to cast off worldly cares before drinking tea. Gravel and stepping stones are prime features. Others are trees, shrubs, and ferns, with their timeless and contemplative character. Ephemeral flowers, do not feature because they reveal the changing seasons and the passing of time.

### Shrubs and bamboos

Bamboos are a characteristic plant in Japanese gardens and many grow well beside streams. Some varieties also grow easily in a large tub or a square, wooden container. Bamboos are described in more detail on pages 218–219.

Two small trees typical of Japanese gardens, and which are ideal in tubs, are the Japanese maples, *Acer palmatum dissectum* and *Acer palmatum d. atropurpurea*, the former with deeply cut green leaves and the latter with bronze-red foliage. They are both deciduous and have a wide, dome-like outline. The evergreen *Fatsia japonica* can also be planted in a large container. Its large, rich glossy green leaves with seven to nine lobes provide a good structural contrast.

▲ Small trees with finely divided green or bronze-purple leaves are instantly associated with Japanese gardens.

▼ Meandering streams, simple bridges, and gravel paths bordered with low-growing plants create a restful ambience.

# surfaces, walls, and trellises

The key part of a garden that hardly ever changes is the structure, and that includes walls, paths, and arbors. They are all extremely important because they have two functions. They divide and shape the garden, creating outdoor rooms, passages, and places to sit, lending atmosphere to the garden, and they add distinctive, attractive features. But before deciding to put up a trellis, think how and where it is to be used, and what you are going to grow it on. These pages look at the wide range of possibilities to be encountered, and the many exciting new materials to use.

# paths for all gardens

*Paths should not just be ribbon-like features providing quick access from one part of a garden to another, they should be attractive in their own right, with surfaces that harmonize with the rest of the garden. These pages explore the many different construction materials available for paths.*

### Why have a path?

Paths are essential in many parts of a garden. An all-weather surface right around a house is especially necessary to link it with a garage, fuel store, and sheds. But even these domestic demands do not mean that a path need be featureless and unimaginative. Areas around cottages can have gray, ribbed-surfaced paving stones spaced 4in/10cm apart in a sea of gravel, or a natural stone path with spaces for low plants. Modern houses need a more formal style, which may be provided by a wide range of plain or mixed surfaces. It is, fortunately, no longer necessary to lay a path alongside a clothes line, thanks to the introduction of compact clothes lines which rotate on a single pole.

### Constraints and opportunities

The choice of materials for the construction of a path is influenced by the garden's topography and shape.

▶ *Crazy-paving paths are right for flat and for sloping gardens because they can hug closely to the most twisting and undulating contours.*

Materials such as square or rectangular paving slabs are ideal for straight paths, whereas crazy paving is more adaptable and can be used for straight and for curved paths. Grass paths, with or without stepping stones running down the center, may be curved or straight, while informal paths of thyme look particularly eye-catching when in flower.

A garden that is undulating or markedly sloped has a strong influence on the selection of materials. Crazy paving is perfectly suited to ground that slopes in several directions, whereas formal paths are best where the ground slopes in one direction. Gravel paths should be reserved for flat areas because the gravel inevitably migrates slowly downhill.

Materials used to construct a path should be in proportion to its width. A path formed of a combination of small, rectangular and square paving slabs looks out of proportion if over 2ft/60cm wide. For a wider path use larger paving slabs. Conversely, narrow paths of crazy paving appear confusing, but look better when wider and irregularly shaped.

## Medley paths

Paths can be formed of several different materials. Those for informal areas could include cross-slices of tree trunks positioned as stepping stones in a sea of coarse gravel, or six-sided concrete slabs with pebbles, while railroad ties spaced 3–4in/7.5–10cm apart in cobbles or gravel also work well. In wild gardens, make gravel or grass paths edged with logs, and in rural gardens where borders are wide, use sections of logs as stepping stones to give access to the entire area.

For formal gardens, the range of materials is much wider. Make patterns from paving slabs of different shapes but similar texture and color, with gaps left for cobbles, but remember that this may make the path very uneven. Bricks and flexible pavers can also be laid in attractive patterns.

### WINTER WARNING

Where plants are positioned in gaps between paving slabs, do not use salt to remove ice, or use a shovel or spade to scrape away snow. Instead, leave these winter hazards alone and let them melt naturally.

▲ *Informal paths formed of a well-drained but firm base covered with shredded bark and with a low, woven edging are ideal for rustic gardens.*

▼ *Concrete pavers are right for straight paths in formal gardens. The pavers can be laid in straight lines or in complex patterns.*

# walls and fences

*Most gardens have a wall or a fence to define boundaries, create privacy, deflect noise, and screen unpleasant views. The main constructional difference is that a wall needs strong foundations along its entire length, whereas a fence requires support only for the concrete or wooden posts.*

◀ *Walls of all types, formal or informal, create secluded and cloistered spots which may have small paved areas for garden furniture.*

### Fence or wall?

Brick walls are much more expensive to construct than fences. A wall 6ft/1.8m high needs to be 9in/23cm thick, with strengthening piers every 6ft/1.8m. Even screen-block walling (blocks 12in/30cm square and 4in/10cm thick, with a latticework design) needs strong foundations and piers every 10ft/3m, and supports at the ends. Screen-block walling can be combined attractively with a traditional brick wall or with bricks of reconstituted stone.

Fences range from white picket fencing to close-boarding. The framework of a close-boarded fence is built from 4–6in/10–15cm wide pales (strips of wood) nailed to arris rails. Such fences are usually 4ft/1.2m to 6ft/1.8m high. Always select a fence to harmonize with the garden. For example, a picket fence is ideal for the front boundary of a cottage garden, whereas wattle fencing and chestnut paling are better suited for the back area. Panel fencing, with 6ft/1.8m long panels from 4ft/1.2m to 6ft/1.8m high, is popular and somewhat cheaper than close-boarding.

Low-slung post and chain fencing is ideal for marking a boundary, but it will not keep people out. The chain is now usually made of strong plastic and needs no maintenance. Ranch-style fencing, with planks of wood 6–8ft/1.8–2.4m long and 6–8in/15–20cm wide nailed to posts, has a modern, open feel. Gaps of about 4in/10cm are left between the planks, but to stop people looking through, nail planks on alternate sides of the supporting posts which are concreted into the ground. These fences can be 3ft/90cm to 6ft/1.8m high.

Cast-iron fencing is ideal for surrounding the front gardens of Victorian, Georgian, and other period town houses. This kind of fence is usually 3–6ft/90cm–1.8m high and painted black. The fences are very attractive and can be used as features on their own, or underplanted with a range of colorful flowers and leafy plants.

## Gates for all gardens

Walls and fences in front gardens are not complete without a complementary gate. White picket fences need rustic wooden gates while an old, weathered brick wall with an arch requires a wrought-iron gate with a round top.

The range of decorative patterns in wrought-iron gates is wide, and this is usually reflected in the cost. Wooden gates vary in style, and apart from the paling type there are overlapping board gates and those with diamond-slatted cladding.

▼ *Choose a fence that suits your garden. Wattle fencing panels secured to stout posts are informal and rustic, and right for a cottage garden style.*

### THIEF-PROOF GATES

Wrought-iron gates are usually hung on peg hinges and can be stolen quickly and easily. To prevent this happening, secure the lower hinge to the post, and with the peg upward, hang the gate and secure the top hinge with the peg downward. Now the gate cannot be lifted off. Wooden gates are usually more secure because the hinge is screwed to the gate and the supporting post.

# decking

*Decking is increasingly popular and creates all-weather leisure areas above ground level. Decking was traditionally laid along one side of a house, often forming a veranda complete with a balustrade. Nowadays it is also built along boundaries or as a free-standing feature.*

◄ *Combining decking with a fountain and a pond creates an attractive feature. Large-leaved, evergreen plants make an ideal background.*

### Constructing decking

The basic construction of a deck is of planks of Western red cedar or another softwood which has been pressure-impregnated with a wood preservative. The planks are attached by galvanized nails to a supporting timber frame, with a ¼–½in/6–12mm space between each pair of planks.

The timber framework supporting the decking is secured to sturdy uprights mounted on metal plates, which are bolted to concrete foundation pads. This allows for sloping ground and demands careful construction and levelling.

Decking can be built from wood bought from a timber yard, but partly constructed units are now available from large home improvement outlets. There are also many companies that specialize in decking and will customize a deck to your specific needs, building the deck and also installing it.

### Economy decking

A deck is expensive and time-consuming to build. Multilevel designs are especially costly. An alternative to decking is to use cinder blocks and fence posts. The blocks need to be half-buried in the ground with their surfaces level, and the fence posts (available up to 3m/10ft long) positioned on top. Pressure-treated gravel boards (normally used for close-board fencing) are then nailed to the fence posts.

### Encircling mature trees

People often want to build a deck in an area where an established tree is growing. This need not be a problem because you can arrange the decking around the tree. Begin by cutting off low-growing branches and then build a square brick plinth around it. This will need strong foundations. Extend the plinth upward until the top is about 15in/38cm above the planned level of the decking. The last stage is to construct the decking around the plinth and to put a capping 6–8in/15–20cm wide on top of the wall, which can serve as a very useful seat.

## WOODEN TILES

These look like decking when laid, but are
formed of 2ft/60cm square units. They are easily
laid. The first stage is to level the ground. Insure
the roots of perennial weeds are dug up, and
then spread and rake level a layer of
horticultural sand 2in/5cm-thick. Place the
wooden tiles on top, with the slatted surface in
a criss-cross pattern. Lay the tiles so they abut
closely, and use stout pegs around the outside
to prevent them being knocked out of position.

◄ *Steps formed of decking and edged with
leafy plants are a practical and attractive means
of leading from one level to another.*

▼ *Old railroad ties laid with their surfaces flush
with the soil's surface, and with gravel between
them, make an attractively uneven surface.*

# steps for all gardens

*Handsome flights of steps that harmonize with the rest of the garden become enduring features of interest. They must, of course, be functional, but there is no reason why they cannot also be attractive. Here is a range of steps that will enhance your garden, whatever its style or size.*

## Informal steps

Log steps are essential for wild gardens on slopes. Thick logs or old railroad ties can be used to form the risers. They have a relaxing appearance and can be enhanced by daffodils naturalized in the grass beside them. Instead of forming narrow ribbons of daffodils, plant them in wide groups, about one-third the width of the steps.

Where peat beds are constructed next to a path and near a flight of steps, use railroad ties rather than logs, especially when the peat needs to be hemmed in.

Consider planting trees on either side of narrow, informal steps set in a steep bank. This will create a light canopy of branches and leaves. Grass steps look good in informal and semiformal gardens. Log steps with grass forming the treads are also informal, but they are not all-weather surfaces. For long flights of steps, a strimmer is essential for cutting the grass, whereas in small areas a pair of hedging shears is sufficient. Semiformal grass steps use bricks at the edges of the treads, with grass behind them.

## Formal steps

Large, wide flights of steps, especially those with wide areas at the top and base, make dominant features. Narrow steps can also be attractive in small gardens, especially when built with unusual materials. Bricks with a chamfered edge can be used as part of the tread, with other bricks as the risers.

▲ *A flight of garden steps, especially when constructed from attractive natural materials, creates a pleasing feature.*

Steps with a semicircular design and a full circle of bricks at the top, are very attractive and always capture attention. The inner parts of the treads can be formed using colored gravels, bricks or grass. Semicircular steps work well as a link between patio or terrace and grass lawn, and between different levels of grass, but do not attempt to form large flights of these steps; usually, three steps on a slight slope is sufficient.

▼ *Wrought-iron spiral staircases create unusual features, either in basement gardens or, when shortened, as steps to a different level.*

## RECYCLING SPIRAL STAIRCASES

Old spiral staircases are very decorative and can be used in basement gardens as a feature. They look good when cloaked in small-leaved *Hedera* (ivy), with supporting pots and small hanging baskets.

# shady patios

*We owe the term "patio" to the Spanish, who used it to describe an inner courtyard, surrounded by a dwelling and open to the sky. Patios are an integral part of the house, providing shade and shelter throughout the day, and they were traditionally planted with leafy plants and colorful flowers.*

### Publicizing patios

The concept of patios spread from Spain to the southern United States and then westward to California, where they were ideally suited to the climate. Later, the term migrated to the temperate regions of Europe, where it is often now used instead of the word terrace.

### The L-shaped patio

Many houses have an L-shaped area outside a rear entrance, and it can be partly enclosed by a fence. An alternative is to use a free-standing trellis, erected about 18in/45cm from the boundary, and with one end forming an L-shape, to create an even more cloistered area. To make an evergreen screen of foliage, erect a trellis and plant a large-leaved variegated ivy such as *Hedera colchica* 'Sulphur Heart' or *H. c.* 'Dentata Variegata'. Both have variegated leaves. For summer foliage the herbaceous

◀ *A secluded patio, shaded from strong sunlight, is an oasis of calm. Tables and benches are essential for outdoor living.*

climber *Humulus lupulus* 'Aureus' (Hops) creates a handsome screen of leaves. Where a flowering screen is desired, plant *Clematis montana*.

## Surfacing patios

An attractive, well-drained surface is essential. It need not be consistent across the entire patio because you can leave spaces for shrubs and small trees. Other areas can be laid with cobbles, with large containers standing on top.

Paving slabs with raised patterns, brick-like slabs positioned together to create a pattern, and granite setts can all be used, but do avoid smooth, highly colored and checkerboard surfaces.

## Healing nature

Part of the enchantment of a patio is the opportunity to have cool, refreshing water splashing from a fountain into a central pond. Repetitive but irregular gentle sound has a therapeutic effect that helps to reduce stress. Also, an enclosed

patio stops the scent of plants from being blown away. *Helichrysum serotinum* (curry plant) may well trigger memories of a visit to Asia, while the unforgettable perfume of lilac may conjure up thoughts of a wedding bouquet. Many fragrances are more personal. A mistress

of the novelist H. G. Wells claimed that his body emitted a honey-like fragrance. She could have recaptured this with the honey-scented bulbs *Crocus chrysanthus* or *Iris danfordiae*. Both can be grown beside paths and also in containers such as pots and window boxes.

---

### ORNAMENTS ON PATIOS

Small statuary and ornamental pots are ideal for creating interest on patios. Large, barrel-like pots make superb homes for *Clematis macropetala*, with its tangled mass of stems and double blue flowers during late spring and early summer. This plant has the bonus of silky, fluffy seed heads.

▶ *An ornamental pond has calming, therapeutic qualities which help to reduce stress, making it a perfect feature for a patio.*

# sunny terraces

*A terrace is an open and usually paved area connecting a house with its garden. It usually has a balustrade or a low wall, especially if raised above the level of the garden. Many houses and bungalows have a flat, all-weather surface like a terrace at the back which may be used to create an outdoor leisure area.*

### Ancient heritage

Terraced landscapes with superb views were known in Thebes, Egypt, in about 1500 BCE. This style of gardening progressed westward to Italy, where terraces were created as status and power symbols, while giving views over the surrounding countryside. During the Middle Ages the viewing equivalent of a terrace was constructed on castle walls, while in 13th-century Spain the gardens on the hill slopes of the Alhambra had similar constructions. The English landscape designer Humphry Repton (1752–1818) was very keen on terracing, and in 18th-century England a variation known as the terrace walk became popular, with a surface of grass rather than paving. Such terraces were often long and especially sited to give views of the surrounding landscape. Grassed terraces were either straight or gently curved.

### Versatile terraces

Most paved areas in temperate climates are terraces. They are usually adjacent to a house, open to the sky and, where possible, positioned to gain the maximum sun (unlike patios, which are features of hot countries where shade is essential). The surface of terraces varies from natural stone paving, ideal for areas around cottages, to paving slabs that suit modern demands. Natural stone paving can be made even more informal by planting prostrate plants between the irregular-sized slabs. For formal terraces that dominate a garden, choose brightly colored, smooth-surfaced slabs perhaps laid in a checkerboard fashion. For other formal areas where plants are cherished as much as they are on the patio, use less dramatically colored slabs, perhaps with a ribbed surface.

Large terraces are still sometimes built and include raised beds. Plant them

◄ *South-facing terraces bask in sun through the summer. A garden pond with a fountain give eye-catching movement and cool the air on hot days.*

with shrubs and small trees to provide some shade. Tubs, ornamental stone sinks, pots, window boxes, and troughs are other worthwhile features.

## Balustrades and walls

In Classical times, terraces had carved stone balustrades. Today, these can be superb features around the edge of a terrace, giving it a hint of Classical style. This type of feature is most appropriate for more formal architecture. Balustrades in this style are totally unsuited to a modern, brightly colored area, for which a wall partly formed of screen blocks with a concrete capping is much more

appropriate. Bear in mind that safety is a priority along the edge of a terrace on a steep slope, especially when young children are likely to use the area. A wall about 2½ft/75cm high is essential.

Wooden balustrades are seldom seen, although a form of ranch-style fencing about 2½ft/75cm high suits terraces surfaced with brightly colored, smooth-surfaced paving slabs. They can be painted white, and built even higher if privacy from prying eyes is an important consideration.

▼ *All-weather surfaces for terraces are essential. They should slope away from the house a little so torrential rain can drain away.*

▲ *Where sunlight is strong throughout summer, attach canopies to the top of patio windows. Insure that they can be taken down in the fall.*

# ards

*Courtyards have a history that extends back more than 1,000 years. They have long been a key functional area in forts and castles, and they were built into the palaces of the Moslem rulers of Arabia, North Africa, and Spain, where they provided pleasant relief from the heat of the sun.*

## Shady and secluded

Today, courtyards in town gardens are usually small, secluded and protected from strong wind, although where gates are on the north side there is a risk of cold winter winds searing the foliage of evergreen plants. Courtyards always have shady areas but this need not be a problem as many plants, including ferns, grow in shade and moist soil (see pages 66–67). You can also grow almost anything, from small trees to bulbs in containers placed to catch the sun.

Seclusion and shade appeal to many gardeners, especially in towns where privacy is hard to find. Shade from strong sun is welcome during the day, but in the late evening the gloom may make the area too dark to use. One solution is to have spotlights and concealed lighting fitted by a qualified electrician.

Basement apartments sometimes have cloistered areas. These can be treated as courtyards, and decorated with plants in containers. If they have stone steps connecting them with ground level, these can be made more attractive by planting trailing plants such as variegated forms of *Vinca minor* (lesser periwinkle), beside them. Plant it toward the top of the steps, so it can trail freely downward. The prostrate *Lysimachia nummularia* (creeping jenny) will also brighten the edges of steps, and grows well in partial shade. For extra color choose the form 'Aurea' with yellow leaves. However, this variety does not thrive in deep shade.

## Flooring a courtyard

A wide variety of paving materials is suitable for terraces. Large, aged, well-worn flagstones are ideal, but they can be difficult to obtain and are usually expensive. Alternatives are brick pavers,

▶ *Courtyards have a secluded and often partly shaded nature. Use plants in pots and tubs and select those that thrive in shaded areas.*

granite setts, and reconstituted flagstones. Cobbles are another possibility but they are difficult to walk on.

## Furniture and gates for courtyards

Wrought-iron or aluminum furniture with an aged, ornate appearance suits a cloistered, shady courtyard. Besides harmonizing with the walls, nonferrous metal furniture does not deteriorate, although it is usually necessary to scrub off lichen and moss in spring. Wooden furniture, such as conjoined benches and tables, are always much in demand. In late fall stand each leg on a brick, and cover the entire table with a plastic sheet tied down securely to protect it from winter weather. Collapsible, slatted furniture has the advantage that it can be taken indoors and stored. Ornate wrought-iron gates make ideal entrances to courtyard gardens. They are not as dominant as wooden doors and allow the outside world to be seen at a glance.

▲ *Courtyards are not complete without furniture; wrought iron is ideal for these small areas because it takes up little space and can often be folded for storage.*

### EARLY MOTELS

In the Near and Far East caravanserais, or caravansary, have been known for many centuries. These were caravan hostels for merchants and travelers built around a large courtyard. They provided a secure and peaceful temporary resting place.

# pergolas, arches, and trellises

*Structures like pergolas were known in warm countries from the earliest times. In Egypt they were probably used to support vines and create shade. The Italians took up the idea and came up with the term "pergola," meaning an arbor, bower, or a walk of bowers covered mainly with vines.*

## Pergolas for all places

Pergolas can be informal, formal, or even oriental. Those constructed from rustic poles, often astride paths, are ideal for giving support to leafy climbers such as *Vitis vinifera*. The leaf shapes look more informal than the leaves of the ordinary vine. If an informal flowering and highly fragrant climber is desired, choose *Lonicera periclymenum* 'Belgica' (early Dutch honeysuckle) or *L. p.* 'Serotina' (late Dutch honeysuckle). *Lonicera japonica* (Japanese honeysuckle) also has a free-flowing show of flowers.

Formal pergolas formed of planed timber, with square-cut uprights and crossbeams, make ideal supports for wisteria. Although wisteria can be grown against a house wall, it is better where the large bunches of flowers can hang freely. It is a vigorous climber, so it soon drains the border soil around a house of any moisture, which can be detrimental to the house and to other plants growing alongside it.

An oriental look can be given to formal pergolas by cutting the underside edges and ends of the crossbeams at a sloping angle. Lean-to pergolas are another variation and can be made to look like an arbor if climbing plants are trained around uprights and crossbeams. Proprietary brackets are available for securing the crossbeams to a wall, with wooden uprights on the other side.

◀ *Most pergolas are straight and straddle paths, but an alternative use is to enclose a rounded area, perhaps devoted to growing bush roses.*

## Arches

At their simplest, arches are just inverted hoops over a path covered in climbers, from roses to the leafy herbaceous climber *Humulus lupulus* 'Aureus' (Hops). However, the ingenuity of gardeners has resulted in arches of all shapes and sizes, including four-way arches at the junctions of paths.

Use arches to create height and focal points, as well as to grow climbers. Metal arches are increasingly used to grow roses over paths and as features on lawns, where, covered in leafy plants, they take on the role of an arbor. Indeed, metal and wooden arches against a wall or a fence will create an attractive and romantic arbor.

## Trellises

Trellises were traditionally secured to walls, but are increasingly used as a free-standing feature to provide privacy and to create smaller areas, each with a different atmosphere. They are also ideal for screening garbage cans.

Rose enthusiasts welcome free-standing trellis as an opportunity to grow more climbers. At the end of a broad lawn erect a line of trellis panels, with shorter panels at right-angles to them. This produces features resembling stalls for horses. Pillar roses, where both climbing and rambling-type roses are grown up rustic poles or tripods of sawn timber, can be integrated into the display to create a variety of shapes.

▲ *Plants that reveal their flowers at eye-level create exciting gardens, with flowers and scent where they can be readily appreciated.*

▼ *Trellises attached to a wall make ideal homes for climbing roses, as well as for other climbers that require a supporting framework.*

# arbors and tunnels

*Arbors and tunnels come in all shapes and sizes, and are mainly admired for their romantic, cloistered leafiness. Arbors are usually smothered in flowering and leafy climbers, while tunnels often have flowering or fruiting trees trained over a wooden or a metal structure.*

▲ *Laburnum trained over metal arches is awash with long, pendulous clusters of yellow flowers during late spring and early summer.*

## Arbors for all gardens

There are arbors for all gardens. There are many suitable for small areas, where they fit into corners or alongside walls. Arbor units are increasingly sold either fully constructed or flat-packed, and are ready to erect, complete with a bench-style seat. Informal types are made of rustic poles, and formal ones of sawn timber. Some are made of wrought iron and have a delicate, aged look that suits roses and less vigorous climbers, such as *Clematis orientalis* (Oriental clematis), *C. tangutica* and *C. macropetala*.

An arbor in the center of a garden is a eye-catching feature. It needs a firm, paved base to provide an area for seats and chairs, and perhaps a small, low table. Some arbors are constructed on a base raised slightly above the surrounding area. This arrangement may suit a more formal garden. An informal arbor with a floor of natural stone paving, may look better if level with the ground. Crazy paving has a semiformal appearance and is also most suitable for an arbor at ground level.

## Tunnels

Tunnels are ideal for channeling people from one part of a garden to another, and if a sundial, an ornamental well or a seat is positioned at the far end of the tunnel, it creates an attractive focal point. A tunnel may have a decorative quality, especially when clothed in laburnum or climbing roses. Apples and pears may also be planted to clothe a series of metal hoops reminiscent of arches. Brambles were traditionally used to make fruiting tunnels. Nut walks were once also popular, but they did not rely for support on large wire hoops. Instead, the branches were pruned to form a kind of tunnel over a rustic path.

Do not make a tunnel long in a short garden, because its length will draw attention to the garden's lack of length. Because they are symmetrical, tunnels are often located in a central position. Where a garden is divided by a crosswise free-standing trellis, bisecting it with a tunnel divides the garden and leads the eye toward another part of it. Feature a herb garden at the end of a fruit tunnel. Alternatively, position a sundial or a seat as a focal point, with a circular gravel path around it with beds for the herbs.

▲ A wrought-iron framed gazebo is an open structure, perfect for climbing roses and for climbers with pendulous flowers.

▲ Cloistered corners, heavily canopied with leafy and flowering climbers, can become secluded and romantic areas in gardens.

◄ A small gazebo is a striking structure, especially when positioned on a firm surface and nestling among shrubs and border plants.

# porches and entrances

*Porches prevent rain saturating people on arrival at a door. Large and ornate porches are often built around a front door, while less decorative and more functional types are at the rear. Rustic or formal arches can also be secured to walls around doors.*

### Brightening porches

A bare area around a front door gives an impression of lack of imagination, or neglect, but when a porch or a structure like a porch is fitted, it brightens the house and garden, especially when covered in leafy plants or flowers. Where a permanent brick-built structure is not possible, an arch may serve. Some may be bought for home assembly. Fit rustic arches around cottage doors and formal styles for more modern houses. Where extra weather protection is needed, secure an unobtrusive piece of wood to the top, to form a flat roof or one with a pitch. This will eventually be covered by the climber. Always secure the arch to the wall and insure that the four posts are concreted into the ground, so that they remain firm. The weight of climbers can be deceptively heavy, and winter winds may loosen weak fixtures.

The insides of large porches can be decorated with hanging baskets with drip trays in their base, and a bright show of tender plants. In summer they can range from *Campanula isophylla* (Star of Bethlehem) to *Chlorophytum comosum* 'Variegatum' (spider plant) and tradescantias. And in summer, the outside can be festooned with hanging baskets

◄ *Climbing plants enrich the outsides of entrances, creating a warm and friendly ambience in the garden and the house.*

suspended from brackets. Take care not to put them where the basket will be knocked, or where water will drip on to plants below. At ground level, hardy plants in containers can be left outside all year. They include narrow conifers, clipped box, and half-standard bay trees planted in tubs.

Not only can flowers and leafy plants make a porch more attractive inside an out but they can keep it colorful through the year. If you have a built porch, secure pieces of narrow trellis to the wall on either side of the door. Position each piece about 9in/23cm from the outer edge of the porch and plant variegated evergreens or plants that flower at different times of year to cover them.

## Brightening gates and entrances

Front gardens bordered by a hedge such as a common privet or yew can be given a fresh identity by training branches to form an arch over a path. The training takes several years and is best performed on a tall hedge. Where paths are long, consider a metal or a wooden arch over the path, positioned about two-thirds of the way along it. Climbing roses clustered over metal arches are suitable for formal and informal areas. Arches constructed from rustic poles are strictly for cottage gardens and are ideal for supporting honeysuckle or jasmine.

Where there is not room for an arch, one or two pillar roses on either side of a path will introduce height to a garden.

▲ *Small porches make a useful and attractive shelter from wind and rain. Linking them with a boundary fence creates a unified feature.*

▼ *Wrought-iron gates and rustic entrances are especially attractive when roses or honeysuckle are trained over an arch.*

# creating
# your garden

# special conditions

Making the most of your garden means knowing how to pick the right plant for the right place. Some plants demand full sun, others need shade, and some can be grown in quite a few different settings. If you have a garden by the shore, for example, you will need to know which plants can survive and even thrive in wind and salt spray. And anyone with a slope will need handy hints on gardening in the apparently difficult conditions it brings. While these important aspects of your garden might be out of your control, there is much you can do to produce a creative show of plants in your garden.

# living with your soil

*All gardeners want an ideal plot of land: one that is well drained, fertile, free from weeds and soil pests, retaining moisture in summer, with a slight southward slope to encourage rapid growth in spring, and sheltered from cold winds. Unfortunately, few gardens have all these qualities.*

### Assessing soil

In broad terms, soil is either light, medium, or heavy, and making an assessment is one of the first things you have to do when taking over a new garden. If the soil sticks to your boots in lumps, it contains clay. Other ways of assessing soil include holding a handful and rubbing some of it between thumb and forefinger. If it forms a smooth, slippery, greasy surface, the soil contains clay, but if it remains gritty between your fingers it is predominantly sandy.

A more scientific assessment may be made by half-filling a screw-top jar with soil, then filling it three-fourths full with water. Shake the jar vigorously and allow one hour for it to settle. Stones will fall to the bottom, and coarse sand, light sand, silt, and clay will settle on top of them. Organic material floats on the surface. The proportions of these layers give a good idea of the soil's composition.

### Improving clay soil

This mainly involves improving drainage and encouraging better aeration. If water remains on the surface, install land drains (see pages 90–91) and, during winter, dig in copious amounts of bulky material, like well-decomposed manure and garden compost. Small areas can be improved by adding horticultural sand, but this is expensive in large gardens. Dust the surface of the soil in winter with hydrated lime or ground limestone to encourage clay particles to stick together, thereby improving drainage. However, do not add fertilizers at the same time, and always check the soil's acidity first to assess the quantity of lime (see below).

### Improving sandy soil

Sandy soils are easy to cultivate, they warm up early in spring and do not become waterlogged. Unfortunately, because water rapidly drains through them, plants quickly become deprived of moisture and nutrients. Improve the soil

◄ *A simple method of assessing soil is by mixing soil and water together and allowing it to settle. Its composition can then be seen.*

| CORRECTING ACIDITY | | |
|---|---|---|
| **Soil** | **Hydrated lime** | **Ground limestone** |
| Clay | 18oz/sq yd 610g/sq m | 24oz/sq yd 810g/sq m |
| Loam | 12oz/sq yd 410g/sq m | 16oz/sq yd 540g/sq m |
| Sand | 6oz/sq yd 200g/sq m | 8oz/sq yd 270g/sq m |

by digging in quantities of manure and garden compost. Other moisture retention methods include maintaining a mulch 3in/7.5cm thick over the soil all summer through to impede evaporation, and installing water sprinklers

## Judging a soil's acidity

The acidity or alkalinity of soil is measured on a pH scale, which ranges from 0–14 with 7.0 as neutral. Figures falling below 7.0 indicate increasing acidity, while those above signify greater alkalinity. The amount of lime needed to make soil less acid depends on its nature (see below), and the type of lime applied.

Assessing soil to see if it is acid or alkaline is quite easy using readily available lime-testing kits. You simply mix some of the soil with water and chemicals and check its resultant color against a color chart. Also available are pH-testing meters which are ideal for gardeners who are red/green color blind.

If your soil is alkaline, dig in plenty of garden compost or manure, and use acid fertilizers such as sulfate of ammonia. Alternatively, grow plants in neutral soil in raised beds, or plant only lime-loving plants. If your soil is acid, apply lime immediately after winter digging. The amount needed depends on the degree of acidity. The quantities indicated left are for every 1.0 pH. Aim for a pH of 6.5.

▶ Add well-decomposed garden compost or manure to the soil just prior to digging in late fall or winter.

# assessing acidity or alkalinity

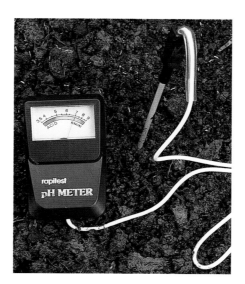

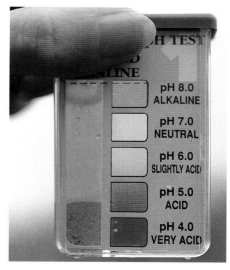

1 Testing the acidity or alkalinity of soil is easy with a pH–testing meter. This device is essential for gardeners who are red/green color blind. When not in use, store the meter in a dry cupboard.

2 Lime-testing kits, in which a soil sample is mixed with water and chemicals, are inexpensive and easy to use. Check the resultant color indicator against a color chart to identify the acid or alkaline levels.

# the ups and downs of gardens

*A level garden has many advantages, especially where easy-access paths are needed for wheelchairs and play areas for young children, but slopes do provide opportunities to create greater visual excitement and mystery. So do not be dismayed if your garden has a slope or steep banks.*

## Practical thoughts

Instead of working against nature and the natural contours of a garden, harness them to your advantage. Moving and leveling vast areas of soil is hard work and time consuming, even when machinery is hired. And there is always the risk of burying topsoil (the upper 1ft/30cm of earth, which is best for plant growth) underneath subsoil. Furthermore, when soil is dug up it initially increases in volume, and fitting it all into a new area may be a problem until it resettles. The natural drainage of the soil may also be destroyed.

### MOVING SOIL UPHILL

Moving large quantities of soil uphill is tiring. Ease the problem by tying a rope to the front of the wheelbarrow so that it can also be pulled by a companion. And, where possible, lay down boards so that the wheel does not dig into the soil.

▶ *On steep slopes construct long flights of steps that cross the area, rather than going straight up, and create resting places at intervals.*

## Paths on slopes

Where sloping ground has been terraced into separate areas, flights of steps are usually built to link them. In addition, try to incorporate a gently sloping path, perhaps as an inconspicuous side feature, so that a wheelbarrow can be moved easily through the garden. Stepping stones may be laid in a grass path, but if you do a great deal of gardening, the grass will suffer. When laying paths on a particularly steep slope, make the surface

firm for winter and use a material that does not become slippery in wet weather. Instead of terracing an entire garden you can build an interesting feature by laying meandering paths around a slope, rather than directly over it. It is always essential to make firm foundations for all paths.

## Steeply sloping banks

A grassy bank is a more economical alternative to a retaining wall. The slope of the bank should be no steeper than 45°. Use a small hover-type mower to trim the grass. Round off the top of the slope slightly to reduce the risk of the mower's blades scalping the grass. Use turf to form the surface because seed may be washed to the base of the slope before it germinates. In formal areas, separate these grassy slopes with a flight of paved or brick steps. In relaxed and informal areas a flight of log steps is cheaper and much quicker to install.

## Retaining walls

Besides containing the soil and separating one level from another, retaining walls offer opportunities to grow rock-garden plants. A drystone wall may be covered in flowers, with bushy and bulbous plants along the top, and trailing plants ones lower down. Do not make the walls more than 4ft/1.2m high.

and fill the rear side with coarse drainage material to prevent the pressure of water pushing it over. Also install weep-holes every 4ft/1.2m along the base of the wall so that water can escape freely.

Another technique for preventing a retaining wall from falling over is to build it so it leans slightly backward. Make certain that its base is firm.

## Sunken gardens

A sunken garden must be in a part of the garden that is low and well-drained. If it is low but badly drained you can install drains to channel the water to a nearby soakaway. This is particularly important if water from the rest of your garden, or from a neighbor's garden, soaks into the area. Most sunken gardens are fairly

formal, with a lawn surrounded by a dry-stone wall about 3ft/90cm high. Do not forget to incorporate access for a lawn mower into your sunken garden.

## Constructing a retaining wall

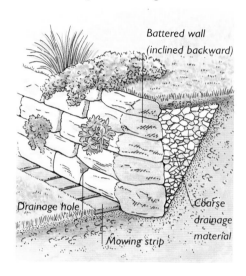

Battered wall (inclined backward)

Drainage hole

Mowing strip

Coarse drainage material

▼ Sunken gardens can be enhanced by installing garden ponds. However, insure that the area is well drained to prevent flooding and fish escaping.

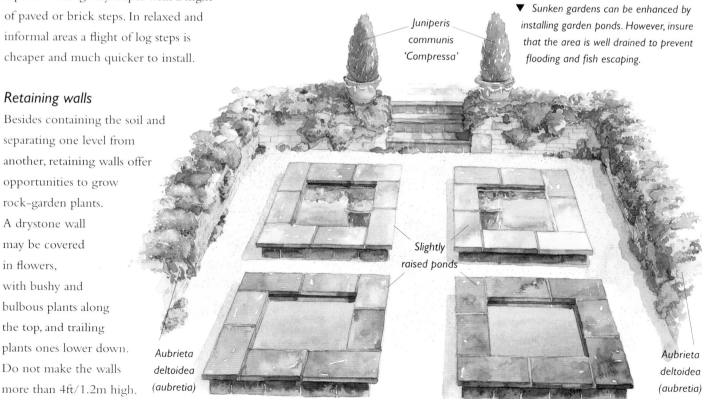

Juniperis communis 'Compressa'

Slightly raised ponds

Aubrieta deltoidea (aubretia)

Aubrieta deltoidea (aubretia)

# shapely gardens

*Whatever the shape of a plot of land—long, narrow, wide, square or even triangular—it can make an attractive garden. Indeed, areas that at first sight appear to have impossible shapes often produce the most interesting gardens.*

### Shaping up

A garden can be as formal or informal as you want, no matter what its shape. For a relaxed atmosphere, consider a lawn with serpentine edges, with a spring-flowering cherry tree and paths that meander. If a formal design is wanted, the lawn might be square or rectangular, and surrounded by flower beds. Clearly, these are just two basic, contrasting examples, and we will look at many more. Other important factors to bear in mind are that trees and shrubs, which form the main garden structure, will eventually mature and may need to be thinned or removed, while the needs of a family usually progress from grassed areas for children to more elaborate, intricate features.

### Creating privacy

As the gardens of newly built houses become smaller, privacy is increasingly difficult to achieve. The problem is that when houses are built close together, the upstairs windows will overlook the gardens. Free-standing trellises drenched with roses and other climbers, tunnels of fruit trees and laburnum, pergolas covered by wisterias, and hedges can all be used to screen your garden. Gazebos also lend privacy.

◄  *Scree beds can be fitted into most gardens but well-drained soil is essential. Add a few small conifers to create height and color.*

Positioning a summerhouse with its back to a boundary wall or a fence and its windows looking out over the garden, is another good way to create privacy, especially if a pergola is linked to it.

### Long, narrow gardens

These are typically town gardens and provide an opportunity to create a series of small, individual areas, each linked but separate. Evergreen hedges can be grown using dark green *Taxus baccata* (English yew), or bright green Monterey cypress, (*Cupressus macrocarpa*) creating year-round seclusion and privacy, and parts of them can be trained and clipped to form arches. Free-standing trellises and arches make an excellent support for climbing

## CHANGES IN SHAPE

Depending on where you stand, the shape of a circular pond appears to change. When seen from a bedroom window at a short distance, a round pond looks circular. But at ground level, and seen from a distance, it appears to be a more interesting oval shape.

roses and other deciduous climbers, which also create summer privacy. And the bright yellow leaved herbaceous climber *Humulus lupulus* 'Aureus' (Hops) gives a superb summer display. Unless a central vista to the end of the garden is desired—and only then if a feature such as a statue can be seen clearly through several arches—change the position of the path within each area. This also adds variety to the garden.

## Short and wide shapes

These need careful design to avoid making the area look exceptionally wide in relation to its depth. The absence of a focal point will confuse the eye. Use a decorative screen so that a central or off-central area meets the eye. Other features should not be so immediately apparent.

Pergolas and trellises give essential privacy from nearby houses overlooking a small garden. In a more open situation, consider installing a sundial or an armillary sphere on a low plinth, encircled by a lawn and rose beds. A summerhouse may also be placed to create a central background feature, with a lawn in front for children to play on.

A freestanding trellis with square or diamond patterning makes a formal screen and can be erected quickly. A rustic pergola entwined with honeysuckle is best in a rural garden. *Clematis montana* is a climber for formal and informal trellis.

▶ *Design the garden so that it cannot be seen at a single glance. Hedges and leafy screens are decorative ways to separate garden areas.*

▼ *Securely constructed arches clothed in leafy climbers help to separate parts of the garden without segregating them completely.*

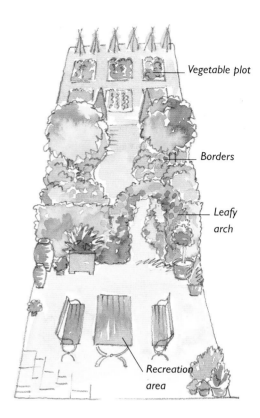

Vegetable plot

Borders

Leafy arch

Recreation area

# gardening in full sun

*Many plants, including hardy annuals, herbaceous perennials, and shrubs, grow well in strong sunlight. Unfortunately, hot sunshine inevitably means dry soil, but this is not an unsurmountable problem. A surprisingly large number of plants grow in these conditions.*

## Living with dry, hot soils

Full sun invariably means dry, impoverished soil unless provisions are made to improve it. These include digging in plenty of well-decayed garden compost or manure to increase the soil's ability to retain moisture. Also, watering the soil thoroughly and then adding a mulch 3in/7.5cm thick mulch improves moisture retention and keeps the soil cool. In a rock garden or on a scree bed, a mulch of pea gravel or stone chippings will keep the soil cool and moist.

## Hardy annuals for full sun

A few hardy annuals grow well in sun or partial shade, but some are especially at home in full sun. Adding well-decayed garden compost or manure to the soil in winter, followed by regular watering through the summer, are aids to success, particularly in hot, dry places. Sun-loving hardy annuals include the following:

► Achillea *(yarrow) flourishes in strong sunlight and contrasts well with hollyhock, a hardy perennial usually grown as a biennial.*

- *Agrostemma githago* 'Milas' (corn-cockle)
- *Argemone mexicana* (prickly poppy)
- *Asperula orientalis* (woodruff)
- *Calendula officinalis* (pot marigold)
- *Carthamus tinctorius* (safflower)
- *Centaurea cyanus* (cornflower)
- *Eschscholzia californica* (California poppy)
- *Godetia amoena* (satin flower)
- *Gypsophila elegans* (baby's breath)
- *Helichrysum bracteatum* (strawflower)
- *Iberis amara* (rocket candytuft)
- *Limnanthes douglasii* (poached-egg flower)
- *Malope trifida* (annual mallow)
- *Nicandra physaloides* (shoo-fly)
- *Nigella damascena* (love-in-a-mist)
- *Phacelia campanularia* (California bluebell)
- *Scabiosa atropurpurea* (pincushion flower)

## Herbaceous plants for sunny borders

Because herbaceous perennials produce fresh leaves, stems, and flowers each year, they need to grow rapidly and without restriction from spring to fall. Many plants native to the Mediterranean region can survive in full sun with dry soil, especially those with silver leaves. Herbaceous perennials that survive in full sun and dry soil include

- *Achillea millefolium* (yarrow)
- *Alstroemeria ligtu* 'Hybrids' (Peruvian lily)
- *Anaphalis margaritacea* (pearly everlasting)
- *Asphodeline lutea*
- *Baptisia australis* (plains false indigo)
- *Buphthalmum salicifolium*
- *Catananche caerulea* (Cupid's dart)
- *Centaurea macrocephala*
- *Echinops ritro* (small globe thistle)
- *Eryngium* (sea holly)
- *Gypsophila paniculata* (baby's breath)
- *Heliopsis helianthoides scabra*
- *Limonium latifolium* (sea lavender)
- *Nepeta × faassenii* (catmint)
- *Solidago* (goldenrod)
- *Stachys byzantina* (lamb's ears).

## Shrubs for dry, sunny borders

Thorough soil preparation is essential before planting shrubs for dry, sunny border. First-rate shrubs for full sun and dry soil include:

- *Artemisia abrotanum* (lad's love, southernwood)
- *Artemisia absinthium* (common wormwood)

- *Brachyglottis* 'Sunshine' (better known as *Senecio* 'Sunshine')
- *Buddleja davidii* (butterfly bush)
- *Caryopteris × clandonensis*
- *Ceratostigma willmottianum* (Chinese plumbago)

▲ *Achillea is an ideal herbaceous perennial for growing in a dry, sunny border. Its flowers are perfect for cutting and displaying indoors.*

- *Choisya ternata* (Mexican orange blossom)
- *Cistus* (rock rose)
- *Cytisus × praecox* 'Warminster' (Warminster broom)
- *Genista aetnensis* (Mount Etna broom)
- *Hebe speciosa* (shrubby veronica)
- *Helichrysum serotinum* (curry plant)
- *Kolkwitzia amabilis* (Beauty bush)
- *Lavandula angustifolia* (lavender)
- *Lavatera* 'Rosea' (tree mallow)
- *Romneya coulteri* (tree poppy)
- *Rosmarinus officinalis* (rosemary)
- *Salvia officinalis* (common sage)—several colored leaf forms
- *Spartium junceum* (Spanish broom)

### CONTAINER GARDENING

Container gardening is popular in hot, sunny countries and a wide range of sun-loving plants can be grown in pots, tubs, and window boxes. If pots and tubs are put in groups, perhaps to one side of a patio, they can be watered more easily. Grouping containers in this way also helps keep them cooler than they would be if positioned separately. If pots and tubs at the back are difficult to reach for watering, tie a stiff bamboo cane, 4ft/1.2m long to the end length of hose pipe so that you can hold it out.

# gardening in shade

*Most gardens have a shady area, perhaps beside a house, a large tree, a fence or a hedge. Such places can be a problem, but they also create opportunities to grow a wider range of plants. In fact, once established, many plants grow in shade, in dry and moist soil.*

### Getting plants established

Plants in dry, shady areas are more difficult to establish than those in moisture-retentive soil. Dig dry areas thoroughly and mix in plenty of well-decayed garden compost or manure.

▲ *Many leafy plants thrive in shade. In this moist area,* Fatsia japonica *forms a perfect corner feature in a border and alongside a path.*

If the soil is impoverished, perhaps under trees or around the bases of shrubs, it will need a dusting of fertilizer. However, take care not to boost the growth of existing plants. Instead, add bonemeal to the planting hole, and a couple of times during the first year fork in a general fertilizer around the stem. Whatever happens, water plants regularly until they are established. Also lay a mulch, 3in/ 7.5cm thick around plants every spring. In moist, shady areas make sure that the soil is adequately drained by adding horticultural sand. The danger is that the plant roots may rot and die.

### Plants for dry shade

Many highly attractive shrubs are sufficiently resilient to survive these conditions, and they include *Mahonia aquifolium* (Oregon grapeholly), which has leathery, glossy green leaves and fragrant, rich yellow flowers in spring. *Ruscus aculeatus* (butcher's broom) is another tough shrub. *Symphoricarpos* (snowberry) and osmanthus are other suitable shrubs. Good herbaceous

perennials include *Anaphalis margaritacea*, with gray-green leaves and pearly white flowers in late summer. Its near relative, *Anaphalis triplinervis*, also grows in dry shade. For a taller and more dominant display, plant *Crambe cordifolia* (colewort), which grows 5–6ft/1.5–1.8m high. It has branching stems with white flowers in early summer. Epimediums grow about 12in/30cm high and will cover the soil with colorful leaves and flowers. *Persicaria affinis* (still better known as *Polygonum affine*) also makes good ground cover.

### Plants for moist shade

Several shrubs flourish in moist soil and shade, including camellias, whose blooms herald the approach of spring, *Elaeagnus angustifolia, Gaultheria shallon, Gaultheria procumbens* and *Fatsia japonica*, with its distinctively large, glossy green leaves. Herbaceous perennials include *Aruncus dioicus* (goatsbeard), *Brunnera macrophylla, Cimicifuga racemosa* (bugbane), the popular hostas, *Lysimachia nummularia* (creeping Jenny), *Pulmonaria angustifolia* (lungwort) and *Rodgersia pinnata*.

## Climbers and shrubs for a shady wall

It is inevitable that one side of a wall will be in shade. Fortunately, there are climbers that grow well, even on the northern, less congenial side of a wall.

*Garrya elliptica* is an evergreen wall shrub that grows on both sunny and shady sides of walls, but it flowers best on the brighter side. *Hydrangea anomala petiolaris* (climbing hydrangea) is a vigorous climber that does well on a north or north-east wall. Its creamy white flowers appear during early summer. *Jasminum nudiflorum* (winter jasmine) also grows well on an almost sunless, north-facing wall, and produces yellow flowers during winter. Several pyracanthas with attractive berries will grow against both sunny and shady walls.

## Shade-loving ferns

Most ferns grow in shade, in damp soil although some will thrive in dry areas that are fully shaded. Visit a specialist nursery and you will find a wide range of plants that are easy to grow and make a very useful addition to the shaded border. Ferns for moisture-retentive soil include *Asplenium scolopendrium* (hart's-tongue fern) (also known as *Phyllitis scolopendrium* or *Scolopendrium vulgare*), *Matteuccia struthiopteris* (ostrich fern); *Onoclea sensibilis* (sensitive fern) and *Osmunda regalis* (royal fern). Ferns for dry soil, as well as modestly moist soil, include the widely grown *Dryopteris filix-mas* (male fern), *Athyrium filix-femina* (lady fern) and *Polypodium vulgare* (the wall polypody).

▼ *Many ferns thrive in shade and moist soil, although some do well in dry soil. Here is a superb example of a fern with* **Fatsia japonica**.

# coastal gardening

*Strong winds and salt-laden sea spray that blows a long way inland are the two main problems encountered by gardeners on the coasts. Fortunately, many plants grow in these conditions, from conifers, shrubs, and herbaceous plants to bulbs and corms—with the help of a resilient boundary hedge.*

## Windbreaks and hedges

In small gardens you may have to rely on existing plants to reduce the wind's speed, but where a new boundary is possible, plant a windbreak formed by the conifer *Cupressus macrocarpa* (Monterey cypress). It eventually forms a hedge at least 30 ft/6m high. The hybrid × *Cupressocyparis leylandii* is sometimes recommended, but is far too vigorous for a small or even a medium-size garden. If you do grow it, be sure to clip it regularly.

## Shrubs for coastal gardens

The range of shrubs tolerant of salt spray is remarkably large and includes the fast-growing hybrid *Elaeagnus* × *ebbingei*, which takes about 12 years to grow to a height of 10–15ft/3–4.5m. Its evergreen, silvery gray leaves form an all-year background for other plants. *Griselinia littoralis* is slower growing and ideal as a hedge or as a specimen shrub in a border. It is evergreen, with thick, lustrous, apple-green leaves, but is often seen in one of its variegated forms such as 'Dixon's Cream', with leaves splashed creamy white.

If you seek a hardy, deciduous shrub with the bonus of bright orange berries from fall to late winter, choose *Hippophae rhamnoides* (sea buckthorn). It can also be planted to create a hedge. The berries are shunned by birds. The New Zealand shrub *Olearia macrodonta* (daisy bush) is evergreen, with leaves like holly leaves and masses of small, white, daisy-like flowers during midsummer, but it is slightly tender and best grown in warm areas. *Olearia* × *haastii* is a hardier form for cooler gardens.

▲ *Many plants help to soften the edges of paths, including the soft and silver-leaved lamb's ears (Stachys byzantina).*

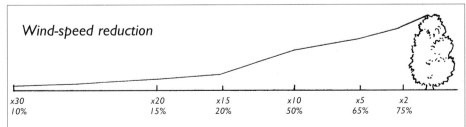

**Wind-speed reduction**

| x30 | | x20 | x15 | x10 | x5 | x2 |
| 10% | | 15% | 20% | 50% | 65% | 75% |

This simplified diagram shows how the benefit of a hedge or a windbreak can be felt up to a distance of 30 times the height of the hedge or shelter belt, although most of the protection is in the first one-third of this distance.

The hardy deciduous shrub *Tamarix tetrandra* (tamarisk) has an appealing wispy look. It grows 10–12ft/3–3.6m high. During late spring it bears bright pink flowers. Because it does not present a solid screen of foliage it often thrives close to the sea, but note that it dislikes chalky soil. If you need something to cover large areas, the suckering, thicket-forming, deciduous shrub *Symphoricarpos albus* (snowberry) has few rivals. It will soon cover a large bank, with the bonus of white berries from early fall to the first frosts. There are one or two superb varieties, including 'White Hedge'. If yellow flowers delight you, plant the deciduous shrub *Spartium junceum* (Spanish broom). Its rush-like green stems make it look evergreen, but it is the tiny bright yellow, fragrant flowers which bloom from early to late summer that have most appeal.

*Pittosporum tenuifolium* is not fully hardy in temperate climates but it is ideal if you want to create a hedge in a mild coastal garden. It is known for its pale-green leaves with wavy edges, which are borne on almost black stems.

## Herbaceous perennials for coastal areas

Once a wind-filtering hedge has been established, many herbaceous plants survive in coastal gardens. The wide range includes plants with attractive flowers, such as *Aster amellus* (Italian aster) and kniphofia hybrids (red-hot poker), and plants with attractive foliage. These include *Stachys byzantina* (lamb's ears) with silver-gray leaves. Other choice herbaceous perennials include:

- *Anemone × hybrida*
- *Centaurea macrocephala*
- *Crambe cordifolia*
- *Cynara scolymus* (globe artichoke)
- *Dierama pulcherrimum* (angel's fishing rod)
- *Eryngium alpinum* (alpine sea holly)
- *Eryngium varifolium* (Moroccan sea holly)
- *Kniphofia* hybrids
- *Phlomis russeliana*
- *Salvia superba*
- *Sedum spectabile*
- *Veronica spicata*.

▲ *Screens formed of laths nailed to a supporting framework will make an artificial windbreak while plants are established.*

### BULBS AND CORMS FOR COASTAL AREAS

- Anemone
- Chionodoxa
- Crocus
- Cyclamen
- Narcissus (daffodil)
- Scilla

▲ Kniphofias (*red-hot pokers*) *are ideal herbaceous perennials for planting in coastal areas. There are many hybrids to choose from.*

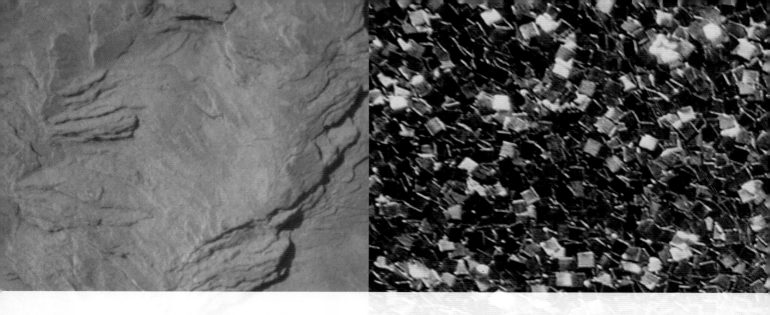

# constructing paths,
# steps, and trellises

*Many garden features, including paths, steps, and wall and freestanding trellises, can be constructed easily. The following pages explain how to lay paths made from many different materials, from paving slabs laid on mortar, which look best in formal gardens, to more versatile and less formal crazy paving, and gravel paths, which need side restraints to confine the gravel. They show how to build steps, from easy-to-construct log steps to paved steps for formal gardens, and erect trellises.*

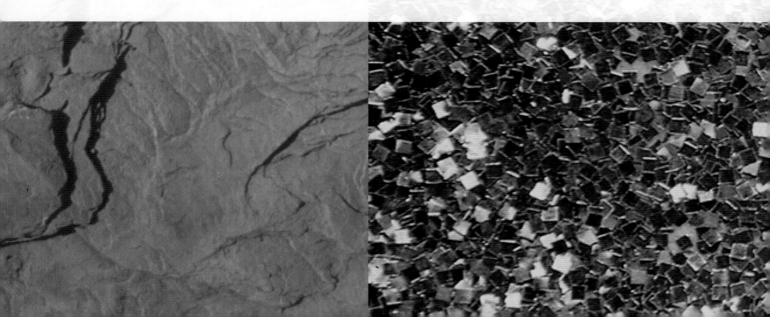

# laying gravel paths and drives

*Gravel paths and drives have an informal nature that blends with many plants and gardening styles. They are quick and relatively inexpensive to construct, and also act as a good alarm system—you can hear anyone coming by the crunch of their feet.*

## Basic construction

Paths and small drives are best made with ¼in/6mm pea gravel. Larger gravel is better suited to drives because it is less likely to spread sideways, and is not so easily picked up on shoes or scattered by the tires of automobiles.

Pea gravel and larger gravel settle in time, so be prepared after a few years to top up with another load. Weeds can be a problem, although weedkillers can be used. Do not use sodium chlorate if there are plants growing nearby because when the soil is constantly wet there is a risk that the sodium will spread through the soil and kill them. Instead, use a specific, non-residual path-clearing weedkiller.

## Constructing a path

You will need to edge the path with a restraint to hold and contain the gravel. In rustic areas you can use stout logs pegged into the soil, while straight paths in formal settings need concrete or wood edgings. Use concrete edging slabs 3ft/90cm long, 6in/15cm deep, and 1¾in/42mm thick, and with rounded tops. Alternative, you can use rough-cut planks, 6ft/1.8m long, 6in/15cm deep and 1in/2.5cm thick, coated with a wood preservative.

Dig out the line of the path, 3–4ft/90cm–1.2m wide and 6in/15cm deep. Place topsoil on shrub borders, but dispose of the subsoil. Put the side edging restraints in place and check that their tops are slightly above the level of the surrounding soil or grass. Use a level to check that the parallel edging is level. Then cement the concrete edging into place, or use stout wooden pegs to secure the wood. Line the base with clean rubble, to about 3in/7.5cm below the tops of the side restraints, and top up with pea gravel to about 1in/2.5cm below the rim.

## Constructing a gravel drive

Check that the area drains freely (see pages 90–91) and, if necessary, install drains. Mark out the area of the drive by using a garden hose and view it from all angles to make sure that it is right. Dig out the area to about 8in/20cm deep, removing perennial weed roots. The depth of the base depends on the weight and usage. If it is a standing area, a depth of 6in/15cm is sufficient.

Strong side restraints will prevent the gravel spreading. Concrete in place a row of bricks, with their tops about ¾in/18mm above the surface of the gravel. Bricks with one side beveled will cause least damage to car tires.

Fill the base with a 3in/7.5cm thick layer of clean, compacted rubble, then top up with gravel.

▶ *Gravel paths can be made more interesting with an attractive pattern of all-weather bricks or paving slabs. Lay these on concrete pads.*

# laying a shingle path

1 Dig out the area of the path 3–4ft/
90cm–1.2m wide and 6in/15cm deep.
Place topsoil on shrub borders, but dispose
of heavy, sticky clay. Make certain that all
perennial weeds are dug out.

2 Install strong side restraints formed of
concrete edging slabs 3ft/90cm long,
and cement them into place. Alternatively,
install strong planks of wood, each about
6ft/1.8m long.

3 Spread clean rubble over the base to
3in/7.5cm below the top of the side
restraints. If all perennial weeds have been
removed, add gravel immediately. If weeds
remain, use a water-permeable membrane.

4 Spread gravel to within 1in/2.5cm of
the top of the side restraints,
smoothing to even the surface. Gravel will
settle eventually, so be prepared to add
more later.

# laying paving slabs

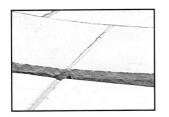

*Paving slabs can be used to create all-weather, firm-surface paths as well as patios. They are widely available, and look good on their own or when attractively combined with bricks and pebbles. Have a look at neighboring gardens for design ideas.*

### Wide range of slabs

Precast paving slabs are available in a wide range of colors, textures, shapes and sizes. Their thickness may also vary, but is usually 1¾–2in/42–50mm. While the most common size is 18in/45cm square, quarter- and half-sizes are available. Other sizes include 24in/60cm square and 30in/75cm long and 24in/60cm wide, but these are difficult for one

▲ *Paving slabs make all-weather surfaces for patios and terraces, helping to create a practical and attractive outdoor living area.*

person to handle. Hexagonal slabs are also available. Note that riven surfaces produce slipproof areas, and that smooth, brightly colored slabs may be used for formal paved areas, perhaps around a pool, but not in informal settings.

If the slabs arrive weeks before you can lay them, do not leave them in a pile. Instead, position two stout boards about 12in/30cm apart on a firm, level surface and at a rightangle to a wall. Position a slab near the wall, leaning against it, and place a piece of wood between the slab and the wall. Continue, with the other slabs, standing each one on its edge.

### Laying a path

Use a garden line to mark out the width and length of the path. Its width should blend with the garden. A path that is too narrow in a wide garden will look like a ribbon. The path needs to be broad enough for two people to walk side by side, but ideally, there should be room for a wheelchair with someone walking alongside it. A path should also be an attractive, eye-catching feature.

### Laying a patio

The preparation for laying a patio is exactly the same as for a path, but on a larger scale. Checking that it is absolutely level is vital. Where a patio adjoins a building it is essential that its surface is at least 6in/15cm below the damp course; this is usually seen as a continuous line of moisture-proof membrane or slate. If this is not possible, leave a 4in/10cm-wide and 6in/15cm-deep space between the slabs and the building and fill the gap with pea gravel to allow drainage.

---

#### CHECK LEVELS

Where levels need to be checked over a long distance, use a hose pipe filled with water and with a piece of clear plastic tubing inserted in  each end. On each piece of plastic tubing, make a mark 3in/7.5cm from the end. Tie one end of the hose pipe to a stout stick, positioning the mark on the plastic at the desired level. Check that the level of water in the hose pipe reaches the marks on the plastic. The unsecured end can then be moved down the garden to check the levels.

# laying paving slabs

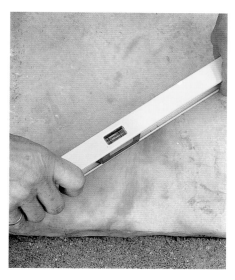

1 Make a 4in/10cm thick base of compacted clean rubble, then spread a layer of horticultural sand 2in/5cm thick. Use a garden rake to spread it evenly to create a firm, level surface.

2 Use the five-blob method to lay each slab: one in each corner and one in the center. This enables easy leveling of the slab and is a good way for beginners to lay slabs. Always wear gloves when cementing.

3 Check that each slab is level by using a level on one of its narrow edges. Next, check carefully that each slab is level with its neighbors by laying a level across each pair of paving slabs.

4 Carefully fill the gaps between slabs, using a stiff, dry mortar mix. Avoid spreading the mortar all over the slabs and clean off any loose mortar immediately as it stains permanently.

▲ *A strong, firm base is essential for all leisure surfaces, especially where edges overlap water features.*

# laying crazy paving

*Crazy paving paths, drives, and patios are traditionally formed from broken paving slabs, usually with a smooth surface and plain coloring. Increasingly, however, pieces of colored paving are being added to make the surface brighter and more attractive.*

### Constructing a crazy paving path

Side restraints are essential to prevent horticultural sand at the base from spilling out. Use wood 6in/15cm wide, 6ft/1.8m long and ¾in/18mm thick, and thinner flexible wood for a serpentine outline.

▲ *Crazy paving is a good material for where a twisting path is needed or where the contours of the ground vary in several directions.*

Begin by securing the side restraints with supporting pegs on the outer edge; this allows the edging to be removed at a later date, should a lawn abut the path. Spread out the crazy paving so that each piece can be seen clearly. Pieces with straight edges should be positioned along the sides. Then dig out the area of the path to about 6in/15cm deep, and install a compact layer of clean rubble 2in/25cm thick. Spread a similar thickness of horticultural sand over this, and rake it level, then lay an ¾in/18mm-thick layer of mortar over it. It is best to tackle long paths in several sections, each about 6ft/1.8m long. This insures that the mortar does not dry before each piece of crazy paving is laid on top.

Place the large, straight-edged pieces of crazy paving along the sides. Fill the gaps between them with smaller pieces, fitting them in like a jigsaw. It is essential that the surface is level, even though it may slope in several directions. Each piece of crazy paving must be laid on a firm bed of mortar. When the path is complete, fill any gaps between the pieces of paving with mortar, taking care not to smear it on the surface of the slab. Work it between the slabs until level with the surface, but with the center slightly lower to allow rain to drain away freely.

### Laying a natural stone path

Of all surfacing materials, natural stone paving creates the most informal effect, especially when plants are grown between the slabs. If natural stone is too expensive. use reconstituted stone. Because of its uneven thickness, natural stone paving is more difficult to lay than crazy paving and unless sawn (when it loses some of its charm) it has an irregular outline. Where plants are to be grown between them, the

---

**A CRAZY PAVING DRIVEWAY**

A slightly thicker base of compacted rubble to a depth of about 4in/10cm is needed for a driveway to allow for the weight of vehicles. Also, a base layer of concrete laid over the sand and compacted rubble is advisable if traffic is extra heavy. The crazy paving is laid on a bed of mortar on top of this.

# laying crazy paving

1 Use strong side restraints (concrete slabs or wood) and dig out the area of the path to 6in/15cm deep. Lay clean rubble 2in/5cm thick, and firm it.

2 Spread a layer of horticultural sand, 2in/5cm thick over the rubble. Leave a 2in/5cm space between the top of the side-restraints and the sand.

3 Spread a layer of mortar over the sand and position large, straight-sided pieces of broken paving along the edges. Check that the edges are level.

slabs can be laid on a 2in/5cm-thick layer of horticultural sand placed directly on firm soil. Alternatively, if a more functional path is desired, it can be laid in a similar way to crazy paving.

When laying a decorative natural stone path, first use strings to mark the edges of the path, then remove soil to about 3in/7.5cm deep. Firm the base, then lay horticultural sand 2in/5cm thick. Each slab is bedded onto the sand to hold it firm, but for extra rigidity lay each slab on five blobs of mortar. Fill the cracks where plants are not being used.

▶ *The relaxed appearance of crazy-paving paths suits informal gardens. Position plants along the sides to cloak the edges*

4 Lay smaller pieces of broken paving in the center of the path and fill the gaps between the stones with mortar to just below the surface.

# laying concrete pavers

*Concrete pavers or paving blocks may be used to construct hardwearing surfaces for paths and drives. They are sometimes called flexible pavers, because they are laid on a bed of horticultural sand and, if necessary, they can be lifted and relaid. Their popularity has increased in recent years.*

### Range of pavers

Pavers come in a wide range of colors and textures. They are usually 8in/20cm long, 4in/10cm wide, and 2in/5cm thick, although some come in 1½–2⅓in thickness. The edges on the upper side of some pavers are beveled. While most are straight-edged, they differ from house bricks in that they do not have recesses on the face side. Some pavers have wavy edges. These are known as fishtails—each brick closely interlocks with its neighbors to produce an extremely strong surface.

### Laying a path

Side restraints are essential to retain the foundations and pavers. Select the type of bond (see below), then form the pattern on a piece of flat ground and measure its width. This will indicate the distance between the two side restraints, which will be concrete, brick, or wood edgings. Dig out the path to the length and width you want it, and to a depth of 6in/15cm, then position the side restraints. Then lay clean, compacted rubble 3in/7.5 cm deep over the dug out area, and spread a layer of horticultural sand over the rubble. This layer should be the thickness of the paver less ⅜in/9mm below the top of the side restraints. This can be achieved by using a piece of wood 5in/13cm deep and a little wider than the path. Measure the width of the path and cut the ends of the board so that its center, when scraped along the sand inside the restraints, leaves the surface of the sand at the right depth. Do not compress the sand at this stage.

The pavers can then be positioned on the sand in the desired pattern. Their surfaces will protrude slightly above the top of the side restraints, and to compact them use a motorized plate-compactor (also known as a plate vibrator), which can be hired, or a thick, flat piece of wood laid on the surface and repeatedly tapped with a club hammer. This hand method is usually adequate for laying a path. When the pavers have been laid, cover the surface of the path with dry horticultural sand and brush it over the entire area. This is best done several times. Finish by watering the surface lightly.

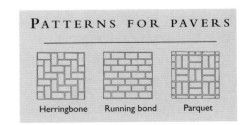

**PATTERNS FOR PAVERS**

| Herringbone | Running bond | Parquet |
|---|---|---|

▲ *Brick paths have a cottage garden informality. Staggering the joints creates a stronger surface than if bricks are laid with joints aligned.*

## Patterns for pavers

Pavers can be laid in several patterns, some of which are illustrated on page 78. Some patterns are complex and laying them requires expertise and skill, but the following are fairly simple to achieve:

❋ Running bond—easy to create and needs only a few half-pavers at the ends to complete the pattern (they can be cut with a hacksaw if a hydraulic stone splitter is not available). Bricks are laid lengthwise, with staggered joints.

❋ Cane-weave bond—creates an attractive surface, and is a pattern that does not require pavers to be cut. It is strong enough for paths, but not for drives. It is formed of rows of three parallel pavers with another paver positioned between and crossing them.

❋ Herringbone pattern—popular for paths and especially suitable for drives, since it forms a strong surface. It involves cutting a large number of pavers.

❋ Basketweave pattern—easy to lay, with two parallel bricks laid at a right-angles to two others. It is ideal for paths, but not for drives.

❋ Squared design—good for rectangular and square areas, for drives with light traffic, and for paths. Whole pavers are laid to form a square, with a half-brick in the center. This pattern requires a great deal of cutting, and a hydraulic stone splitter will be needed if you intend to pave a large area.

❋ Fishtail weave—forms a strong surface and is especially suitable for informal garden areas.

# laying concrete pavers

1 Dig out the area of the path to 6in/15cm deep and install strong side restraints. Compact a layer of clean rubble 3in/7.5cm thick in the base. The rubble needs to be broken up evenly.

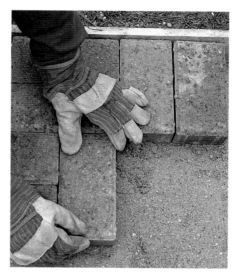

2 Spread horticultural sand loosely over the rubble, so that its surface is the same thickness as the paver less ⅜in/9mm below the top of the side restraints. Lay the pavers on top of the sand.

3 Compact the pavers by using a motorized plate-compactor (also known as a plate vibrator) or a thick piece of wood laid on the surface and hit with a club hammer repeatedly.

4 When the surface of the pavers is level with the side restraints, cover them with dry horticultural sand. Brush the sand over the surface. Repeat this once, and then water the entire area.

# choosing and installing edgings

*Edgings should be both functional and attractive, marking the edges of borders, lawns, paths, and drives, and harmonizing with their surroundings. Edgings range from corrugated plastic strips to bricks, concrete, and logs, and some are quickly installed while others need to be mortared in place.*

### Bricks and paving blocks

Frost-resistant bricks and concrete pavers create attractive edgings alongside flower beds and gravel drives and paths. They are placed upright and concreted into position, and because they are only 4in/10cm wide they can be used around curved as well as straight edges. Bricks make an informal edging if they are placed at an angle of 45°, with one brick leaning against another. Between half and one-third of each brick is buried in the soil, and this keeps the edging in position without any need for mortar.

### Tiles

Glazed and unglazed tiles, usually 9in/23cm long and 6in/15cm deep make decorative edgings. Placed directly in the soil they do not need mortar.

### Strips

These are varied, ranging from shaped concrete edging to plastic strips. Concrete edgings are usually 3ft/90cm long, 6in/15cm deep, and 1¾in/42mm thick, with rounded or crenated (notched) tops. They are ideal for edging straight gravel paths and drives, and must be concreted into place. Corrugated green plastic edging strips, bought in rolls and in several depths, are best used to edge borders. Their corrugated shape prevents the edges of lawns from being cut straight.

▲ *Log rolls create attractive edgings for informal borders. They are easily installed and can be bought in several heights.*

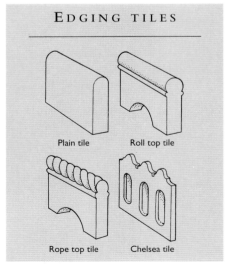

**EDGING TILES**

Plain tile

Roll top tile

Rope top tile

Chelsea tile

# installing edging tiles

1 When installing an edging for a straight border, first stretch a garden line along the edge. Dig out a narrow trench 3–4in/7.5–10cm deep.

2 Position the tiles so that two-thirds will be buried when the job is complete. Check that each tile is upright and extends uniformly above the border.

3 Draw soil around the base of each tile and firm it to the level of the surrounding soil. Take care not to push the tiles out of line.

## Wooden edgings

These range from log rolls, which blend with informal areas, to planks of wood, used to edge straight paths. To insure these planks have a long life, use a wood preservative.

Log rolls make an attractive edging especially for meandering paths in informal and rustic gardens. They are made by securing one-third to half-sections of logs to galvanized wires, They are available in 3½ft/1m lengths and in several heights, including 6in/ 15cm, 12in/30cm, and 18in/45cm. These rolls are installed very simply by inserting the log roll into a narrow trench to about half the depth of the edging, and firming the soil around it.

Whole logs make attractive edgings for straight and meandering paths in informal gardens. Select logs about 4in/10cm thick. Make a shallow depression at the side of the path to be edged, put the logs in position along it, and firm the soil. Secure the logs with wooden pegs.

### GRAVEL GULLEYS

Gulleys, often seen around bowling greens, may be dug around a lawn and filled with pea gravel. A gulley 6–12in/15–30cm wide makes an attractive edge and improves a lawn's ability to drain freely. Where there is a risk of the lawn edge being trodden on and crumbling, install planks of wood with their surfaces level with the lawn. Then fill the gulley with pea gravel to within 2in/5cm of the lawn's surface.

▲ Bricks placed at a shallow angle make attractive edging in an informal garden. They do not need to be cemented into position.

# constructing garden steps

*Garden steps can be more than just a safe and convenient way of getting from one level to another. They should form attractive features, with proportions and style that unify them with the rest of the garden, and materials that harmonize with their surroundings.*

### The structure of steps

To be sure that steps are easy to walk on they must have the right proportions. Steps have their own technical vocabulary:

⚙ Base stone—the stone at the bottom of a flight of steps. It is essential where steps lead directly onto a lawn.

⚙ Flight—the complete run of steps.

⚙ Landing—an extra wide area of tread, often used as a resting area on a long flight of steps.

⚙ Overhang (also known as the "nosing") the distance by which the edge of a tread overhangs the riser. An overhang gives steps a professional appearance.

⚙ Riser—the distance between the tread on one step and the tread of the one above. Usually, 4–7in/10–18cm.

⚙ Tread—the surface which is walked on. A tread is usually 12–18in/30–45cm deep, with a slight slope from back to front so that water drains away freely.

⚙ Width of steps—for two people to use the steps side by side, steps need to be at least 4½ft/1.3m wide. For one person, 3ft/75cm is sufficient.

### Types of steps

There is a wide range of styles to choose from for garden steps, from formal to rustic, and they may be made in many different materials.

⚙ Cut-in steps—built into slopes and made easily from paving slabs and bricks. The shape of the steps has to be cut in, allowing slightly more depth for strong foundations. The paving slabs form the treads, with bricks as the risers.

⚙ Free-standing steps—required where a bank is almost vertical, and the steps are built on a level surface but with the top step abutting and level with the top of the bank. Paving slabs and bricks are the easiest materials to use. These steps need more foundation material and concrete than cut-in types, so take longer to make.

⚙ Log steps—ideal for rustic gardens, and used mainly on gentle slopes. The level areas between the steps can be formed of grass, but for all-year use a thin coating of gravel is better. The steps (risers) are formed of logs 4–6in/10–15cm thick, or stout, roughly cut pieces of wood coated in plant-friendly wood preservative.

Start from the base of the slope and bed the first log slightly into the soil to give it greater stability. Secure it in position with two stout pegs. Place gravel behind the log, compact it, level the surface, and secure another log. Shredded bark can be used instead of gravel, but birds often scatter it and bark can be slippery in wet weather and on a steep slope.

---

## MEASURING STEPS

To make steps comfortable to use, it is essential that the depth of the tread and the riser are right. Before deciding on these distances, try walking up and down steps in gardens belonging to friends. Take the measurements and use them to build your steps.

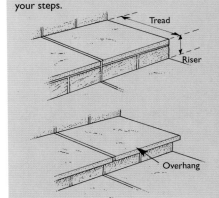

# making cut-in steps

1 Start at the base of the flight of steps and dig out the soil to a depth of about 6in/15cm. Lay clean rubble 2–3in/5–7.5cm thick evenly over the entire area, and firm it.

2 Spread a layer of horticultural sand 2in/5cm deep over the rubble. Firm it and rake level, using a level. Set paving slabs on top, each one on a layer of mortar.

3 When the mortar has set, use bricks to form the riser which will support the next step. Check that they are level. Dig out and prepare the base for the next level.

▲ A flight of steps built of frost-resistant bricks makes an attractive yet practical feature in a cottage garden or an informal area.

4 Lay and firm clean rubble at the bottom, then lay and firm a layer of horticultural sand. Use a long, straight-edged piece of wood to check that the surface is level.

# erecting trellis

*Trellis has several roles in a garden. It provides a good opportunity to grow more climbers, and a freestanding trellis erected near a boundary creates privacy. It can also be used inside a garden to form an arbor and as a screen, separating one garden area from another.*

### Erecting a wall trellis

Direct your attention to the wall before securing the trellis. Check that it is sound and will hold wall-fixings when drilled. Repaint the wall if necessary. Measure it and buy trellis to fit the area,

▲ *Trellis is an attractive feature when covered with plants. It is easy to attach trellis to a wall and to build a freestanding trellis structure.*

and make sure that the eventual spread of the climbers you intend to plant will equal the dimensions of the trellis. A vigorous climber on an inadequate trellis is a recipe for disaster.

The trellis needs to be positioned against the wall so that its base is 9–12in/ 23–30cm above the soil. Use a level to get its positioning right, and when you are satisfied that it is level, mark the positions of the corners of the trellis on the wall and the spots where the holes need to be drilled, so it can be returned to the same place. Remove the trellis and drill the holes, countersinking them to make certain that the head of each screw will be flush with the surface of the wood. Reposition the trellis against the wall, insert a screw into each hole, and tap each one gently to mark its position.

Remove the trellis and use a masonry drill to make each hole, then insert a wall-fixing. Put the trellis back in position and screw it into place. Tighten each screw just partially at first, then when all screws are in position, tighten them fully. Always use galvanized screws to secure trellis.

Plants with a scrambling habit are best grown on a trellis fixed to battens that position it 1in/2.5cm from the wall. The stems can then entangle with the trellis.

### Constructing freestanding trellis

Square- and diamond-shaped trellis panels may be used for a freestanding trellis, but they must have wooden battens, secured to upright posts, 4–5in/10–15cm square, cemented at least 18in/45cm into the ground. To create a screen 6ft/1.8m high, posts measuring 8ft/2.4m long are needed, with trellis panels 6ft/1.8m long and 5ft/1.5m high. Use a garden line to indicate the position of the trellis and mark 12in/30cm square holes every 6ft/1.8m apart for the posts. Dig holes 18in/45cm deep.

#### ON SLOPING GROUND

Where ground slopes it is usually necessary to step the trellis panels. The top of the post on the lower end needs to be 1in/2.5cm above the top of the trellis. Each piece of trellis needs to be level and aligned with its neighbors.

The easiest way to begin erecting a free-standing trellis is to lay two posts on the ground and secure the trellis to it, using galvanized nails, so that its top is about 1in/2.5cm below the top of each post. Then, with the help of two people, lift the trellis and position each post in a hole. Use a level to check that the posts are upright and the trellis is level. Wedge each post upright with pieces of wood.

Prepare the next panel by nailing it to a post. Put the post in a hole and secure the trellis to the post erected just before it. Continue erecting the trellis in this way. Recheck the alignment of trellis and posts with a level, then mix some concrete and pour it into the holes around the posts. Finally, about a week later, nail a cap to the top of each post. This helps to prevent water entering the end grain of the wood and rotting it.

# erecting a wall trellis

1 First, check that the trellis fits the area of the wall and is not too large. Position the trellis and mark the drilling holes on it, then take the trellis down and drill the holes.

2 Position the trellis on the wall, level it, and mark the positions of the drilling holes on the wall, using a pencil, a bradawl. or just the tip of the drill.

▲ *The range of ornamental trellis is wide and includes patterns with diamond-shaped squares, as well as the traditional pattern of squares.*

3 Drill each hold marked on the wall and insert a wall fixing, tapping it gently into position. The fixing must be the same size as the screws that will be used to secure the trellis to the wall.

4 Screw the trellis to the wall, using a normal screwdriver or a drill that can double as a screwdriver. When the screws are in place, do not tighten them excessively since this can damage the trellis.

# getting the basics right

You do not need many gardening skills to create a good garden, but it helps if you know how to improve the soil and plant trees to give them an excellent start. Here is a guide to the best way to garden, with ideas on digging and draining, making compost piles, and staking tall plants. You will also find tips on assessing the soil, lighting up the garden, knowing when you might need to apply lime, and how to stock your shed with all the right equipment for your needs. In short, everything you need to know that will get your garden off to a good start.

# the tools you will need

*Garden tools should be a pleasure to use, as well as being functional. Buy the best quality that you can afford and, if possible, always handle pieces of garden equipment before buying them to check that their weight and size suit you. Looking after your tools will insure that they last for many years.*

### Digging and forking tools

✿ Garden spades—in several sizes, with blades about 11in/27cm long and 7½in/19cm wide; border spades have blades 9in/23cm long and 5½in/14cm wide. Some spades have blades with tread-like ledges that enable more pressure to be applied by foot to force the blade into the soil. Most spades have handles 28in/72cm long (the distance between the top of the handle and the top of the blade). Some are longer at 32in/82cm.

✿ Garden forks—for heavy digging and for breaking down large clods of soil in spring. Also for shallow digging between shrubs and herbaceous plants. There are several sizes: digging forks have four tines (prongs), each 11in/27cm long, while the tines on border forks are 9in/23cm long. Potato forks have flat-sectioned tines about 11in/27cm long.

### Hoeing tools

✿ Draw hoes—a handle of plastic or wood, 5–6ft/1.5–1.8m long is attached through a swan-like neck to a sharp-edged cutting blade. Have several uses, including forming shallow drills into which seeds can be sown, and severing annual weeds at ground level.

✿ Weeding hoes—wood or plastic handle 5–6ft/1.5–1.8cm long is attached to a forward-pointing blade used to sever weeds and to create a fine tilth. When using a weeding hoe, walk backward.

✿ Onion hoes—resemble draw hoes, but are only 12–15in/30–38cm long and are used to sever weeds around young plants.

### Raking

✿ Metal rakes—sometimes called iron rakes, are used for leveling soil. They have heads 10–12in/25–30cm wide, each with 10–14 teeth 2½–3in/6–7.5cm long. The wood or plastic handle is 5–6ft/1.5–1.8m in length.

✿ Landscape rakes—used to level large areas. They have a wooden head, 28in/72cm wide with 3in/7.5cm long tines spaced 1½in/36mm apart.

### Planting tools

✿ Hand trowels— a metal scoop attached to handle 6–12in/15–30cm long.

✿ Dibbles—range in size and are used to make planting holes for cabbages and other brassicas in vegetable plots, and small holes for seedlings in seed trays.

✿ Bulb planters—are for planting bulbs in grass, they remove a core of turf.

◄ *Garden spades and forks have multiple uses, including digging the soil in winter, in preparation for sowing and planting in spring.*

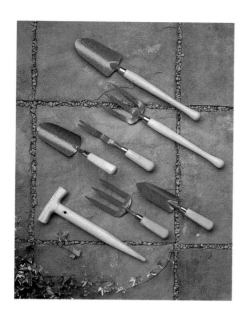

▲ *Trowels, hand forks and large dibbles are used to plant small, ornamental plants and cabbages, cauliflowers, and Brussels sprouts.*

## Cutting and sawing

✲ Pruners—these are designed to cut stems and they have two cutting actions: the anvil type has a blade that cuts against a firm, flat surface, while the bypass pruner has two parrot-shaped blades that cross each other.

✲ Saws—range from Grecian saws (with a curved blade and teeth that cut on the pull stroke) to large saws for cutting thick wood.

## Lawn tools

✲ Rakes—are used to rake debris. Range from spring-tined types to rubber and plastic-tined models.

✲ Half-moon edging irons—used to cut lawn edges, so need to be kept sharp.

✲ Edging shears—used to cut long grass at the edges of lawns. They have strong handles usually 32in/82cm long and shears about 8in/20cm long.

✲ Hand shears—used to cut hedges as well as long grass.

▲ *Essential tools for pruning and clipping are the long-handled saw (top), garden shears (center), and hand saw (bottom).*

◄ *Weeding and draw hoes are used for weeding and digging seed drills, while edging irons are for straightening lawn edges.*

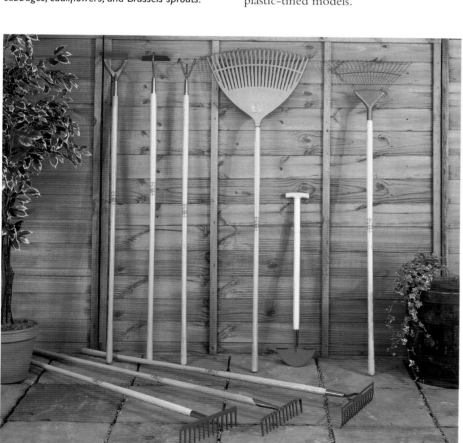

# draining soil

*If soil is constantly saturated with water, the roots of many cultivated plants will decay. Some plants thrive in moisture-saturated soil and they can be grown in bog gardens, but most garden plants need soil that is well-drained to a depth of 2ft/60cm through most of the year.*

### The need for drains

If water is continually seen on the soil surface, drains are needed. Rushes and reeds growing in an area are also signs of excess water. The need for drains can also be established by digging a hole 4ft/1.2m deep, in the fall, and monitoring the level of water in it through the winter. If the water remains within 9in/23cm of the surface, land drains are required.

### Drainage options

There are choices between rubble drains, clay pipes, and perforated plastic tubing.

⊛ Rubble drains—relatively cheap to install if you have sufficient rubble available. Only one main drain is usually needed, with minor drains feeding into it, leading to a soakaway or a ditch. The spacings between side drains depend on the soil: 12–15ft/3.6–4.5m for clay soils and 40ft/12m for sandy ones. Dig the trenches 12–18in/30–45cm wide and 2–2½ft/60–75cm deep, with a minimum slope of 1 in 90 toward the outlet. Fill the trenches about half-full with rubble, and place thick polyethylene over it to

prevent the soil clogging it up. Add soil until level with the surface, then firm it.

⊛ Clay pipe drains—a traditional way of draining soil. Use unglazed clay pipes 12in/30cm long and 5in/13cm wide to form main drains, with 4in/10cm-wide pipes as side drains. Like rubble drains they are laid in trenches  Lay gravel 3in/7.5cm thick in each trench. Place the pipes on top and cover the joints with pieces of broken tiles or sheets of double-thick polyethylene. Over this lay shingle 4in/10cm thick, and strong polyethylene sheeting, and add a layer of well-drained soil. Clay pipes are now difficult to find and plastic tubing may have to be substituted.

⊛ Perforated plastic tubing—quicker to install than pipe drains, this is corrugated for extra strength and bought in 82ft/25m rolls with a 4in/10cm or 3in/7.5cm bore.

### Soakaways or ditches

It is essential to direct surplus water into a soakaway or a ditch. If you are fortunate enough to have a ditch, allow the end of the pipe to extend into the ditch and

cover it with netting to keep out vermin. However, most gardeners have to construct a soakaway at the lowest point. Dig a hole about 4ft/1.2m square and deep; its base must be 12in/30cm below the lowest part of the trench. Fill to half its depth with clean rubble, then to within 12in/30cm of the surface with gravel. Cover this with double-thick polyethylene and fill up with soil.

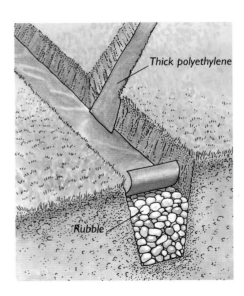

Thick polyethylene

Rubble

▲ *Rubble drains are relatively inexpensive, especially in a new garden and where a builder has left a mass of clean rubble.*

# installing plastic drains

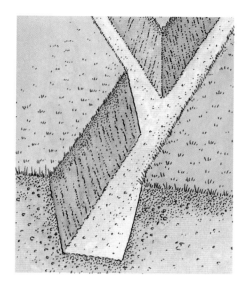

1 Use string to indicate the width and position of the main and side drains. Dig out the drain trenches, making a slight slope toward a drainage ditch or a sump. Take care not to break the edges of the trenches.

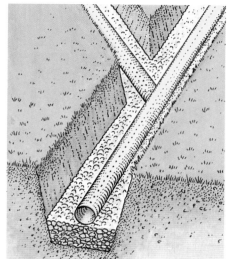

2 Spread a layer of clean gravel 3in/7.5cm deep in each trench and lay the plastic pipe in the center. Where each side drain meets the main pipe, cut its end at an angle so they fit together snugly.

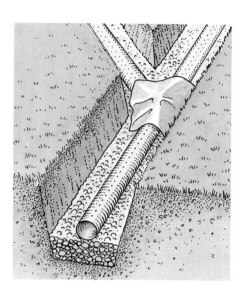

3 Spread a double thickness of strong polyethylene over the joints to prevent soil entering the pipes and blocking them. Use a little gravel to hold the polyethylene in place while the other joints are covered.

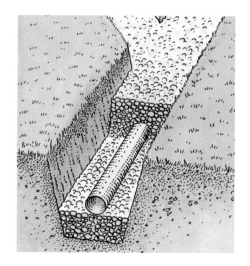

4 Cover all the pipes with a layer of gravel 3in/7.5cm deep. Over this position a layer of strong polyethylene and then top up with well-drained soil. Mound the soil a little to allow for settlement.

▲ Well-drained soil is essential for most garden plants. If their roots are perpetually in water, they will decay and will eventually die.

# preparing the soil

*Digging is a traditional part of gardening and is mainly performed in late fall or early winter to prepare the soil for crops during the following year. Single-digging (to the depth of a spade's blade) is the normal way to prepare soil for planting.*

## Why dig?

Apart from making a garden neat and tidy, digging has several other benefits. It enables air and water to penetrate the top 10in/25cm of soil, and drains excess water into the subsoil. However, if lower layers are impervious, water may remain on the surface. If this happens, install drains (see pages 90–91).

When the topsoil is broken up, roots are better able to penetrate the soil. Also, annual weeds become buried and perennial weeds can be removed. Digging also allows garden compost and well-decayed manure to be mixed with the soil. The process of digging usually leaves large lumps of soil on the surface, and winter weather will break them down to a fine tilth by spring. Digging may also leave soil pests such as the larvae of craneflies and cockchafers on or near the surface for birds to pick off.

## Single digging

Digging is a systematic activity, and one you will soon master. Do not dig too quickly, or for too long at a time. As you progress, you will find your own rhythm and the work can becomes satisfying and less strenuous.

## Rotating crops

If vegetables of a similar type are grown continuously on the same piece of land, it depletes the soil of the plant foods necessary for the healthy growth of those vegetables, while encouraging the build up of pests and diseases. Rhubarb and asparagus are permanent crops and are left in the same place, but for other types of vegetables the plot needs to be divided into three and the different groups of vegetables in the following order.

❀ Root crops—when preparing the soil, do not add lime or manure. Instead, rake in a general fertilizer a couple of weeks before planting or sowing. Root vegetables include beetroot, carrots, Jerusalem artichokes, parsnips, potatoes, salsify, and scorzonera.

❀ Brassicas—dig in well-decayed manure or garden compost if the soil lacks humus. If it is acid, apply lime in late winter and a general fertilizer prior to sowing or planting. Brassicas include broccoli, Brussels sprouts, cabbages, cauliflowers, radishes, rutabagas, and turnips.

❀ Other crops—dig in well-decayed manure or garden compost. If the soil is acid, dust it with lime in late winter and rake in a general fertilizer before sowing or planting. Vegetables include eggplants, beans, bell peppers, celery, leeks, salad vegetables, marrows, onions, peas, corn, and tomatoes.

### NO-DIGGING PHILOSOPHY

This has many advocates but is successful only where the soil is light, well drained and aerated, and free from perennial weeds. Crops are grown on top of compost laid regularly on the surface of the soil. However, it can be expensive to buy compost each year. Where soils have a high percentage of clay there is no alternative but to dig, and to mix in well-decomposed compost or manure.

▶ *Digging flower and vegetable beds in winter improves the soil, and makes the entire garden look tidier during the winter months.*

# single digging

1 The first step is to dig a trench 10–12in/25–30cm deep and 12in/30cm wide across one end of the plot of land. Move the soil to the other side of the plot.

2 Skim off weeds and grass from the adjacent strip of soil and place them in the trench. Add well-decomposed manure or garden compost to the trench.

3 Insert the blade of the spade into the soil, at right-angles to the trench and the width of the blade. This will enable a block of soil to be removed easily.

4 Push the blade into the soil and parallel to the trench, lift out the block of soil, and place it upside down in the trench. Repeat this action all along the trench.

# compost piles

*Digging in garden compost made from kitchen waste and soft, non-woody parts of garden plants is an inexpensive and environmentally friendly way to feed and aerate the soil and aid moisture retention. Compost can be dug into the soil in winter, or be used as a mulch in spring and summer.*

### Making garden compost

Garden and kitchen waste can just be placed in a pile on the ground and left to decay, but this is not the best way to make compost. Instead, place it in layers in compost bins. It is best to have three bins: one being filled; another that was filled months before and whose contents are rotting down; and a third holding decayed compost that is being emptied and used currently in the garden.

Compost bins that measure 3–4½ft/1–1.3m high and are square—allowing air to enter the compost without rapidly drying it out—are best. Proprietary types are available, while home-made bins built from planks of wood 6–9in/15–20cm wide with 2in/5cm-wide gaps between them, work extremely well. Wire-netting bins can be used, but they need to be lined with punctured black polyethylene sheets to prevent rapid drying.

### Filling a compost bin

Place a compost bin on a well-drained piece of soil and put a thick layer of coarse material such as straw, 9–12in/ 23–30cm thick, at the bottom. Tread it firm, then add vegetable waste such as grass cuttings, spent annuals, weeds, and soft parts of plants, in a layer 6in/15cm thick. When using only grass cuttings, make each layer thinner because thick layers become compacted, excluding air.

The next stage is to lay garden soil 2in/5cm thick on top. Finally, water it thoroughly and dust it with sulfate of ammonia at 2oz/14g per 1sq yd/1sq m. Alternatively, you can buy proprietary compost activators and use as instructed.

◀ *Circular compost bins made of wire netting are easily made. Line the sides with punctured polyethylene to keep the compost moist.*

Continue building up the layers and, when the heap reaches the top of the bin, water the contents thoroughly and cover with 1–2in/2.5–5cm of soil. Place a plastic sheet over the top and secure it to prevent the compost from becoming too wet or dry. After about six months in winter (less in summer) the compost will be ready to be used.

## Medley of waste

In addition to soft garden plants, other materials can be added to a compost heap, including newspapers (but not glossy magazines), crushed eggshells, pea pods, potato peelings, and tea bags. Do not use grass cuttings if the lawn has been treated recently with a hormone weedkiller. Do not add perennial weeds to the compost.

Mix up the waste as it is put into a compost bin because thick layers of the same material can prevent air from entering the mixture.

Well-decomposed
garden compost,
ready for use

Decomposing
compost

Compost bin
currently being filled

▲ Use three compost bins in a sequence to insure a regular supply of well-decomposed garden compost.

### LEAF MOLD

The leaves of deciduous shrubs and trees can be collected in the fall and placed in layers 6–9in/15–23cm thick in a compost bin, with a sprinkling of sulfate of ammonia between them. Leaves from evergreen shrubs and trees are unsuitable, while leaves from poplar, plane, and sycamore take longer to decompose than those from beech and oak.

Leaves can also be encouraged to decay by putting them in perforated bags of black polyethylene (a good way to decompose leaves in small gardens). Add a sprinkling of sulfate of ammonia between the layers, and, when the bag is full, add water and seal the top. About six months later the leaf mold can be used as a mulch or dug into the soil. It is an excellent reconditioning treatment for soil.

▲ The range of proprietary composters is wide and includes this green design which is attractive yet practical for a small garden.

# staking and supporting plants

*Many plants, from hardy annuals to fruit trees, need support. Those used to support ornamental plants must be unobtrusive, whereas for fruit trees they need to be strong, functional, and durable. Here is a good range of ways to support plants in your garden.*

### Hardy annuals

Each year these plants grow from seed and create spectacular summer displays. Many of them benefit from support.
⚙ Twiggy supports—also called pea sticks, these are cut from beech, hornbeam, or birch trees and are needed in several sizes, from 12in/30cm to 4ft/1.2m long. Insert them among young plants immediately after their final thinning. Push them firmly into the soil, and use pruners to trim their tops to just below the expected height of the fully grown plants.

### Herbaceous perennials

These are plants that die down to soil level in the fall and develop fresh shoots in the spring. Not all herbaceous plants need support but when they do, try:
⚙ Twiggy sticks—like those used for annuals, but usually stronger and longer. Insert them around young plants in spring and early summer. Many herbaceous perennials are self-supporting but others, especially those with a multitude of stems, require support.
⚙ Stakes and string—a good way to support dahlias. Push three stakes, 4ft/ 1.2m long about 9in/23cm into the soil to form a triangle around a plant. Then encircle the plant with several tiers of string looped tightly around each stake.
⚙ Metal supports—several proprietary types are available, one of the most popular having two halves, each with a curved top to form a circle, which encloses the stems.

▲ *Support sweet peas on a framework of sticks tied together with garden string, or with a twiggy stick. Pole beans also need support.*

**Herbaceous supports**

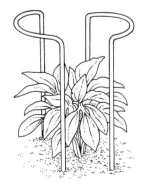

*Sticks and string*          *Twiggy sticks*          *Metal supports*

## Trees

Strong supports are essential to prevent wind breaking branches and trunks. Choose from the following:

⚙ Vertical supports—the easiest way to support ornamental and fruit bearing trees. Use a stake of stout ash, spruce, or chestnut, which, when knocked about 12in/30cm into the soil will have its top slightly below the lowest branch. Knock the stake into the hole before the tree is planted. Position the stake on the windward side, using proprietary ties to secure the trunk and prevent it rubbing against the stake. This is the best way to support an ornamental tree in a lawn, allowing grass to be cut neatly close to the tree and its support.

⚙ Oblique supports—this involves inserting a stake at a 45° angle into the soil, with its top slightly below the lowest branch. The top of the stake must face into the prevailing wind. This is often used to replace a broken stake.

⚙ H-stakes—used after a tree has been planted. Knock two stakes into the soil, one on each side of the trunk, and secure a cross-stake to each of them, a little below the lowest branch. Secure the cross-stake to the trunk.

## Vegetables

Supports for vegetables need to remain strong through summer. Some vegetables need support into the fall as well.

⚙ Pole beans—use bean poles 8–9ft/2.4–2.7m long inserted about 12in/30cm apart, in two rows 18–24in/45–60cm apart, with their tops inclined toward each other and crossed, making an inverted V-shape. Position a horizontal pole along the top and tie it in place. An alternative method is to use three or four poles to form a wigwam up which plants can clamber.

⚙ Peas—use twiggy sticks or large-mesh wire netting, 3ft/90cm to 4ft/1.2m high, held upright by canes.

⚙ Fava beans—insert a stout stake at the ends of the row, and encircle the plants with strong string tied to it.

▶ *Herbaceous perennials with masses of stems can be supported with twiggy sticks pushed into the ground when plants are young.*

### Tree supports

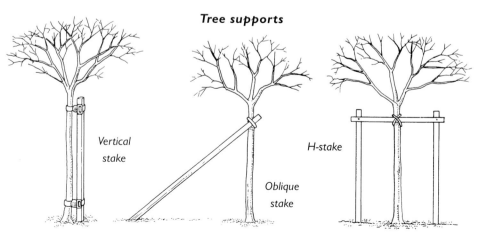

*Vertical stake*

*Oblique stake*

*H-stake*

### SUPPORTING HEAVILY LADEN FRUIT BRANCHES

Sometimes, branches of fruit trees become so heavily laden with fruit that they bow downward. Where this happens use Y-shaped pieces of wood knocked into the soil beneath a laden branch to give it support. Alternatively, drive a stake 10ft/3m long into the soil near the trunk, from which branches can be supported by stout strings.

# choosing and erecting a shed

*A dry, vermin-proof shed is essential in a garden to store gardening tools and a wide range of other equipment. Always buy the largest shed you can. The average size is about 8ft/2.4m by 6ft/1.8m. Before erecting or installing it, level the site it is to stand on, and firm the ground.*

### Range of sheds

Sheds come in many shapes and sizes, some with a traditional apex roof (the ridge along the center), others with a roof that slopes from front to back. A few have a combination of a back-sloping roof and a greenhouse area at one end. There are also summerhouses that combine garden room with storage space. When choosing a shed, its style should suit the style of your garden, even if it is to be sited at the far end of your garden (if gasolene or kerosene is to be stored in your shed, do not locate it close to your house). Put your shed on a patch of poor soil or position it to hide unsightly features. You could camouflage an unattractive shed by putting a freestanding trellis in front of it. You will need an all-weather path to connect the shed to the house.

Most sheds are made of wood. Rigid PVC is an alternative, but it is not always considered attractive. Wooden sheds are made of a timber frame and clad with overlapping or tongue-and-grooved planks of wood. The type of wood influences the price of the shed and its longevity. Softwood (usually deal and often fir or pine) must be pressure-treated with a preservative, while more costly timber such as western red cedar has greater resistance to water but still needs to be coated regularly with cedar oil.

### Erecting a shed

A firm, level base is essential. First, clear the area of vegetation and overhanging branches. A shed can be erected directly on timber bearers, usually 2–2½in/ 5–6.5cm square, pressure-treated with a wood preservative, and laid directly on soil. However, it is better to lay paving slabs. Mark out on the ground an accurately square area for the shed. Use a level to check its horizontal alignment. Then use flat paving slabs, 18in/45cm square or 2ft/60cm-square to form a

base. Space the slabs 12–18in/30–45cm apart, and in three rows. The timber bearers are laid on top, and at right angles to the timbers that secure the floor of the shed.

If the shed is made of softwood, coat all surfaces and edges thoroughly with a wood preservative. Then position the flow and recheck the levels. Two or three people will be needed to build the shed quickly and easily. Screw or bolt the sides into position, holding each piece in place until it is secure, then position the roof and secure it. Cover the roof in roofing felt and to stick the edges of the felt together with adhesive. The windows will need glazing. Non-opening window panes can be secured by glazing sprigs (or panel pins). Windows that open are more securely bedded in a layer of putty.

## GAZEBOS

These are distinctive features which, by definition, let people gaze out onto a garden. They have a long history. In early Persian gardens they evolved from dovecotes which were located close to each corner. Gazebos make beautiful focal points when positioned toward the end of a large, broad lawn. Alternatively, position the gazebo in a corner from where there is a wide view of the garden. A gazebo generally has a wooden frame, with wooden latticework at the back, and an ornate roof. Simple ones can be made from four stout, upright posts supporting a pitched roof. The back and roof are clad in latticework painted white.

◀ *Plant shrubs and climbers and tall biennials, around a shed to blend it into the garden and harmonize with the plants growing there.*

# erecting a shed

1 The base of a shed can be laid directly on strong timber bearers. However, laying paving slabs first and then laying the bearers on top makes a more substantial and frostproof base.

2 Ask a couple of friends to help you put the sides and ends of the shed into position. These may be screwed or bolted together. The finished construction must be square and upright.

3 When the ends and sides are in position, put the roof in place. Lodge the ends of the roof firmly in their sockets, and check all round the shed to ensure that it overhangs evenly around the sides.

4 Place the roofing felt in position: it can be laid longitudinally or across the ridge. Use galvanized, large-headed nails to secure it, and coat the overlaps with a roofing adhesive.

# electricity in a garden

*Electric power in a garden means you can use a wide range of equipment, including heated propagation units in greenhouses, lights in sheds, fountains, ponds, and decorative lights on a patio. But the wiring must be installed correctly and safely by a qualified professional electrician.*

◄ *Garden ponds, with spotlights illuminating fountains and subdued lighting on other areas, are attractive in the evenings.*

### Lights on a patio

Warm summer evenings provide the perfect opportunity to linger on patios, especially if lighting is installed. Lights are also a good way of deterring burglars, especially if an infrared detector is

**Types of lighting installation**

Solar-powered floodlight

Wall-mounted light

Tiered light

Globe light

attached. This works when it is dark. It responds to body heat by turning on the light. It can also be fitted to a spotlight circuit at the front of a house to light a drive or a path, but it should not be activated by people walking on a nearby sidewalk, or it may be turning on and off all night. The range of patio lights is wide and includes low-level spotlights and lights mounted on the top, at the sides, and at the base of a walls. Some can be placed among the plants in patio borders.

## Pond power

In ponds there are two choices of power: mains electricity or low-voltage power. In most areas in a garden, from patios to greenhouses and garden sheds, mains electricity is best because it provides strong lighting and power, but in or near ponds many gardeners prefer the safer lower voltage supply (a transformer reduces the power) for lights and a small fountain. If you need power to run several fountains, a waterfall, and strong lighting, you will need mains electricity, but note that it is far more expensive to install a mains supply than a low voltage system. You can also buy solar-powered water fountains. These are easy to install, but your garden will need regular sunshine if you want a fountain running on solar power to work constantly.

## Greenhouse power

Mains electricity is useful in a greenhouse, especially if electrical tubular heaters are installed. Fan heaters and propagation units also need this power. Small mist-

propagation units are now available for amateur greenhouses, and they too require mains electricity.

Have the power installed by a qualified electrician, with a mains board fitted near the door and at least 4ft/1.2m above the ground. Tack a loose sheet of plastic over it to keep off water droplets, but maintain good air circulation around it. In addition, have a Ground-Fault-Interrupter (GFI) fitted into the circuit to cut off the power if a fault occurs.

## Power in sheds

This is not essential but it makes life easier, especially in winter when lawn mowers and other equipment need to be serviced. Have a mains board fitted, so that the power supply can be isolated from the main house supply.

▲ *Lights at ground level and flush with the surface are ideal for illuminating plants around paved areas. Containers can be placed on top.*

### SAFETY IN GARDENS

The top five tips are:
❂ Consult a specialist when installing electricity in a garden. Do not take short cuts or use inferior materials.
❂ Where cables are buried, keep a record of their position. Have all buried cables installed in a conduit. If you sell your property, inform the new owner about the position of underground cables.
❂ Have all equipment checked each year. Equipment must be specified as being designed for outdoor use.
❂ Never use mains electricity without a Ground-Fault-Interrupter fitted into the circuit. This especially applies when using mains operated lawn and hedge cutters.

# lawns and their care

Lawns are too often taken for granted, yet in most gardens they are the biggest, most eye-catching feature. Lawns provide essential places to play, sit, and eat, areas that link different sections of a garden, and foils for a wide range of plants. Looking after them is not difficult, but you have to know what to do. Here are some essential tips on feeding and watering, and on repairing holes, hollows, and bumps, along with ideas on creating chamomile lawns to give a stylish look.

# creating a lawn from seed

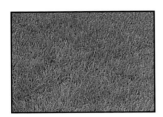

*In temperate regions there are two main ways to create lawns: sowing seed or laying turfs. There are other methods, however. In warm climates, dibbling tufts of grass about 3in/7.5cm apart is successful. In a tropical climate, spreading a mud plaster of chopped grass, water, and soil works well.*

### Preparing the site

Whether you create a lawn from seed or by laying turfs, preparation of the soil is the same. First, check that the ground is well drained (pages 90–91) and, if necessary, install drains. In winter, dig the soil (pages 92–93), removing perennial weeds. A few weeks before sowing seeds, rake the area level or with a slight slope. Firm the soil by shuffling sideways over the whole area, so that it is uniformly firm. Do not use a roller. Rake the soil to create a fine tilth.

### Sowing lawn seed

About a week before sowing lawn seed (usually in late spring, or from late summer to early fall), scatter a general fertilizer evenly over the area at 1½oz per sq yd/50g per sq m. Use a metal rake to mix it lightly into the surface. Wait for a day when the surface soil is dry, and use string to section the area into strips 3½ft/1m wide. Then use a couple of bamboo canes 4ft/1.2m long to form a 1m/3½ft square at one end of the strip.

Into this area sow lawn seed at the rate of 1½oz per sq yd/50g per sq m. Sowing less than this amount results in a thin, sparse lawn, while too much produces masses of tightly bunched seedlings susceptible to disease.

Next, move one of the canes to form another square and sow with more seed, continuing in this way until the whole area has been covered. Then, standing on a plank of wood, rake the seed lightly and evenly into the surface. It is important that you do not walk on newly sown areas of lawn because this depresses the soil and seed may stick to your shoes. If the weather forecast indicates a dry period, water the soil lightly but thoroughly. Also provide protection from hungry birds by stretching black thread about 6in/15cm above the surface and 6in/20cm apart. An alternative method which is unlikely to harm birds is to lay large sheets of black polyethylene on the sown surface to give protection and retain moisture. However, the sheets must be removed immediately once the grass seeds have germinated.

► *Lawns provide a natural foil that shows off plants to perfection. Grass paths may also be sown to connect parts of a garden.*

---

### ADVANTAGES OF SOWING SEEDS

❀ Cheaper than laying turfs.
❀ Lighter work than laying turfs.
❀ Easier to create intricately shaped areas.
❀ There is lawn seed for almost every part of the garden, from sunny sites to shady areas, and from play areas to ornamental lawns.

### DISADVANTAGES OF SOWING SEEDS

❀ It takes from 3–4 months before a lawn can be used.
❀ Cats often disturb the sown surface, and dogs and toddlers may tread on it.
❀ Perennial weeds can be a problem if the area has not been prepared thoroughly.

---

### HINTS AND TIPS

Always buy a little more seed than you will need. Small bare areas often occur and it is useful to have the same type and batch of seed handy to resow them.

# lawns from seed

1 Level the soil and remove any large stones. Work in a general fertilizer at 1½ oz per sq yd/50g per sq m using a garden rake or a metal-tined lawn rake.

2 Stretch two garden lines across the area to be sown, a yard apart. Then, place two garden canes 4ft/1.2m long to form a square yard.

3 Scatter seed evenly into each square at the rate of 1½ oz per sq yd/50g per sq m. Take care to sow each part of the square, not just the center.

4 When the square has been sown, move one of the canes to form another square. Then repeat the sowing until the row is complete. Use a garden or lawn rake to work the seed lightly into the surface.

# creating lawns from turfs

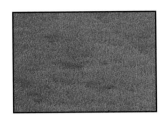

*Lawns made of turfs are thought to be instant features, but be warned, you will have to wait at least four weeks before they are established and can be used. Soil preparation is exactly the same as when creating lawns from seed (pages 104–105).*

## Laying turfs

Turfs can be laid from spring to fall, although early fall is the most popular period because the soil is warm and usually moist. After preparing the soil thoroughly, use a metal rake to level the surface and, about one week before laying turfs, scatter a general fertilizer at 2oz per sq yd/70g per sq m. Rake it lightly into the surface.

Mark out the area to be laid and stretch a garden line down one edge. As an insurance against dry weather and damage to the edges, make the area about 3in/7.5cm wider than required. Should the edges become dry the lawn will not be spoiled because it can be cut back to the desired size.

Start laying the lawn by positioning a row of turfs along the garden line, closely abutting their ends. Then, place a plank of wood 8in/20cm wide and 8–10ft/2.4–3m long on top of the turfs. Stand on this plank (moving it as necessary) to lay another row of turfs. Stagger the joints. Again, move the plank and lay another row, continuing until the whole area is covered.

Always insure that each turf is in close contact with the soil by using a firming device made from a thick piece of wood, 18in/45cm square, attached at its center to a vertical handle, usually a thick, 5ft/1.5m-long pole. Gaps will inevitably occur between the turfs, at their ends and their sides. Trickle a mixture of equal parts of sieved soil and fine peat into the gaps. When the area has been turfed, use a sprinkler.

## Types of turf

Two main types of turf are used to make garden lawns. One is meadow turf cut 3ft/90cm long, 12in/30cm wide, and 1½in/36mm thick; but expect variations. It comes from pasture and is usually the cheapest way to buy turfs.

Cultivated turf is the other type and is sometimes known as seeded turf. It is grown especially for sale, costs more than meadow turf, and is sold in rolls, but before buying it is important to check the exact size because it can vary.

### ADVANTAGES OF LAYING TURFS

⊛ A usable surface is usually created about four weeks after laying.
⊛ Eliminates problems with birds, cats, and dogs.
⊛ Ideal for families with young children.
⊛ Turfs can be laid from spring to fall, but not when the soil is dry. If it becomes dry, regular watering is essential.

### DISADVANTAGES OF LAYING TURFS

⊛ More expensive than sowing seeds.
⊛ Much heavier work than sowing seeds.
⊛ Turfs have to be laid within 24 hours of delivery. If left rolled up, the grass becomes yellow and the edges begin to dry. If laying is delayed, be prepared to unroll the turfs and water them.

### HINTS AND TIPS

Always buy a few more turfs than you need. This is important where the sides of a lawn are curved. Also note that because turfs are laid in a staggered pattern there is always some wastage at the ends.

# laying turfs

1 Prepare the soil thoroughly and rake in a general fertilizer. Stretch a garden line along one side of the planned lawn and lay a turf alongside it. Lay other turfs, with their ends butted against each other.

2 Put a wide, strong plank on top of the laid turf and stand on it to lay another line, closely abutting the first row and with the end joints staggered. Never stand on the turf because it causes indentations.

3 Improvise a firmer by tapping on a plank of wood with the heel of a hammer, or fashion one from a thick piece of wood 45cm/18in square, with a vertical pole 1.5m /5ft long, fixed at its center.

4 Trickle a mixture of sieved soil and peat into the joints and use a broom or a besom to work it into the cracks. When the lawn is complete, use a sprinkler to soak the lawn area gently but thoroughly.

▲ A well-maintained lawn creates a sense of space and highlights plants and other ornamental garden features.

# looking after lawns

*Lawns are essential garden features creating attractive, restful and permanent foils for ornamental plants. They also unify a garden and provide recreational areas for children and pets. With a little care, lawns can be kept in peak condition and will withstand most household wear and tear.*

### Repairing lawn edges

After a few years it is inevitable that the edges of lawns become damaged and unsightly, but it is quite easy to repair them. (See opposite page.)

### Repairing holes in lawns

Where a lawn is used as a play area for young children and pets, holes soon appear. Make repairs as soon as possible, so that the damage does not become any larger. (See opposite page.)

▲ *Lawns need regular attention the year round to keep them tidy and smart. If a lawn is neglected it becomes an eyesore.*

### Leveling bumps and depressions

An uneven lawn with bumps and depressions can easily be leveled if these are less than 5ft/1.5m wide. Stretch a garden line over the center of the depression or bump, and use an edging iron to cut a line about 2⅓in/6cm deep along it. Then measure 12in/30cm-wide strips at rightangles to the center line and cut along them. Use a garden spade or a turfing iron to cut under the turfs, from the center outward, and roll them back to expose the bump or depression. Then either remove excess soil or fill and firm compost over the area, so that it is level. Replace the turf and firm it. Sprinkle compost between the cracks and water the area thoroughly.

### Bare areas

These usually result from excessive wear. Fresh grass can be encouraged to grow by placing wire netting over the bare area and keeping it moist, but if the soil is compacted, more radical treatment will be required. Fork the area to about 6in/15cm deep and add some

horticultural sand. Level, refirm and sprinkle lawn seed over the area at 1½oz per sq yd/50g per sq m. Water the area lightly, allow the surface to dry slightly, then place clear polyethylene sheet over it. Remove the sheet when the grass seedlings are growing strongly.

---

## LAWN ROUTINE

Lawns are often neglected, yet with regular care they can be transformed into areas that enhance the whole garden. Three tips guaranteeing success are:

⚙ Mow the grass regularly from early spring to early or mid-fall. Use a grass box to collect the cuttings, except when the weather is hot and dry.

⚙ Feed lawns during spring and early summer. Use quick-acting fertilizers and apply them every six to eight weeks except during dry periods. In late summer and early fall use slow-acting fertilizers. Always follow the application rates recommended by the manufacturer.

⚙ Aerate lawns in late summer. To do this, push the tines of a garden fork 4in/10cm deep and 3in/7.5cm apart into the lawn surface, or use a proprietary hollow-tine fork. Then rake a top-dressing compost mixture into the soil. Prick the surface of the lawn in spring before adding fertilizers.

# *repairing the edges of lawn*

1 Place a piece of wood, 8–9in/20–23cm wide, 12in/30cm long and ½–³/₄in/ 12–18mm thick over the damaged area and place one of the narrow ends flush with the lawn's edge.

2 Now use a half-moon edging iron to cut about 2½in/6cm deep into the lawn, not omitting to cut the corners. Remove the piece of wood and use a spade to lift the turf and reverse it.

3 The broken area will now be toward the lawn's center, with the cut part flush with the edge of the lawn. Fill and firm the damaged area with compost, and sow it with lawn seed.

# *repairing a hole in a lawn*

1 Dogs and children often make holes in lawns; but repair is easy. Place a piece of wood 10–12in/25–30cm-square over the hole and then cut round it using a half-moon edging iron.

2 Remove the damaged piece of turf. Use the same wood to cut a healthy piece of turf from an out-of-the-way position. Put it in position and level it to align it with the surface of the surrounding grass.

3 Firm the turf gently to ease it into position and dribble compost carefully between the cracks all the way round. Then water the area thoroughly and repeatedly until the turf starts to grow.

# chamomile lawns, thyme paths

*These lawns and paths are unusual and colorful features that can be fitted into most gardens, whatever their size. Chamomile lawns have a long history and were popular in Elizabethan England, when bowls were played on their scented surface. The aroma of thyme adds a dimension to a garden walk.*

## Chamomile lawns

These lawns are planted with *Chamaemelum nobile*, formerly and widely known as *Anthemis nobilis*, a prostrate, mat-forming herbaceous perennial with finely dissected leaves that release a fruity scent when bruised and walked on. The non-flowering variety, 'Treneague' has a scent rather like bananas.

Weeds can be a problem in new chamomile lawns and thorough preparation is necessary. Dig the area 12in/30cm deep in winter and remove all perennial weeds. Leave for 12 months, pulling or digging up weeds as they appear. In the second winter, dig the soil again, and plant in the spring.

## Planting a chamomile lawn

Rake the area level and shuffle sideways over the surface to firm it evenly. Then, rake again to remove footprints. If the lawn is dry, water the soil thoroughly and wait until the surface is dry and crumbly before planting.

You can plant the lawn in late spring or early summer. Space the plants 6–8in/15–20cm apart in staggered rows, and use a trowel to make holes that do not constrict the roots of each plant. Check that the crown of each plant is just below the surface, then firm the soil and water the whole lawn lightly but thoroughly. When the plants start to grow into a lawn, trim them with sharp hedging shears.

## Thyme paths

Use *Thymus serpyllum* (English or wild thyme) to form a colorful, scented path. It is evergreen and carpet-forming, with richly fragrant gray-green leaves, and bears flowers ranging from white to pink to red flowers through much of the summer. When established, this thyme has a 18–24in/45–60cm spread, but for rapid cover set the plants closer together.

## Creating a thyme path

During winter, mark the width of the path and dig the area thoroughly to remove perennial weeds. Leave the surface rough so that the weather will break down the surface to a fine tilth. In spring, rake the soil and place stepping stones on the surface (check that the spacing is right for everyone who will use the path). Set the stepping stones into the ground so the surface of each stone is about ½in/12mm above the soil surface. To promote quick covering, set the plants 9–12in/23–30cm apart. Firm the soil around them and water the whole lawn thoroughly. Until the path is established, water it regularly, especially at the edges where the soil tends to dry out.

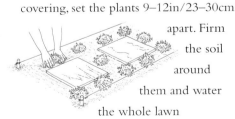

▲ *Chamomile lawns, formed of finely dissected midgreen leaves with all the fruity fragrance of chamomile, always attract attention.*

▶ *Thyme paths become decorative ribbons of color throughout summer and are ideal for linking one part of a garden with another.*

## SCENTED SEATS

These are an original feature in a small garden. They are raised, planted structures about 18in/45cm high, 4–6ft/1.2–1.8m long, and 20–24in/50–60cm deep, planted with chamomile or thyme. Because the bed is raised the soil tends to become dry, especially if the weather is hot and sunny, and so regular and thorough watering is essential. A variation on this type of seat is to intersperse the plants with small paving slabs. As well as providing sitting positions, the slabs help keep the soil moist and cool.

# water and rock gardens

*Water gardens are becoming increasingly fashionable, and there is little excuse for not having a water feature, whether it be a wildlife pond with frogs and newts, a wall fountain dribbling water onto a shiny group of colored pebbles on the ground, or for the more adventurous, a bog garden with permanently moist soil for growing some special plants. However, rock gardens, with quick-draining soil and exquisitely beautiful small plants may be more your style. All these are quite easily made, with the aid of a few practical tips.*

# water gardens

*Water introduces tranquillity and movement to a garden. Established garden ponds, perhaps nestling in an open, sunny corner of a garden, create a restful atmosphere, especially when covered with waterlilies, and with dragonflies hovering over the surface.*

## Water features for all gardens

It is quite possible to have a water feature in your garden without digging a pond, and in a garden to be used by young children, an alternative is often welcome. There may be a fountain splashing over pebbles, or water in a shallow trough being recirculated by a pump. Such a feature may be quite small and so there is often room for one on a patio.

A pond can be built to any desired shape or size. The water surface can be level with the surrounding ground or raised by about 18in/45cm. A pond at ground level with an informal outline can be merged with a bog garden or a wildlife area. Several decades ago, ponds were nearly always square or rectangular, and made of concrete. Building one was hard work, and unless it was reinforced it soon cracked. Modern bowl-shaped ponds with gently sloping sides are a popular choice and more durable.

Today, ponds are mainly formed using a flexible liner (also called a pond liner) or come as a rigid liner (called a preformed pond or a molded shell). Flexible liners are used to line holes dug

▲ *Garden ponds introduce tranquillity and peace into a garden. The range of plants is wide, from waterlilies to fragrant marginal plants.*

### SELECTING FOUNTAINS

⊛ The spray should not fall on waterlilies or marginal plants.
⊛ The height of the spray should not be more than half the width of the pond.
⊛ In windy areas, use fountains that produce large droplets of water.
⊛ Do not allow water droplets to disturb floating plants.

to the desired shape and depth. Their durability depends on the material used to make them. Polyethylene liners are low cost and have a relatively short life, especially when exposed to sunlight. Butyl rubber sheeting is the most durable, lasting for over 20 years, but it is also the most expensive.

Liners must be laid on an underlay to prevent the water pressure from puncturing them on sharp stones. Ready-made rigid liners are sunk into a hole. The cheapest type is made of plastic, which has the shortest lifespan. Glassfiber shells are more costly but will last for 20 years or more.

## Choosing waterlilies

These plants need careful selection to insure that vigorous varieties do not dominate and overcrowd small ponds. Waterlilies are usually put into four classifications: dwarf; small; medium; and vigorous. Dwarf types suit ponds with a depth of 4–10in/10–25cm; small lilies need a 6–18in/15–45cm depth; the medium lilies need a depth of 1–2ft/ 30–60cm, and the vigorous type need a water depth of 1½–3ft/45–90cm.

To plant a waterlily (*Nymphaea* spp), put it in a plastic mesh container with soil and cover it with a layer of clean pea gravel 1in/2.5cm thick. Soak the soil and place the container in the pond. Using bricks as a stand for the container, position it so that the waterlily leaves float on the surface. Remove the bricks progressively as the plant grows, always keeping the leaves on the surface.

## Miniponds on patios

Even a patio in the smallest garden can have a water feature. Stout wooden tubs are ideal summer homes for miniature waterlilies and other aquatic plants. They contain only a small volume of water, so unfortunately must be emptied or moved to a greenhouse or a conservatory during winter. First-rate miniature waterlilies include:

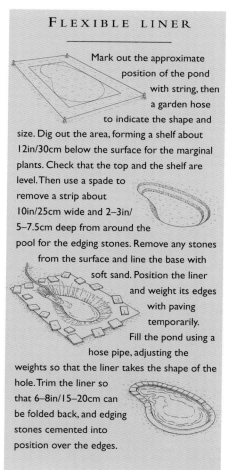

*Nymphaea* 'Aurora'—pinkish-yellow, then orange and later red.
*Nymphaea* 'Indiana'— orange, with orange-red stamens.
*Nymphaea tetragona*— white, with yellow stamens.
Marginal aquatics include:
*Carex elata* 'Aurea'— narrow, golden leaves.
*Scirpus latifolia* 'Zebrinus'—quill-like stems banded green and white.

▲ *A raised pond creates a distinctive feature on a patio. It needs to be built with materials that harmonize with other garden structures.*

### FLEXIBLE LINER

Mark out the approximate position of the pond with string, then a garden hose to indicate the shape and size. Dig out the area, forming a shelf about 12in/30cm below the surface for the marginal plants. Check that the top and the shelf are level. Then use a spade to remove a strip about 10in/25cm wide and 2–3in/ 5–7.5cm deep from around the pool for the edging stones. Remove any stones from the surface and line the base with soft sand. Position the liner and weight its edges with paving temporarily. Fill the pond using a hose pipe, adjusting the weights so that the liner takes the shape of the hole. Trim the liner so that 6–8in/15–20cm can be folded back, and edging stones cemented into position over the edges.

# bog gardens

*Moisture-loving plants may be planted beside an informal garden pond or in naturally occurring wet spots in the garden to make a bog garden. The range of bog garden plants is wide and includes border primulas, moisture-loving ferns, and many colorful herbaceous perennials.*

### Creating a bog garden

Few gardens have an area where soil naturally remains moist throughout the year. A bog garden built in a dry area is usually better than one planted in naturally wet ground. This is because soil mix in a specially constructed bog garden is constrained within a plastic liner, and this helps to retain moisture throughout the year, whereas soil in what appears to be a naturally moist area usually becomes dry in hot weather. There are a few constructional "musts"

and they include keeping the bog garden small enough so that you can reach plants without standing in the soil, which causes unnecessary compaction. To keep the soil mix moist but not waterlogged, the plastic liner should be punctured. When constructing a bog garden, check that the top of the soil is slightly below the surface of water in the adjacent pond. It is important to have a water sprinkler at hand during spring and summer to water the soil during dry weather.

### Step-by-step construction

Mark out an area to one side of an informal pond. Use a garden hose so that the shape of the bog garden can be changed several times during its planning stage. Create an attractive outline, perhaps irregular, but still allowing all parts to be reached easily.

Dig out the area, putting the topsoil to one side (ready for refilling), and barrow away the subsoil. A depth of 15–18in/38–45cm is about right. Line the hole with a layer of moist sand 1in/2.5cm thick, and place the liner in the hole. Tuck it under the edge of the pond liner or shell.

Next, puncture the base with holes ½in/12mm wide every 2½–3ft/75–90cm to insure that excess water can escape. Lay clean gravel or pea gravel 2in/5cm thick over the liner, then top up with soil mix consisting of three parts topsoil, three parts peat, and one part clean, lime–

◀ Hostas *thrive in bog gardens and their large leaves can be used to soften the edges of straight-sided ponds in a formal style.*

free grit. Firm the soil gently. Put large stones around the edges of the bog garden to cover the plastic sheeting,

### Planting and plants

Spring or early summer is the best time to put in the plants. First, dust the surface with a general fertilizer and fork it lightly into the soil. Then space out the plants on the surface, so that they look attractive. Use a trowel to plant them, from the center of the bed to the edges. Firm the soil around the roots and water over the area gently but thoroughly. Good plants to consider for the bog garden include the following primulas, ferns, and herbaceous perennials.

### Primulas

*Primula denticulata* (drumstick primrose)—dense, globular flowerheads in spring. The color range includes white, blue and mauve.

*P. florindae* (giant cowslip)—fragrant, bell-shaped flowers in early and midsummer. The color range is light orange to blood red.

*P. japonica* (Japanese primrose)—flowers borne in whorled tiers on upright stems from late spring to midsummer. The color range includes white, magenta-red, pink, and bright red.

### Ferns

*Onoclea sensibilis* (sensitive fern)—2ft/ 60cm high with pale green fronds.
*Osmunda regalis* (royal fern)—4–6ft 1.2–1.8m high with pea-green fronds.

### Herbaceous perennials

*Astilbe × arendsii*—lax spikes of red, pink, or white flowers during summer.
*Hostas* (plantain lilies)—large range, many with single-colored leaves, others variegated.
*Iris sibirica* (Siberian iris)—blue flowers during early summer.
*Lysichiton americanum* (skunk cabbage)—bright yellow, arum-like flowers during spring and early summer.
*Rodgersia pinnata*—large, deep-green leaves, sometimes tinged brown.
*Trollius × cultorum* (globe flower)—globe-like flowers during late spring and early summer. The range of colors varies from yellow to orange.

### Constructing a bog garden

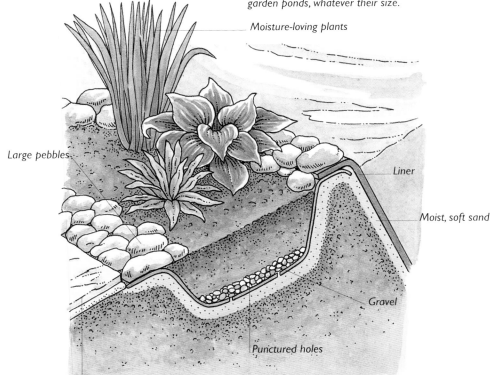

▲ *Waterfalls, with cascading water that sparkles in the sunlight, create an extra dimension to garden ponds, whatever their size.*

Moisture-loving plants

Large pebbles

Liner

Moist, soft sand

Gravel

Punctured holes

Paving slabs

# building a rock garden

*Rock gardens make delightful features in small gardens, especially as a large number of small plants can be grown in them. A rock garden can be grown on a gentle slope and on a freestanding mound created from well-drained soil, with stones added in stratified rows.*

## Rock gardens

If you are fortunate enough to have a garden with a slope toward the south or west, a rock garden is easily created with pieces of natural stone such as limestone or sandstone positioned to resemble stratified rows. For a rock garden with an area of about 15sq yd/4.5sq m you will need between 1–2 tons of stone.

The range of plants for rock gardens is wide and includes alpines and small herbaceous perennials, dwarf bulbs, and miniature and slow-growing conifers. Dwarf shrubs such as *Cotoneaster linearifolius* grow about 12in/30cm high and 20in/50cm wide and give a permanent structure. There are many other shrubs including thyme, the glorious yellow-flowered *Hypericum olympica*, and *Zauschneria californica* (Californian fuchsia) with red, tubular, fuchsia-like flowers during late summer and early fall.

## Freestanding rock gardens

These have natural stone in stratified layers, like a rock garden on a slope. They often provide more space for plants than a rock garden built on a slope because it is possible to plant the front and the two sides. Since the front is usually small, do not dominate it with large, shrub-like plants but use miniature, columnar, and slow-growing conifers to create the impression of height. These include *Juniperus communis* 'Compressa'

### STAR PLANTS

| | |
|---|---|
| Aubrieta deltoidea | Sedum acre |
| Aurinia saxatilis | Saponaria ocymoides |

◀ *Rock gardens that are harmonized with a gently flowing stream are immediately more interesting than when on their own.*

(18in/45cm high after 10 years) and *Juniperus scopulorum* 'Skyrocket' (6ft/1.8m high after 10 years). Where interest is needed at the base of the rock garden to give the impression of extra width, plant *Juniperus squamata* 'Blue Star' (15in/38cm high and 24in/60cm, wide after 10 years) or *Juniperus* × *pfitzeriana* 'Gold Coast' (20in/50cm high and 30in/75cm wide after 10 years).

## Drystone walls

These walls look wonderful when their sides are covered by colorful flowers. Several rock garden plants can achieve this effect, but perhaps none better than *Aurinia saxatilis*, better known as *Alyssum saxatile*. On a dry-stone wall it spreads 12–18in/30–45cm wide, and trails golden-yellow flowers more than 24in/60cm). There are several attractive varieties. *Aubrieta deltoidea* is an evergreen perennial that bears cross-shaped flowers in shades of rose-lilac to purple in spring and early summer.

Plants may also be grown along the top of the wall so their tumbling foliage softens the wall's sharp outline. Such plants include *Saponaria ocymoides,* with pale pink flowers through most of the summer that trail to about 2ft/60cm, and *Sedum acre* 'Aureum', which has bright yellow flowers and spreads to 2ft/60cm. Raised beds are similar to drystone walls, but with the wall encircling a bed 1½–3ft/45–90cm high up to 5ft/1.5m wide.

## Scree beds

Scree beds are often placed around rock gardens. However, in very small gardens they are lovely on their own. Suitable plants range from miniature and slow-growing conifers to dwarf bulbs and perennials such as aethionema, erodium, *Phlox douglasii* and silene.

▲ *Scree beds are ideal for small gardens and can be added to an existing rock garden or constructed as features on their own.*

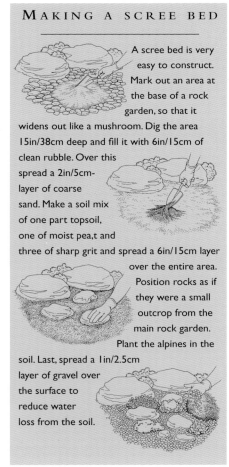

## MAKING A SCREE BED

A scree bed is very easy to construct. Mark out an area at the base of a rock garden, so that it widens out like a mushroom. Dig the area 15in/38cm deep and fill it with 6in/15cm of clean rubble. Over this spread a 2in/5cm-layer of coarse sand. Make a soil mix of one part topsoil, one of moist pea,t and three of sharp grit and spread a 6in/15cm layer over the entire area. Position rocks as if they were a small outcrop from the main rock garden. Plant the alpines in the soil. Last, spread a 1in/2.5cm layer of gravel over the surface to reduce water loss from the soil.

# wildlife ponds

*These ponds create havens for wildlife including aquatic insects, small mammals, amphibians, and birds. Fish such as goldfish and shubunkins, which normally enrich ornamental ponds with color and vitality, should not be put in a wildlife pond because they soon become meals for birds.*

### Creating a wildlife pond

Wildlife ponds are sometimes thought suitable only for rural gardens, but they are also extremely important in towns where they provide feeding, bathing, and watering places for birds.

A flexible liner, most often butyl rubber sheeting, is usually used. Dig out to a varying depth of 2–2½ft/60–75cm.

This is essential to give pond life a chance of survival when the surface water freezes. Create an irregular outline, with space at one side to form a bog garden (pages 116–117) filled with moisture-loving plants. The pond should also include a gentle slope so that any wildlife can get in and out. Lay moist sand 2in/5cm thick and place the

flexible liner on top. If a path is to be built, allow an overlap of 9in/23cm so that paving slabs can be laid on top. Add another layer of sand to cover the liner, and top with a layer of heavy soil 2–3in/5–7.5cm thick.

Place large pebbles or another material along the edge of the liner to cover it. Fill the pond carefully by standing a bucket on the soil with the end of a hosepipe in it. Allow water to trickle gently over the sides of the bucket into the pond. Oxygenating plants can be planted directly into soil at the bottom of the pond, but waterlilies and marginal plants are best planted in plastic-mesh containers.

### Looking after a wildlife pond

Your pond should reflect nature left to its own devices and appear as natural as possible. However, it will need some maintenance, and excess blanketweed,

◀ *Wildlife ponds create restful places in gardens. They attract and create homes for birds, amphibians, and small mammals.*

## Constructing a wildlife pond

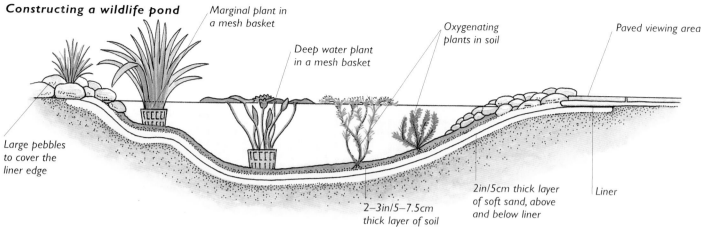

Marginal plant in a mesh basket

Deep water plant in a mesh basket

Oxygenating plants in soil

Paved viewing area

Large pebbles to cover the liner edge

2–3in/5–7.5cm thick layer of soil

2in/5cm thick layer of soft sand, above and below liner

Liner

duckweed, and fall leaves should be removed along with stems and leaves, if too many appear above the water surface. When the pond is newly filled, introduce aquatic life with a few buckets of water from an established pond.

### Protecting wildlife

◉ Never use pesticides or any garden sprays on plants growing in or near to garden ponds. Frogs, toads, and newts are highly susceptible to garden chemicals.
◉ Do not use weedkillers on lawns surrounding a pond.
◉ Put ramps at the pond edge giving easy access to small animals and amphibians.
◉ Where possible, keep a clear area around a pond to reduce the chance of a cat creeping up on birds.
◉ Keep the area free from overhanging deciduous trees. If left, fall leaves will decay and produce toxic gases.
◉ Do not put your pond near trees with poisonous berries or fruits, like laburnum.

▶ *Many moisture-loving plants can be planted around a wildlife pond. Ferns are especially attractive and many are suited to moist areas.*

# propagating plants

Within every gardener there is a desire to produce new plants, whether from seeds, cuttings, division, or by layering low-growing stems on shrubs. Many of these methods are easy and involve little time or expense. However, sowing half-hardy annuals in early spring requires a warm greenhouse; the young seedlings are transferred to seed trays and later planted into borders when all risk of frost has passed. Hardy annuals are sown outdoors in late spring where they are to germinate and grow.

# simple propagation

*The desire to increase plants is a passion for most gardeners, especially if it can be done easily and cheaply. Some ways are almost instant and include dividing clump-forming plants such as some herbaceous perennials. Other methods, such as layering, take longer before a fresh plant is produced.*

## Dividing plants

After about five years, herbaceous plants become congested and woody, with bare centers. In fall or spring cut down all stems to ground-level and use a garden fork to dig up the clump. Insert a couple of garden forks, back to back, into the clump and lever their handles together, so that the clump is loosened and can be pulled into several pieces. Select healthy young parts from around the outside, and replant them in a border. Discard the old woody pieces.

<table>
<tr><td colspan="2" align="center">SHRUBS AND TREES<br>THAT CAN BE<br>LAYERED</td></tr>
<tr><td>Amelanchier</td><td>Euonymus</td></tr>
<tr><td>Azalea</td><td>Forsythia</td></tr>
<tr><td>Calluna (heather)</td><td>Hamamelis</td></tr>
<tr><td>Camellia</td><td>Jasminum nudiflorum</td></tr>
<tr><td>Chaenomeles</td><td>Magnolia</td></tr>
<tr><td>Chimonanthus</td><td>Pieris</td></tr>
<tr><td>Cornus (dogwood)</td><td>Rhododendron</td></tr>
<tr><td>Cotinus</td><td>Rhus (sumac)</td></tr>
<tr><td>Cotoneaster</td><td>Vaccinium</td></tr>
<tr><td>Erica (heath)</td><td>Viburnum</td></tr>
</table>

## Layering shrubs and trees

This is a simple way to increase plants, although it may take more than a year before roots form and the new plant can be severed from its parent. It suits woody plants with low-growing branches that can be lowered to soil level. Layering can be done at any time, but spring and late summer to early fall are the best times of year.

## Hardwood cuttings

This is an easy way to increase many shrubs and soft fruit bushes. All that is needed is a nursery bed, a spade and horticultural sand. Once taken and inserted in the ground they require little attention. These cuttings are taken in early or mid-fall, and consist of the current year's growth. Shrubs increased in this way include berberis, deutzia, forsythia, *Ilex* (holly), *Ligustrum* (privet), philadelphus, spiraea, and weigela.

To increase blackcurrants (*Ribes rigrum*), in mid-fall cut a shoot 8–10in/20–25cm long slightly above and below a bud, and insert it in a straight-sided trench, so that two buds are above the soil. Space them 3–4in/7.5–10cm apart and position them on a layer of horticultural sand. Firm the soil around them. Take gooseberry cuttings in mid-fall by cutting a shoot 12in/30cm long slightly above and below a bud. Remove all but the top four buds and insert the cutting about 6in/15cm deep in a straight-sided trench. Space the gooseberry cuttings 3–4in/7.5–10cm apart and place them on a layer of sharp sand. Firm the soil around them. Whitecurrants and redcurrants are increased in the same way.

<table>
<tr><td colspan="2" align="center">HERBACEOUS PLANTS<br>TO DIVIDE</td></tr>
<tr><td>Achillea</td><td>Geranium</td></tr>
<tr><td>Alchemilla mollis</td><td>Helenium</td></tr>
<tr><td>Anaphalis</td><td>Leucanthemum</td></tr>
<tr><td>Aruncus</td><td>x superbum</td></tr>
<tr><td>Astilbe</td><td>Lysimachia punctata</td></tr>
<tr><td>Campanula</td><td>Monarda</td></tr>
<tr><td>Coreopsis</td><td>Perennial asters</td></tr>
<tr><td>Echinacea</td><td>Rudbeckia (coneflower)</td></tr>
<tr><td>Erigeron (sea holly)</td><td>Solidago (goldenrod)</td></tr>
<tr><td>Filipendula</td><td>Tiarella (foamflower)</td></tr>
</table>

# dividing herbaceous perennials

**Hardwood cuttings (privet)**

*Select a mature, healthy shoot 10–12in/ 23–30cm long, and trim beneath a leaf joint.*

*Remove all the other leaves except the top six to eight.*

1 To divide the roots of a large clump, insert two forks into the clump, and lever the handles together to force the roots apart. Remove the forks and discard the older, central part of the roots.

2 Pull and tease the young parts carefully from around the outside of the clump, making several pieces. Do not separate off tiny pieces which will take a long time to grow into plants that give a good display.

*Make a trench 6–8in/15–20cm deep, with one straight side. Sprinkle sharp sand in the base, stand the cutting on it, and firm the soil around it.*

# layering shrubs

1 Select a long, low-growing, vigorous stem, up to two years old. Make a trench 3–6in/ 7.5–15cm deep, 9–18in/ 23–45cm from the tip of the stem.

2 Lower the stem into the trench and bend it upright, 9in/23cm from its end. At the bend, cut halfway through it or make a tongued cut.

3 Use a wooden or metal peg to secure the stem in the soil and insert a cane, without damaging the stem. Carefully firm the soil around the stem.

4 Tie the stem to the cane, but do not constrict it. When the shoot develops new growth, remove the soil, sever the stem, and transfer to a nursery bed.

# sowing hardy annuals

*Hardy annuals have a relatively short life; they are sown in flower beds in the spring and grow, flower, and die by the onset of cold weather in the fall. Although short lived they create spectacular displays, either in borders specially devoted to them or as fillers in flower beds.*

### Preparing hardy annual borders

In late fall or early winter, single-dig the soil (to the depth of a spade) and mix in decayed manure or compost, bury annual weeds, and burn perennial weeds. Leave the surface rough but even enough to allow the winter weather to break it down to a friable tilth. In mid- to late spring, shuffle sideways over the soil to consolidate it and rake it level.

▲ *Hardy annuals are often used to fill bare patches in herbaceous or mixed borders during their early years before plants are established.*

### Sowing hardy annuals

Hardy annuals are not sown before mid- to late spring, when the soil has warmed up, because the seeds will not germinate in cold, wet soil. Use a trickle of sharp sand to mark areas of different sizes and shapes into which different species and varieties are to be sown. Those at the front of a border should be shallower and smaller than those at the back.

Some gardeners sow annuals by scattering seed on the surface, but this is wasteful. Instead, use a pointed stick to dig straight drills /¼–½in/6–12mm deep and 9in/23cm apart. Make the direction of the rows in each sowing area different from its neighbors. Sow the seeds thinly and evenly, and use the back of a metal rake to push and draw friable soil gently over them. Then firm the soil by using the head of a metal rake. When sowing is complete, use small sticks to mark the ends of each row. This later makes weeding much easier as the rows of annuals can be seen easily. Label each group of seeds with the name and date of sowing. Keep the soil moist.

Birds are often a problem, but they can be deterred by stretching black thread over the area. After germination, when the seedlings are large enough to handle, they must be thinned. The exact spacing depends on the species and variety (check the packet). Thin the seedlings in two stages, first to half the recommended distance, and then to the full spacing.

### RAISING BIENNIALS

These are plants that produce flowers during their second season of growth. In late spring or early summer sow biennial seeds in a nursery bed in drills ½in/12mm deep and 9in/23cm apart. Sow the seeds evenly and thinly. After germination, when the seedlings are large enough to handle, thin them or transplant them to another nursery bed. Thinning is better than transplanting if the seeds were sown thinly. For example, thin small biennials such as daisies to 3–4in 7.5–10cm apart, and wallflowers and other tall flowers to 5–6in/13–15cm apart. Where seeds were sown thickly, fork up the clumps and select the strongest seedlings. Replant them 6–8in/15–20cm apart in rows 12in/30cm apart. In late summer or early fall, transplant the established plants into beds or containers.

# sowing hardy annuals

1 Dig the soil in winter and in spring rake the surface level. Firm the surface by shuffling sideways to cover the whole area. Rake the surface level and use horticultural sand to mark the sowing areas.

2 Use a straight-edged piece of wood to mark the positions of the drills and a pointed stick to make drills ¼–½in/6–12mm deep and about 9in/23cm apart. Align the drills at a different angle for each sowing area.

3 Sow seeds evenly and thinly in each drill. Do not sow the seeds in clusters because this will result in overcrowding and poor growth. Take care not to waste seeds that fall between the drills.

4 *When each group of seeds has been sown, use the back of an iron rake to draw and push friable soil over the seeds. Firm the soil over the drill of seeds by pressing downward with the head of the rake.*

▲ *Hardy annuals are easy to grow and produce a wealth of blooms in many colors and shapes throughout summer. They die down in the fall.*

# sowing half-hardy annuals

*Half-hardy annuals, sometimes called summer-flowering bedding plants, produce bright, summer-long displays in borders, window boxes, wall baskets, hanging baskets, and tubs. These plants are tender nature, which means that they are easily damaged by frost.*

### Sowing half-hardy annuals

Because these plants are slightly tender they need to be sown in gentle warmth in greenhouses or conservatories in late winter or early spring. Sowing them is not complicated, and the first stage is to fill a seed tray with seed-starting mix and to firm it gently, especially around the edges. Mix that is left loose soon becomes dry.

Add more mix to the seed tray and use a straight-edged piece of wood to tap the surface level. Firm the surface by using a soil presser; this is a piece of wood, 5–6in/13–15cm square and ⅜in/18mm thick with a handle on one side. Firm the mix to about ½in/ 12mm below the rim of the seed tray. To sow seed, tip a few seeds into piece of stiff card folded into a V-shape, hold it over the mix and tap its end lightly so

## sowing half-hardy annuals

1 Fill a plastic seed tray with seed-starting mix. Using a soil-presser, level and firm it to about 12mm/½in below the top of the tray.

2 Tip a few seeds into a piece of paper folded into a V-shape and tap its end to sow seeds evenly and thinly over the surface, but not near the sides.

3 The thickness of mix covering the seeds varies between species. Check the seed packet instructions and use a sieve to cover them evenly.

4 Water the mix by standing the seed tray in a bowl of water until moisture seeps to the surface. Remove and allow excess to drain away.

that the seed falls evenly over the surface. Do not sow seed within ½in/ 12mm of the tray's edge. Cover the sown seed with mix shaken through a horticultural or domestic sieve to give a fine, even covering. The thickness varies with the species (check the seed packet) but it is usually ⅛–¼in/3–6mm. Water the seed by standing the seed tray in a bowl filled with 1in/2.5cm of clean water. When moisture seeps to the soil surface, remove the seed tray.

Gentle warmth (61–70°F/16–21°C) is needed to encourage germination. This varies for different species, so check on the seed packet. Cover the seed tray with a plastic lid or a sheet of glass, then with a sheet of newspaper, because most seeds need darkness to germinate, although a few do require light.

Check the mix regularly to keep it moist, and wipe the glass to remove any condensation that forms on the underside. Depending on the species, germination takes between 7 and 21 days. As soon as the seeds germinate, remove the newspaper and lift off the glass or plastic cover for longer periods each day. Also, slowly reduce the temperature so that the seedlings adjust to normal weather conditions.

---

### HINTS AND TIPS

Use only clean starting mix when sowing seeds or pricking off seedlings. Soil directly from a garden contains pests and diseases that soon damage seedlings. Also, it may be badly drained and result in root rot.

---

# *pricking off seedlings*

1 After germination, seedlings grow rapidly and if left, become congested and damaged. As soon as they are large enough to handle, transfer them to wider spacings.

2 Use a small dibble to make holes in the growing mix, 1–1½in/25–36mm deep and 1½in/36mm apart, leaving a margin around the container ½in/12mm from the edge.

3 Use a spatula or an old kitchen fork to loosen a cluster of seedlings. Place them on a piece of moist newspaper so that their roots do not become dry.

4 Hold each seedling gently by one of its leaves, not by its stem, and lower the roots into a hole, so that the roots are at about the same depth as before.

5 Use a dibble to firm the mix gently around the roots, taking care not to squash them. Then level the surface of the compost carefully.

6 Stand the seed tray on a level, well-drained surface. Water the seedlings with a fine rose to settle the mix around the roots.

# increasing plants from cuttings

*Taking cuttings is a popular way to increase plants and because it is a vegetative process each new plant is identical to its parent. Hardwood cuttings are easy to root and no special equipment or artificial warmth is needed. Softwood and semihardwood cuttings are raised differently.*

## Softwood cuttings

The tips of fresh growth are used to propagate many houseplants and herbaceous perennials, and they are called softwood or sometimes soft-stemmed cuttings.

Softwood cuttings can be taken from soft-stemmed greenhouse plants through the year, although spring and early summer are the best times. Softwood cuttings from herbaceous perennials are taken in early and midsummer. However, there are exceptions. To encourage the development of soft chrysanthemum shoots early in the year, dormant roots are boxed up in compost during early winter, and kept warm and moist. They produce soft shoots which can be used as cuttings. During late winter or spring; trim them to 2–3in/5–7.5cm long and insert three or four cuttings about 1in/2.5cm deep in pots of equal parts moist peat and horticultural sand. Firm the mix around the cuttings, water them, and keep the pots at 55°F/13°C. Hormone rooting powders also encourage rapid rooting.

## Semihardwood cuttings

These firmer cuttings are also called half-ripe and semimature cuttings and are more mature than softwood cuttings. The method is shown opposite.

## Hardwood cuttings

Many hardy shrubs and soft fruits can be increased with cuttings from the mature shoots of the current season's growth. In fall to early spring when plants are dormant, cut a firm shoot 9–15in/23-38cm long, depending on the shrub. Trim just above a bud at the top of the shoot and just below a bud at the other end. Take a spade and make a trench with one side vertical in a nursery bed, and plant each cutting two-thirds of its length deep and about 4in/10cm apart. Firm soil around them. Hardwood cuttings take about a year to form roots. When rooted, transfer them individually to wider spacing in a nursery bed.

◀ *The hardy deciduous shrub* Chaenomeles *(flowering quince) can be increased from heel-cuttings during mid- and late summer.*

# softwood cuttings

**Semihardwood cuttings**

*Take half-ripe cuttings during midsummer to the early part of late summer. Select a shoot 4–5in/10–13cm long, with a heel at its base.*

1 Spring and early summer are the best times to take softwood cuttings. Fill a pot with equal parts moist peat and horticultural sand, and firm it, especially around the edges.

2 A plantpot about 3in/7.5cm wide will hold three or four cuttings comfortably. Use a dibble to make holes approximately ½in/12mm from the sides of the pot and about 1½in/36mm deep.

*Use a sharp knife to trim off the lower leaves and to remove whisker-like growths from the heel.*

*Insert the cuttings 1½–2in/36–50cm deep in equal parts moist peat and horticultural sand. Firm the mix around them and water gently.*

3 Use a sharp knife to trim the base of each cutting, just below a leaf-joint. Also, cut off the lower leaves. Insert one cutting into each hole, then firm the soil around it and water the cuttings gently.

4 To encourage rapid rooting, insert three to five thin stakes, 6–8in/15–20cm into the soil and draw a clear plastic bag over them. Seal around the pot securely with a rubber band.

## RAISING SHRUBS FROM SEMIHARDWOOD CUTTINGS

*Abelia*
*Camellia*
*Ceanothus* (Californian lilac)
*Chaenomeles* (flowering quince)
*Chimonanthus* (wintersweet)
*Cistus* (rock rose)
*Cotoneaster*
*Escallonia*
*Potentilla*
*Viburnum*

# care of trees, shrubs, and climbers

*Careful planting is essential for all garden plants and especially for long-lived trees, shrubs, and climbers; constricted roots or poor soil will restrict the establishment and subsequent growth of plants. Hedges, evergreen and deciduous, also need careful attention. Pruning is important for ornamental shrubs, trees, and climbers and for fruiting bushes and trees. Roses need yearly pruning with different techniques for hybrid tea, floribunda, climbers, and ramblers.*

# planting trees and shrubs

*Since they form a permanent framework in a garden, always buy strong and healthy trees and shrubs from a reputable nursery or garden center. Inferior plants are never satisfactory and will be a continuing disappointment, whereas healthy plants will give pleasure for many years.*

### Planting container-grown shrubs

Plant these at any time when the soil is neither frozen nor waterlogged. However, spring is best because it gives the plant all summer to become established before the onset of winter.

Prepare the soil a week before planting by forking a dressing of fertilizer lightly into the surface. The day before planting, stand the plant—still in its container—on a well-drained surface and water the soil. The next day, dig a hole to accommodate the roots, make a shallow mound at the bottom of the hole, and firm the soil around it. Stand the plant on the mound, with its most attractive side facing toward the front of the bed. Adjust its height so that the top of the rootball is slightly lower than the surrounding soil. This can be checked by placing a straight piece of wood across the hole. Draw soil around the rootball and firm it down in layers. Continue to fill the hole, firming the soil with the heel of your boot. When planting is completed, rake or lightly fork the soil to remove foot marks, and water the plant.

### Planting bare-rooted trees

Deciduous, bare-rooted trees can be bought from garden centers, nurseries, and through mail-order companies. They are sold leafless during winter and will have been dug up from nursery beds during their dormant period. They too can be planted whenever the soil is neither frozen nor waterlogged.

The first stage in planting begins immediately you get the plant home. Remove all packaging and stand the roots in a bucket of water for about one day. Then plant it or, if the soil is not suitable, heel it into a trench about 12in/30cm deep. Place the roots in the trench, and cover with soil. Before planting, trim long, thin or damaged roots, and any misplaced or damaged branches. Dig a hole large enough to accommodate the roots and follow the steps illustrated on page 135, making sure the friable soil is between the roots.

When supporting a tree by using a vertical stake, knock this into the soil on the windward side before planting the tree, but check that its top will be slightly below the lowest branch. Secure the stake to the tree. Other ways to support trees are described on pages 96–97.

---

#### ADVANTAGES OF CONTAINER-GROWN SHRUBS AND TREES

Since the introduction of garden centers in the early 1960s, plants have been increasingly sold in containers. They have many advantages.
- Plants receive little check when planted.
- They can be inspected before they are bought.
- They make an instant garden.

#### ADVANTAGES OF BARE-ROOTED TREES

- They are often cheaper to buy than container-grown plants.
- Their roots are usually less constricted than those of container-grown plants.
- Unusual species of trees and shrub are not always sold as container-grown plants, but may be available only as bare-rooted specimens from specialist nurseries.

# *planting a container-grown shrub*

1 About a week before planting the shrub, fork a light dressing of a general fertilizer into the soil. Work the fertilizer evenly into the area that is to be planted.

2 The day before planting, thoroughly water the soil in the pot. Dig a hole to accommodate the roots. Make a mound of soil at the bottom and firm it.

3 Lower the rootball into the hole. Use a straight-edged piece of wood to check that the rootball is positioned slightly lower than the level of the surrounding soil.

4 Draw soil around and over the rootball and use the heel of your boot to firm it. Rake the surface level and water the plant and the soil around it thoroughly.

# *planting a bare-rooted tree or shrub*

1 Before planting, thoroughly soak the roots in water. Dig a hole and check that the old soil mark on the stem will be slightly deeper than before.

2 Some shrubs have a "face" side, one that is more attractive than others. Insure that this is positioned to face toward the front of the bed.

3 Spread friable soil over and around the roots and firm it in layers. When planting is complete, rake the soil level to remove all foot marks.

4 When the planting is completed, water the soil and spread a 2–3in/5–7.5cm-thick mulch of garden compost over the soil.

**135**

# hedges and windbreaks

*Hedges have many uses, from creating boundaries and windbreaks to separating and making sheltered gardens for tender plants. Creating privacy and diminishing noise are other roles for hedges, which can be formed of both evergreen and deciduous trees and shrubs.*

## Multipurpose hedges

Hedges fulfill many roles, some functional, others decorative. Keeping out unwanted animals is important, in country and in urban areas. Several shrubs and trees which make good hedges also have spines or prickly leaves and will keep out most intruders. They include holly, pyracantha and berberis, and all can be encouraged to form low dense growth.

Marking a boundary has always been important, using plants such as beech, privet, and yew, but internal hedges are equally useful for edging paths and separating parts of a garden. Good candidates include lavender and *Buxus sempervirens* 'Suffruticosa' (dwarf box).

Forming a windbreak is important in exposed areas, and the benefits can be felt up to a distance of 30 times the height of the hedge, although most of the protection is in the first third (see page 68). Protecting plants in coastal areas from strong, salt-laden wind is also important. Hedging plants that survive these conditions include tamarisk, and *Hippophae* and *Escallonia* varieties.

Privacy from neighbors is increasingly important. Conifers and privet will provide year-round screens. Reducing road and neighbor noise is also important, and conifers and evergreen shrubs do the job well. When noise is a real nuisance, plant a staggered, double row of hedging plants. Finally, use hedges to make an attractive background for other plants. Yew, for instance, makes a superb backdrop for herbaceous borders, and white flowers stand out well against the dark green leaves.

## Planting bare-rooted, deciduous plants

These are planted during their dormant period, from late fall to early spring. Encourage bushiness by cutting back each plant by one-third to a half immediately after planting.

◀ *The slightly tender evergreen shrub* Choisya ternata *(Mexican orange blossom) has flowers and leaves fragrant with the scent of oranges.*

# planting a conifer hedge

1 Dig a trench 1ft/30cm deep and 1½ft/30—45cm wide. Water the plants in their pots and place them in the trench. Use a straight edge to check that the top of each rootball is slightly lower than the soil level.

2 Remove the pot and spread friable soil between and around the rootballs. Firm the soil in layers and check that each plant remains upright. Using the heel of your boot firm the soil around the plants.

3 Use bamboo canes to support the conifers, tying one to each plant. Tie a piece of string to the cane, then around the conifer, without restricting the stem. During the first year regularly check the ties.

4 Water the soil thoroughly to settle it around the roots. Add a 3—4in/7.5—10cm thick mulch around the plants and along the sides of the row. Water the plants regularly through the first summer.

## SIX POPULAR HEDGES

*Buxus sempervirens* 'Suffruticosa' (dwarf box)
Hedge height: 8—15in/20—38cm
Hedge width: 6—9in/15—23cm
Plant: 6—8in/15—20cm apart
Dwarf, evergreen shrub, ideal for forming a miniature hedge as part of a knot or herb garden. Bears small, shiny, deep-green leaves.

*Cupressus macrocarpa* (Monterey cypress)
Hedge height: 6—10ft/1.8—3m
Hedge width: 3½—4ft/1—1.2m
Plant: 18—24in/45—60cm apart
Evergreen conifer with densely packed, bright green foliage. Young plants are sometimes damaged in very cold areas and may need some protection until they are mature.

*Escallonia* 'Donard Seedling'
Hedge height: 5—6ft/1.5—1.8m
Hedge width: 4—5ft/1.2—1.5m
Plant: 15—18in/38—45cm apart
Slightly tender evergreen shrub with a lax nature, and apple-blossom pink flowers in early and midsummer.

*Fagus sylvatica* (beech)
Hedge height: 8—12ft/2.4—3.6m
Hedge width: 3½—5ft/1—1.5m
Plant: 18—24in/45—60cm apart
Deciduous, with bright-green leaves when young, then mid-green and yellow and russet tints in the fall.

*Lavandula angustifolia* 'Hidcote' (lavender)
Hedge height: 1—2ft/30—60cm
Hedge width: 1½—2ft/45—60cm
Plant: 9—12in/23—30cm apart
Evergreen shrub, often short-lived as a hedge, with silvery gray leaves and deep purple-blue flowers from mid- to late summer. Ideal as an internal hedge.

*Ligustrum ovalifolium* (California privet)
Hedge height: 4—6ft/1.2—1.8m
Hedge width: 2—2½ft/60—75cm
Plant: 12—18in/30—45cm apart
Bushy shrub, usually evergreen but partially evergreen in cold areas, with oval leaves. 'Aureum' is a yellow-leaved form.

# pruning ornamental shrubs

*Few gardening tasks are cloaked in as much mystery as pruning. Its aims, however, are quite simple, and with ornamental shrubs include better flowers and an attractive shape. Pruning also insures good health by removing any congested and diseased shoots.*

## When to prune?

The timing of pruning often causes confusion. In temperate areas it is influenced by the cold winter weather and if gardeners did not have to concern themselves with this period, the optimum pruning time for flowering plants would be immediately after their flowers fade. However, as pruning encourages the development of young, tender shoots these would be damaged if late summer-flowering shrubs were pruned immediately their flowers faded.

## Deciduous flowering shrubs

These shrubs can be put into three groups according to the time of year they flower—winter, spring, early to midsummer, and late summer. Good choices include:

**Winter flowering**—*Hamamelis mollis* (Chinese witch hazel), *Cornus mas* (cornelian cherry) and winter-flowering viburnums. They need little pruning, other than cutting back damaged shoots to healthy buds in the spring. Also cut out thin, twiggy shoots and those that grow towards the plant's center.

**Spring and early to midsummer flowering**—they flower on shoots that were produced during the previous year and include forsythia, philadelphus and weigela. They are pruned immediately their flowers fade.

**Late-summer flowering**—these plants flower on shoots that develop during the current year and include *Buddleja davidii* (butterfly bush), *Caryopteris* × *clandonensis* and *Spiraea japonica*. In spring, as soon as all risk of frost has passed, cut out the previous year's flowering shoots to encourage strong new shoots.

◀ Buddlja davidii *(butterfly bush) develops large, tapering spires of flowers from midsummer to fall. Prune them in early spring.*

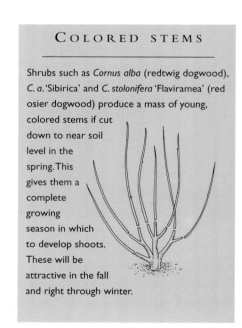

### COLORED STEMS

Shrubs such as *Cornus alba* (redtwig dogwood), *C. a.* 'Sibirica' and *C. stolonifera* 'Flaviramea' (red osier dogwood) produce a mass of young, colored stems if cut down to near soil level in the spring. This gives them a complete growing season in which to develop shoots. These will be attractive in the fall and right through winter.

▶ *Weigela florida* 'Foliis Purpureis' *reveals a wealth of pink flowers amid purple-flushed leaves. It is an ideal shrub for small gardens.*

## Pruning shrubs

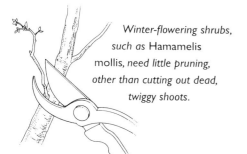

*Winter-flowering shrubs, such as Hamamelis mollis, need little pruning, other than cutting out dead, twiggy shoots.*

*Cut out crossing and dead shoots that congest the shrub's center.*

*Buddleja davidii (butterfly bush), a deciduous shrub with flowers from midsummer to fall, is pruned in early spring.*

### Evergreen shrubs

These are in leaf all year and require little pruning. In spring, or early summer in cold areas, cut out weak, diseased and misplaced shoots. If the shrub flowers in spring, delay pruning until these fade.

### Conifers

Most conifers are evergreen but a few are deciduous and include *Ginkgo biloba* (maidenhair tree) and *Larix* (larch).

Conifers bleed profusely when pruned in spring and summer, and are therefore best cut in late fall or early winter, when there is not an active flow of sap.

### Pruning ericas (heath) and callunas (heather)

These evergreen shrubs are kept neat by trimming them with hedging shears. The time to prune depends on when they flower. Remove all the clippings.

✸ *Callunas* and summer-flowering ericas—trim in spring, before growth begins. Cut off dead flowers to form a neat and undulating outline. Plants pruned in this way include *Erica cinerea* (bell heather), *E. vagans* (Cornish heath),

*E. terminalis* (Corsican heath), *E. tetralix* (cross-leaved heather) and *Calluna vulgaris* (Scottish heather, ling).

✸ Winter and spring-flowering types—they are trimmed as soon as their flowers fade to create a neat outline. They include *Erica × darleyensis* (Darley Dale heath), *E. erigena* better known as *E. mediterranea* (Mediterranean heath), and *E. carnea* (spring heath or winter heath). *Daboecias*—trim off old flower heads and lax shoots in late fall, after flowering has finished. In cold areas leave this task until early spring.

Tree heathers—they need little pruning but in late spring, after their flowers fade, remove straggly shoots.

# pruning climbers

*Many climbing plants need regular pruning to restrain growth or to encourage the regular development of flowers. Deciduous climbers grown for their attractive foliage require little pruning, other than restricting their size, whereas those with attractive flowers need annual attention.*

### Pruning climbers and wall shrubs

These plants are so varied in their nature, flowering time, and size that pruning is best described individually.

❀ *Actinidia deliciosa*, still known as *A. chinensis* (Chinese gooseberry)—

▲ *Leafy climbers create privacy and are ideal for separating parts of a garden. This enables cloistered areas to lead directly on to lawns.*

deciduous climber. In late winter, use pruners to thin out and restrict growth.

❀ *Actinidia kolomikta* (variegated kiwi vine)—deciduous climber. If space is restricted, cut back shoots in late winter.

❀ *Akebia*—evergreen climber in mild winters, but usually semievergreen. Thin out and shorten straggly shoots in late winter or spring.

❀ *Berberidopsis corallina* (coral plant)—slightly tender evergreen shrub. Use pruners to thin out overcrowded plants in late winter or early spring.

❀ *Carpenteria californica*—slightly tender evergreen shrub. No regular pruning is needed, other than cutting out straggly shoots after the flowers fade.

❀ *Ceanothus* (California lilac)—many evergreen species can be grown against a wall. Little pruning is needed, but reduce the previous year's growth in spring.

❀ *Clematis macropetala*—deciduous climber. Cut out dead and thin shoots in early spring.

❀ *Clematis montana*—deciduous climber. Little pruning is needed, especially if it is given plenty of space. However, when

pruning is needed to restrain growth, cut back as soon as the flowers fade.

❀ *Clematis flammula*—deciduous climber. From late winter to early spring, cut out weak and dead shoots. Also, cut back to healthy buds any shoots that flowered during the previous year.

❀ *Clematis orientalis* 'Orange peel'—deciduous climber. This is pruned as for *C. flammula*.

❀ *Clematis tangutica*—deciduous climber. Prune as for *C. flammula*.

❀ *Eccremocarpus scaber* (Chilean glory flower)—evergreen sub-shrubby climber. Use pruners to cut out frost-damaged shoots in late spring. If it is severely damaged, the best course of action that you can take is to cut all shoots back to their bases in spring.

❀ *Fallopia baldschuanica* (Russian vine)—deciduous climber. Cut back rampant plants in spring.

❀ *Hedera* (ivy)—evergreen climber. Wide range, from small-leaved types to those with leaves 6in/15cm wide or more. As necessary, cut back rampant plants in spring.

# pruning winter-flowering jasmine

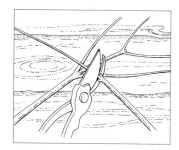 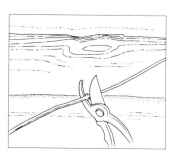 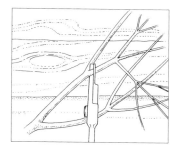 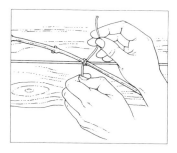

1 Use sharp pruners to cut out crossing shoots; cut each one back to a strong bud.

2 Cut back sideshoots to strong buds to encourage the development of new growth.

3 Where shoots are congested, cut them back to a strong shoot or bud.

4 The last task is to tie all sideshoots to the supporting wires. Use soft string.

❀ *Humulus lupulus* 'Aureus' (yellow-leaved hop)—herbaceous climber. Cut down to ground level all shoots in fall or late winter.

❀ *Hydrangea anomala petiolaris* (Japanese climbing hydrangea)—deciduous climber. No regular pruning is needed, other than trimming to shape and cutting out dead shoots in spring.

❀ *Jasminum nudiflorum* (winter-flowering jasmine)—deciduous shrub. After flowering, cut out weak and old shoots. Also, cut back flowered shoots to 2–3in/5–7.5cm of their bases.

❀ *Jasminum officinale* (common white jasmine)—deciduous climber. After the flowers fade, thin out flowering shoots to their bases.

❀ *Lonicera* (honeysuckle)—deciduous, semievergreen or evergreen climber. No regular pruning is required, other than thinning out congested shoots after the flowers fade.

❀ *Parthenocissus*—deciduous climber. No regular pruning is required, other than

cutting out overcrowded and dead shoots in spring.

❀ *Passiflora caerulea* (passion flower)—slightly tender evergreen climber. In late winter, cut out any tangled shoots to their bases or to soil level. Also, cut back side-shoots to about 6in/15cm of the main stems.

❀ *Vitis coignetiae* (crimson glory vine)—deciduous climber. No regular pruning is needed, but where necessary to prevent the plant from becoming invasive, trim excessive growth in spring.

❀ *Wisteria*—deciduous climber. Prune established plants in winter and summer. In late winter, cut back all shoots to within two or three buds of the point where they started growing during the previous season. In the latter part of midsummer, cut the current season's young shoots back to within five or six buds of the base.

▶ *The dramatically colored* Humulus lupulus 'Aureus' *(yellow-leaved hop) is a herbaceous climber and each year produces fresh leaves.*

# pruning fruit bushes and trees

*Bush, cane, and tree fruits differ in the way they produce fruits. Some develop fruit on young, newly produced shoots, others on an existing framework. Therefore, pruning must encourage the development of suitable shoots, as well as allow light and air to reach the plants.*

## Bush fruits

These popular fruits for small gardens need little space and produce fruit within a few years of being planted.

⊛ Blackcurrants—on planting, cut all stems to one or two buds above the soil. During the following year, stems develop, which are left to grow and bear fruit. Between late fall and early spring the following year, and thereafter, prune by cutting to ground level all shoots that produced fruits. Also, cut out thin, weak and diseased shoots to allow light and air to enter the bush.

⊛ Gooseberries—established bushes have a permanent framework upon which short, fruit-bearing spurs develop. Newly planted gooseberry bushes without a framework of branches should be pruned in winter by cutting back all shoots by half. Prune established bushes in winter; cut out diseased, damaged, and overcrowded shoots. Also, cut back by half all shoots produced during the previous season, and reduce side-shoots to about 2in/5cm long.

⊛ Redcurrants and white currants— they have a permanent framework and are pruned like gooseberries.

## Cane fruits

Being upright these will fit into narrow positions, perhaps alongside a path.

⊛ Summer-fruiting raspberries—they fruit on upright canes produced the previous year. Prune established plants in the fall by cutting out all canes that produced fruit in the summer. Leave the young canes tied to the supporting wires to fruit the following year.

⊛ Fall-fruiting raspberries—they fruit on canes produced earlier the same year. Prune established plants in late winter and cut all canes to ground level. In spring, as the canes grow, cut out weak

▲ *Cane fruits, such as raspberries, need yearly pruning to encourage the growth of young canes that will bear fruit during the following year.*

ones at the base and tie the remaining ones to the supporting wires.

✹ Blackberries and hybrid berries—they fruit on canes produced the previous year. Immediately after picking the berries, cut down to the base all canes that produced fruit. Then spread out the remaining young canes and tie them to the supporting wires.

## Tree fruits

It usually takes several years before a framework of branches and fruiting spurs is formed. Where space is limited, plant cordon, espalier and fan-trained forms against a wall, or secure them to a framework of tiered wires.

✹ Apples and pears—during the first four years it is essential to develop healthy, well-positioned branches. Once they are established, pruning creates a balance between maintaining and renewing the framework and retaining a proportion of the existing fruiting wood and spurs, while developing others. Creating and maintaining this framework is a task best tackled in winter. However, when apples and pears are grown as cordons and espaliers, pruning will also be needed during the summer to retain the shape and inhibit the growth of unnecessary shoots. Do not be in a hurry for the tree to bear fruit.

✹ Cherries—never prune cherry trees in winter when they are not growing strongly and are unable to prevent the entry of bacterial canker through cut surfaces. They are ideal for growing as a fan against a wall.

*▶ Apple trees need regular pruning to encourage the development of fresh fruiting spurs to replace old ones. Old wood can also be removed.*

✹ Plums—these are usually grown as bushes or fans. When creating a framework of branches in a young tree, prune in mid-spring, just as the sap is rising. Try to create three to five strong branches. Later, prune in early summer, removing dead and diseased wood to keep the tree healthy and not congested. With fan-trained trees, prune in spring to create short side-shoots that grow from the framework.

✹ Figs—these are often inherited in old, town gardens and are easy to cultivate when their growth is limited by restricting their roots. Prune established plants in early summer. Pinch back all young shoots leaving only five leaves to encourage the development of new, fruiting shoots. In early fall, thin out the young fruits (about the size of a pea). These will develop into fruits that can be picked during the following year.

### Pruning gooseberries

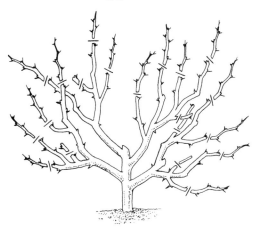

### Pruning raspberries

Summer fruiting | Fall fruiting

# pruning bush and species roses

*There are many strongly held opinions about the best way to prune roses involving the timing, method, and severity. Here we give the basic philosophy, but you might have to amend your approach according to the rose variety, soil type, and weather.*

### Large-flowered bush (hybrid tea) and cluster-flowered bush (floribunda) roses

These need regular pruning to keep them healthy and flower-bearing, but there is some disagreement about how and when to prune. Although pruning can be done at any time during a rose's dormant period, in cold areas it is best left until early spring. The optimum time is when growth is beginning and the uppermost buds are starting to swell, but before leaves appear. Rose bushes planted in late fall and during winter are also best pruned in spring. Because leaving pruning until early spring puts bushes at risk from winter wind damage, when their roots might be loosened in the soil, it is best to cut back long shoots in late fall or early winter.

Bush roses respond in distinct ways to the severity in which they are pruned. If they are hard pruned (sometimes called low pruning), with stems cut back to three or four buds, they produce vigorous shoots during the following season. This suits newly planted bushes and weak-growing varieties. Also, it is a technique often used when growing exhibition blooms. Where large-flowered bush roses are grown close together in beds, hard pruning is the best method. It results in a mass of strong stems.

◄ *Most rose bushes need yearly pruning to create glorious displays of flowers and to keep the plant healthy and not congested with shoots.*

If moderately pruned (sometimes called medium pruning), with stems cut back by about one half, growth develops. This suits most bush roses.

When bush roses are lightly pruned (sometimes called long or high pruning), cutting back stems by about one third, only a little growth develops. This suits vigorous varieties and roses growing in light, sandy, and impoverished soils. When light pruning is carried out over

## WHEN MAKING CUTS

Take care to make pruning cuts in the right position. A cut too high above a bud encourages a shoot to die back, but if the cut is too close it will damage the bud. Make a sloping cut about ½in/6mm above an outward-facing bud. Use sharp pruners with a good action. Ragged cuts with blunt blades make it easier for infections and diseases to enter the stem, and cause it to die back.

several years, it often results in spindly bushes that bear inferior flowers. Encourage better growth by feeding, mulching, and watering plants.

## Shrub and species roses

These need very little pruning and none at all during the first two years after being planted. During this period allow the shrub to build up growth. Thereafter, each spring, cut out dead, weak, thin, and diseased shoots. If, after several years of growth, the shrub becomes congested, remove older shoots to enable young ones to grow.

## 'New English Roses'

These are repeat-flowering shrubs. The aim is to build up an attractively shaped shrub and to encourage the regular development of young shoots. These shrubs vary in size so beware of pruning too severely. When you buy a 'New English Rose' it will probably have been pruned so no more will be needed during the first year. Each spring cut out weak, thin, twiggy and diseased growth. After a few years, also cut out congested growth so that young shoots can grow strongly. Cut the remaining shoots to half their size, but take care not to spoil the shape of the shrub. Some 'New English Roses' can be treated as bushes or climbers.

### *Pruning hybrid tea and floribunda roses*

**Hard pruning**

*Cut back all stems to three or four buds from their base.*

**Moderate pruning**

*Cut back strong, healthy stems by half. Cut weak ones back further.*

**Light pruning**

*Cut back stems by about one third. Also, cut back sideshoots.*

▶ *Roses are equally attractive whether planted in borders with a rich medley of other flowers or on their own in separate beds and borders.*

# pruning climbers and ramblers

*These roses may appear to be similar, but they have different natures. Climbers have a permanent framework and large flowers borne singly or in small trusses during the latter part of early summer and into midsummer. Ramblers produce small flowers in huge trusses, in midsummer.*

## Pruning climbers

There are two main ways to prune climbers, and these are influenced by the variety. Pruning takes place in early spring, when growth is just beginning.

Method one—little pruning is needed except for cutting out dead, diseased and old, exhausted wood. Cut back to 3in/7.5cm long all side-shoots that flowered the previous year. Varieties needing this treatment include 'Casino', 'Climbing Ena Harkness', 'Climbing Étoile de Hollande', 'Madame Grégoire Staechelin', and 'Mermaid'.

Method two—little pruning is needed except for cutting out dead, diseased, and old, exhausted wood. Also cut off withered shoot tips. Varieties suitable for this treatment include 'Compassion', 'Golden Showers', 'Joseph's Coat', 'Parade', 'Madame Alfred Carrière', 'Maigold', 'Meg', 'Pink Perpetue', and 'Zéphirine Drouhin'.

## Pruning ramblers

There are three main ways to prune ramblers and, as with climbers, the appropriate method is influenced by the variety. Pruning is in late summer or fall, as soon as flowering has finished. Cut stems of newly planted ramblers to soil level. The following information applies

◄ *Climbing Rose 'Mermaid' has large, single, sulfur yellow flowers and amber-colored stamens. This rose is superb when seen in bright sunlight growing against a wall.*

to established ramblers that will have young shoots bearing flowers the following year, and to shoots that produced flowers in the current year.

Method one—having removed all stems that produced flowers during the current year, tie the young shoots to a supporting framework. However, if insufficient new shoots were produced, leave a few old stems and trim back their lateral shoots to 3in/7.5cm long. Varieties suitable for this treatment include 'American Pillar', 'Crimson Shower', 'Dorothy Perkins', 'Sander's White Rambler', and 'Seagull'.

Method two—cut back all flowered stems to new growth, and cut back one or two old stems to about 12in/30cm above soil level. Where plants are congested and it is impossible to take down stems, cut back lateral shoots to 3in/7.5cm long. Varieties suitable for this treatment include 'Albéric Barbier',

'Albertine', 'Paul's Himalayan Climber' and 'Veilchenblau'.

Method three—pruning is very simple because all you need do is cut out dead and old wood, and cut back the tips of lateral shoots that have flowered. Varieties that have proved suitable for this pruning method include 'Emily Gray', *Rosa filipes* 'Kiftsgate', and 'Wedding Day'.

▲ *Climbing Rose 'Madame Grégoire Staechelin', has long, shapely buds that open to reveal semi-double, glowing pink flowers.*

## PRUNING TOOLS

Pruners are ideal for cutting sideshoots on climbers and ramblers, but when severing stouter stems, stronger equipment is essential. Long-handled loppers—with an anvil or bypass cutting action—will cut stout stems from a distance, reducing scratching. A Grecian pruning saw with a curved blade that cuts on the pull stroke is also useful when dealing with neglected ramblers. Wear thick gloves to protect your hands. Place all the pruned stems in a wheelbarrow, or collect them on a large piece of hessian on the ground.

# gardening under glass

A greenhouse extends the range of things you can do in your garden. For example, instead of buying half-hardy annuals as bedding plants, you can grow them from seed. Many useful devices make greenhouse gardening easy. They include automatic ventilators, extractor fans, and heated propagation frames. The following pages explain the technicalities of greenhouse gardening. They also show you how to utilize cloches, cold frames, and poly-tunnels, all alternatives to the greenhouse, and especially useful in the vegetable garden.

# greenhouse gardening

*Greenhouses add a dimension to gardening in a temperate climate, enabling a wider range of plants to be grown. Summer-flowering bedding plants can be sown in gentle warmth in late winter and early spring for later planting in borders and containers when all risk of frost has passed.*

## Range of greenhouses

Greenhouses range in shape, structure, and size, giving a very wide choice. Where possible, choose the largest greenhouse you can afford that will fit into your garden. Growing plants in greenhouses often becomes a passion demanding ever more space.

❀ Even-span—also called full-span greenhouses, have a traditional outline with a ridged sloping glass roof. Traditionally made of wood, they have a low brick or wood-paneled base, and glass above. Wooden designs are available but aluminum types are popular; these have glass from the ground to the apex.

Even-span greenhouses about 8ft/2.4m wide have a central path, and 3ft/90cm-wide areas on both sides that can be used for staging or growing plants such as tomatoes at ground level. Where a greenhouse is 6ft/1.8m or 7ft/2.1m wide, the spaces will be smaller but still thoroughly practical.

❀ Lean-to greenhouses—these are designed in width and length to suit the wall they are constructed against. Most lean-to greenhouses are glazed from soil level to the top, but with a brick surround to about 2½ft/75cm high they begin to look like a conservatory, especially where there is direct entry into the house.

❀ Hexagonal greenhouses—these have a more modern design and are becoming increasingly popular. They are usually constructed of aluminum with glass. Staging can be bought to fit.

❀ Mini greenhouses—these are for gardens with only enough room for a

◀ *Wood-framed lean-to greenhouses are ideal for mature and informal gardens. Aluminum-framed types have a rather more clinical look.*

tiny lean-to structure, which can be positioned against a garden wall, a stout fence, or the house. Proprietary staging is available and young plants can be raised in them in spring. However, because the volume of air inside is small, dramatic fluctuations in temperature can occur when the front is closed.

## Wood or metal?

Greenhouses were traditionally built with a wooden frame, but increasingly aluminum is now used.

❀ Timber—the type of wood used markedly influences its longevity. Baltic red wood, also known as yellow deal, is used but needs regular painting. Western red cedar is more durable and, instead of being painted, is regularly coated in linseed oil. The Victorians used long-lasting oak and teak, but nowadays their high cost usually makes them prohibitively expensive.

❀ Aluminum—this is widely used and, when glass is added, creates a strong structure. The extruded aluminum is designed so that both shelving and insulation brackets can be attached. Because the glazing bars are narrower than those of wood, much more light enters the greenhouse.

▶ *Aluminum-framed greenhouses are available in many interesting shapes, including a wigwam (right) and a hexagonal shape.*

▼ *The all-glass, aluminum-framed greenhouse enables the maximum amount of light to enter the structure.*

---

## POSITIONING A GREENHOUSE

Choosing the right position in a garden for a greenhouse can reduce fuel bills. Try to:

❀ Position full-span greenhouses so that the span runs east to west. Position lean-to types, against a south- or west-facing wall. Where

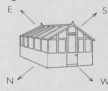

possible, position doors on the side away from the prevailing wind. If the door is hinged insure that it does not open directly into the wind; similarly, if it slides, check that it first opens on the side away from the prevailing wind.

❀ Avoid positions under overhanging trees which block out light. A snapping branch could also cause damage.

❀ Because strong winds in late winter and early spring soon cool a greenhouse, plant an evergreen hedge several yards away on the north or windward side.

# equipment for greenhouses

*Successful greenhouse gardening needs a few pieces of equipment. Shading is essential during summer, while heating is needed to germinate seeds and root cuttings. Although tomatoes in growing bags can be placed directly on soil at ground level, staging is needed for seed trays and pots.*

### Ventilators

Good circulation of fresh air is essential to maintain healthy plants within a greenhouse, especially during summer when the temperature can rapidly rise. A ventilator is really needed on both sides of the roof. In small greenhouses only one ventilator is usually fitted, and this should be on the south side. In large greenhouses, side-ventilators are definitely an advantage.

Ventilators are usually operated by hand, but automatic ones can be fitted. An extractor fan can also be fitted into the gable end of a greenhouse.

### Shading

Strong sunlight dramatically increases the temperature and can damage some plants. There are several ways to provide shading and the cheapest and easiest method is to coat the outside in a proprietary whitener. Paint only the central two-thirds of each pane of glass. During summer it wears off and cracks. Wash it off in the fall and reapply the following early summer. Roller blinds fitted to the inside of a greenhouse are expensive, but they can be rolled up during cloudy periods.

### Benches and shelving

If you want to sow seeds in spring and early summer, permanent or temporary staging is essential along at least one side of a greenhouse. It also enables plants to be displayed throughout the year. A wide choice of staging is available.

✿ Wooden staging—this is usually fitted in wood greenhouses and has a supporting framework with a surface formed of slatted wood, with 1in/2.5cm gaps between. This allows the free circulation of air around the plants, and free drainage from them.

◀ *Electric-powered heaters and propagation units make raising and growing plants in a greenhouse easy and trouble-free.*

❀ Metal staging—aluminum-framed greenhouses, with glazing bars made of extruded metal, are inevitably fitted with metal benching. The bench can usually be folded down to enable crops to be grown in soil at ground level. The staging is made of aluminum and thick, plastic-coated wire, which allows air to circulate around pots and plants.

❀ Solid staging—this is rarely seen now. It traditionally consisted of a solid base covered with a layer of pea gravel. It is ideal in summer because humidity can be encouraged around the plants by keeping the gravel moist.

❀ Temporary staging—in spring, when seeds are sown and seedlings pricked out, extra space can be created by using strong wire to suspend planks of wood, from wooden glazed bars. These can be used to support seed trays. When watering plants on temporary shelves, insure water does not drip onto plants underneath, because it can damage fragile seedlings. Aluminum greenhouses have proprietary fittings.

### SEASONAL CLEANING

❀ In late fall or winter, thoroughly clean the inside and outside of a greenhouse. Clean glass is essential to enable light to enter, while dirty glazed bars may harbor pests and diseases. Always:
❀ Replace cracked panes of glass.
❀ Remove all plants and scrub surfaces with hot water and a disinfectant. Leave the door and ventilators open until the inside is dry.
❀ Check electrical fittings and equipment, ready for next spring.

### Insulating a greenhouse

Preventing warm air escaping is essential, especially in late winter and spring. Check that ventilators and doors fit well, and secure bubble-wrap insulation to the inside of the greenhouse. In wooden structures it can be stapled or pinned to the glazing bars. Aluminum greenhouses have proprietary fittings. Remove the bubble-wrap in late spring.

▶ Slatted, wooden staging is a traditional way to display plants in a wooden greenhouse. It allows drainage yet keeps the soil relatively warm.

▼ In spring a greenhouse enables a wide range of half-hardy annuals to be raised from seed, until they are ready to be planted out.

# heating greenhouses

*In temperate climates, heating is needed in greenhouses during late winter and spring if summer-flowering bedding plants are to be grown from seeds. Tomato plants can be planted in growing bags or large pots in early spring in a heated greenhouse.*

## Methods of heating

There are two main ways to heat a small greenhouse, by kerosene or electricity.

⊛ Kerosene heaters—these are popular and relatively inexpensive to buy and operate, although it is necessary to have space in a lockable shed away from your house for cans of fuel. The heaters can be moved from one greenhouse to another, and removed in early summer, cleaned and stored. The amount of heat they produce depends on the size of the heater and the length of wick allowed to burn. If the length of the wick is excessive, it will result in black smoke. Single- and double-burner heaters are available, in a range of sizes.

When a heater is being used, check it each evening to make sure that there is sufficient kerosene to burn through the night. Use a small dip stick to check the kerosene level and never tip the heater on its side, especially when it is alight. Kerosene, when it is burnt, produces an equal volume of water vapor, consumes oxygen and also gives off gases, so it is essential to leave a ventilator slightly open at all times.

▲ *Electrical and kerosene propagating units are available and both types are suited for use in a small greenhouse.*

### HEATED PROPAGATION CASES

These provide the right conditions for seeds to germinate and cuttings to root without having to heat the whole greenhouse. They are heated by electricity or kerosene, and are available in several sizes. At the end of each season, clean and store the propagation case in a dry shed. Check all electrical cables and connections.

Electricity is a clean, efficient way to heat a greenhouse, but the cables and sockets must be installed and maintained by a professional electrician. Electricity and water are a dangerous duo, so do not take any risks.

A thermostat controls the heater, and there are two main types to consider. Tubular heaters are usually secured to a wall, about 10in/25cm above the ground. They create a gentle flow of rising warm air. If installed under a solid-surface bench, insure that a 4–6in/ 10–15cm gap is left at the back to let warm air escape and circulate.

Fan heaters also create a good circulation of warm air, which helps to prevent the onset of diseases encouraged by damp, static air. Check that hot blasts of air do not blow directly on plants. Finally, do not use domestic fan heaters in a greenhouse because they are unsafe in a humid atmosphere, and especially where water may be inadvertently splashed on them.

## Conserving heat

Since heating a greenhouse is expensive, whether by kerosene or electricity, you must conserve heat. Site a greenhouse so that the maximum amount of sunlight enters, especially in late winter and spring. A hedge positioned on the cold windward side also reduces the heat loss.

The cost of heating does not actually rise in direct proportion to the desired temperature but increases dramatically with each extra degree of heat that is generated. Therefore, assess the optimum temperature required for all the plants and set the thermostat accordingly.

In the fall, check that doors and ventilators fit their frames, and replace any broken panes of glass. Fit draft excluders around doors, and make sure that they cannot be blown open. Also, install bubble-glazing. In exceptionally cold areas, place a large sheet of clear polyethylene over the cold, windward side of a greenhouse. It will need to be securely pegged down to withstand winter weather. Lastly, always check for broken panes of glass after a storm.

▼ *Kerosene heaters are relatively cheap to buy and easy to install in a greenhouse. Both single- and double-burners (below) are available.*

# cloches, frames, and tunnels

*Cloches and poly-tunnels are frequently used in vegetable gardens to enable early crops and extend their growing or ripening periods into the fall. Cold frames are mainly used to harden off summer-flowering bedding plants. Low-growing vegetables can also be grown in them.*

## Cloches

The range of cloches is now wide. Once they were all made of glass, but flat and corrugated PVC kinds are extremely popular now for reasons of cost and safety. Note that cloches must not be airtight; a gentle flow of air is essential.

❀ Glass cloches—these allow more light to reach plants than those made of plastic, and they conserve more warmth.

▲ *Bell-jars have a traditional and cottage garden-like aspect that makes them features of interest as well as a way to protect plants.*

There are several types and sizes to suit most crops. The barn cloche is a good choice, formed of four sheets of glass clipped together: two sheets form the sides, with the other two creating a tent above them. Barn cloches are ideal for covering plants up to 12in/30cm high. The other main type is the tent cloche, with a simpler construction and two sheets of glass in a tent-like shape. They are lower than barn cloches and are ideal for young plants and small salad crops such as lettuces and radishes. Less frequently seen are tall, frame-like structures about 2ft/60cm high and 4–5ft/1.2–1.5m wide. They allow a good circulation of air over plants. Instead of glass, some are covered in rigid, clear plastic.

❀ Corrugated PVC cloches—these are extremely strong and resilient and, although they do not transmit as much light as glass, they are less likely to break and are safer to use. Metal hoops hold the corrugated plastic in a half-circle, in close contact with the soil, and prevent it being blown away. PVC is also used to construct barn-type cloches. Clear PVC is used for the top, with opaque PVC often employed along the sides of the cloche and at the ends.

❀ Bell-jars—traditionally made of glass, but modern versions are made from transparent PVC. Alternatively, large, clear plastic bottles with the base cut off can be placed over individual plants or seedlings. Glass jelly-jars are also useful, especially for covering marrow seedlings.

### Cloches, tunnels, and bell-jars

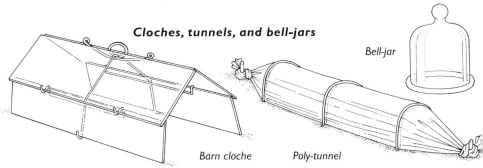

*Bell-jar*

*Barn cloche*   *Poly-tunnel*

## Poly-tunnels

These have a simple construction, with metal hoops inserted into the ground and polyethylene sheeting drawn over to form a tunnel. Plants underneath require ventilation and therefore it is a daily task to open the front. Unfortunately, polyethylene sheeting has a life-span of only two or three years. Sunlight soon causes deterioration, but it is a cheap way to protect low-growing plants.

## Cold frames

English pit lights are now part of garden history, but are still occasionally seen. They were heavy to move and needed a permanent framework on which they could be rested. Later, Dutch lights became popular, as they are much lighter and easier to handle. They consist of a single piece of glass in a frame about 4ft/1.2m long and 2ft/60cm wide. They rest on a wood or brick framework,

12–18in/30–45cm high at the back and 6–12in/15–30cm high at the front. Make sure that the front side faces south or southwest so that plants receive the maximum amount of light. Cold frames are mainly used to acclimatize plants raised in gentle warmth in late winter or spring, to outdoor conditions. Alternatively, they are very useful for growing tender salad vegetables that need a slightly sheltered environment.

▲ *Cold frames are useful in spring, when they protect plants while the weather is cold and before they can be planted into a garden.*

# growing your own food

One of the joys of gardening is to eat food fresh from your own garden. Even in small gardens this is possible by growing salad crops such as lettuces, scallions, radishes, and tomatoes. Fresh herbs, grown in cartwheel herb gardens or pots on a patio or a terrace, are also welcome. Large fruit trees are not practical in small gardens but espalier and cordon apples and pears, and fan-trained peaches and nectarines, are possible. Dwarf apple trees can be grown in large pots in small paved areas and will bear a large crop of fruit.

# apples and pears

*Apples are among the easiest tree fruit to grow in temperate climates. Pears are also popular, but they are a little harder to grow. Dessert varieties need a sunnier and more wind-sheltered position than apples. In small gardens, grow apples as cordons or espaliers.*

## Planting and growing apples

In the past, apple trees often grew 20ft/6m high or more, and were difficult to prune and harvest. Today, a dwarf bush apple on an M27 rootstock is ideal for a small garden, where it grows about 6ft/1.8m high and produces 12–16lb/5.4–7.2kg of fruit each year. Cordons, when grown on a similar rootstock and planted 18in/45cm apart, produce 5–7lb/2.2–3.1kg of fruit. Espaliers planted about 14ft/4.2m apart bear 20–30lb/9–13kg of fruit. Bushes demand less pruning than cordons, while espaliers need more attention.

Choose a frost-free site in full sun with shelter from strong wind. Sun is essential to ripen highly colored dessert varieties. Apples usually flower in the early part of late spring; in areas where frosts repeatedly occur at that time, select a late-flowering variety.

Well-drained moisture-retentive soil is essential, especially for dessert varieties. Cooking apple trees grow well on heavier soil. Bare-rooted trees are planted during their dormant period in winter. When planting out, mix in plenty of well-decayed garden compost or manure.

Container-grown trees are planted whenever the soil and weather allow; planting them is fully described on pages 134–135. Support cordons and espaliers with galvanized wires tensioned between strong posts 8–12ft/2.4–3.6m apart; space the wires 15–18in/38–45cm apart to about 7ft/2.1m high. Check the posts every spring for wind damage.

◄ *Apple trees can be grown in tubs or large pots, but plant only those growing on dwarf rootstocks.*

### APPLE TREES IN TUBS

An apple tree in a container on a patio is the best way to grow fruit in a small garden. Dwarf rootstocks such as M27 (trees in containers grow to about 5ft/1.5m high) and M9 (up to 8ft/2.4m) make this possible, using 15in/38cm-wide wooden tubs or pots.

Well-drained, moisture-retentive compost is essential and in summer regular watering is needed, sometimes every day. During winter it may be necessary to wrap straw around the tub to prevent the roots freezing and getting damaged. A plastic sheet can also be used to prevent the soil from becoming too wet. Repotting every other late winter is essential, as well as feeding during summer. Large crops are not possible but good varieties to seek include 'Gravenstein', 'Fiesta', 'Liberty', and 'Sunrise'.

## Planting and growing pears

The range of rootstocks for pears is limited so that it is not possible to grow pears on trees as small as dwarf apples. Few gardens can accommodate pear trees up to 20ft/6m high, and therefore in small areas it is best to grow pears as cordons or espaliers. Cordon pears planted 18in/75cm apart each produce 4–6lb/1.8–2.7kg of fruit a year, while an espalier yields 15–25lb/6.8–11.3kg.

The same methods are used for planting and supporting pears as for apples, but pears are more susceptible to drought than apples, so be prepared to water the soil copiously during dry periods. It is probably better to select a dessert variety than a cooker, but it will need a compatible pollinator that will flower at the same time. For example, 'Conference' is partly self-fertile and needs other varieties, such as 'Seckel' or 'Harrow Delight'. Alternatively, if you have a warm garden plant the superb 'Comice', also 'Highland' (this has the bonus of keeping the fruits from late fall to early winter).

### Cordon
Single, inclined stem

### Espalier
Tiered branches

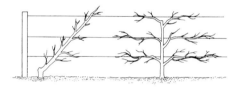

### Espalier supports

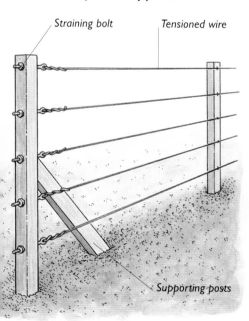

Straining bolt    Tensioned wire

Supporting posts

▶ *Pears grown as cordons or espaliers are best for planting in a small garden. The fruits are easily picked without using stepladders.*

# peaches, nectarines, and plums

*Peaches and nectarines need a warm climate. They are closely related; nectarines are smooth-skinned sports (mutations) of peaches, which have fuzzy skins. Nectarines are less hardy than peaches and have smaller yields. Plums are easily grown stone fruits.*

## Growing peaches and nectarines

In temperate climates, with the likelihood of frost in early and mid-spring and a general lack of pollinating insects at that time, it is often difficult to grow peaches and nectarines successfully.

Where conditions are least favorable, choose a peach rather than a nectarine, and always grow it as a fan trained on galvanized wires against a warm, sunny, south or southwest facing wall rather than as a bush.

Choose a reliable variety such as 'Harbrite' or 'Reliance'. Fortunately, peaches and nectarines are self-fertile.

Construct tiers of galvanized wires before planting a peach or nectarine. Position the lowest wire 1ft/30cm above the ground, with others 8in/20cm apart to a height of about 6ft/1.8m. Secure the wires 4in/10cm from the wall. Because peaches and nectarines are best grown against a wall it is essential to thoroughly prepare the soil by adding plenty of moisture-retentive, well-decayed garden compost or manure. Prepare an area 18in/45cm deep and 3½ft/1m square and position the main stem about 9in/23cm from the wall. Plant bare-rooted specimens in late fall or early winter, and container-grown plants at any time when the soil and weather allow. Choose a two- or three-year-old plant with eight or more branches.

Rather than tie stems directly to the wires, secure them to bamboo canes, and then to the wires. The two main arms should be at an upward 45° angle, with other stems spaced out.

▲ *Plant a fan-trained peach tree against a warm, sunny wall. To maintain the shape, secure the branches to tiers of galvanized wires.*

Always prune peaches and nectarines in late winter or early spring, when growth begins, but never tackle this task in winter. Initially, the purpose of pruning is to encourage the development of a fan. Pruning a two- or three-year-old plant is much easier than creating a fan from a rooted shoot with no side-shoots. On an established plant, cut back each arm of the fan by about one third, making cuts slightly above a downward pointing bud. In the following summer, shoots develop on each arm; allow three to form and tie each of them to a cane. Also, use a thumb to rub out buds growing toward the wall. During late summer, when each of these shoots is 18in/45cm long, nip out their growing points. Picking and storing peaches and nectarines is described on pages 168–169.

## Growing plums

These are popular fruits. Because they flower early in the year and are vulnerable to frost, plant them in a mild, frost-free area. Dessert plums especially need a warm, sunny position to encourage good flavor. Plums can be grown in several forms, including standards, half-standards, bushes, and

pyramids, but in small gardens a fan-trained form is better.

Prepare the soil in the same way as for peaches and nectarines, and with a similar arrangement of tiered wires against a wall. Also, plant and prune fan-trained plants in the same way.

See pages 168–169 for information on picking and storing plums.

### Fan trained

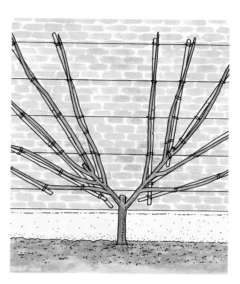

▼ *Plum trees flower early in the season and therefore need a warm, sheltered position against a wall. This is an ideal form for small gardens.*

### HAND POLLINATING

Peaches and nectarines flower early in the year when pollinating insects are scarce. Therefore, use a soft brush or loose ball of cotton wool to gently dab each flower every other day from the time the buds open until the petals fall.

# growing soft fruits

*It is surprising how many different types of soft fruits can be grown in a small garden. Raspberries grow vertically, while blackcurrant bushes take up only a little space. Strawberries may be grown alongside paths to be easily accessible, but if space is restricted they can be grown in a barrel.*

## Strawberries

There are several forms of these popular, easily grown fruits, including perpetual and alpine, but the summer-fruiting varietes are most widely grown. Once planted, they are usually left for three or four years before being discarded, with fresh beds prepared for new plants. It is possible to grow summer-fruiting types as an annual crop producing high quality fruit, but they will not grow as prolifically as well-established two- or three-year-old plants. Plant bare-rooted, summer-fruiting varieties between midsummer and early fall, and container-grown plants at any time when the soil is workable. In practice, however, they are best planted at the same time as bare-rooted plants.

Prepare strawberry beds by digging the soil in late spring or early summer, and adding well-decomposed garden compost or manure. Remove and burn perennial weeds. Just before planting, dust the surface with a general fertilizer. When planting bare-rooted plants, spread out the roots over a small mound of soil at the bottom of the hole, and check that the crown of the plant is level with the surrounding ground. Firm the soil around the roots. With container-grown plants do not bury the crown but keep it level with the soil surface. After planting, water the soil thoroughly and pull up weeds regularly.

During the following spring, sprinkle a general fertilizer around the plants, water the soil and add a mulch of straw to keep fruit off the soil. When the fruits are red all over, pick them with the calyx attached early in the morning.

## Raspberries

There are two types of raspberry: summer- and fall-fruiting. Established summer-fruiting varieties produce most fruit. Pruning the canes is described on pages 142–143, and picking and storing on pages 170–171.

A tiered framework of wires is essential, using strong posts (up to 12ft/3.6m apart) with galvanized wires strained between them at a height of 3ft/75cm, 3½ft/1m and 5¼ft/1.6m above ground. Plant bare-rooted canes during late fall and early winter, or in early spring, spacing them 18in/45cm apart. Immediately after planting, cut all canes to 9–12in/23–30cm high just above a healthy bud.

During the first year, young canes develop and will fruit the following year.

▲ *Blackberry 'Oregon Thornless' has medium-sized fruits in late summer and early fall and can be planted against a trellis or an arch.*

## Blackcurrants

These are borne on deciduous bushes for picking during the latter part of midsummer and late summer. Position each plant slightly deeper than usual to allow for soil settlement, and encourage the development of shoots from below. Space plants 5ft/1.5m apart, and cut all stems to about 1in/2.5cm above the surface. Plant young, container-grown bushes at any time of the year when the soil and weather allow. If you plant in summer, wait until the fall and cut out all the old shoots to soil level. Prune fall to spring planting immediately.

### STRAWBERRIES IN BARRELS

For more than 100 years strawberries have been grown in wooden barrels with holes cut in their sides. Good drainage is essential. Drill drainage holes in the bottom of the barrel, add clean rubble, and place a 4–6in/10–15cm-wide wire-netting tube filled with drainage material in the center. Fill the barrel with well-drained soil mix, and put a plant into each hole.

▲ *Growing strawberries in pots is popular in small gardens. It is a good way to prevent slugs and snails damaging the fruits.*

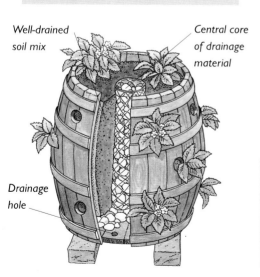

Well-drained soil mix

Central core of drainage material

Drainage hole

### Planting blackcurrants

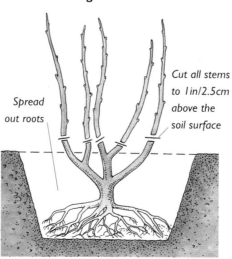

Spread out roots

Cut all stems to 1in/2.5cm above the soil surface

### Planting strawberries

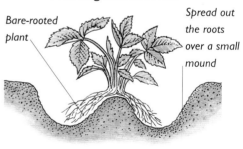

Bare-rooted plant

Spread out the roots over a small mound

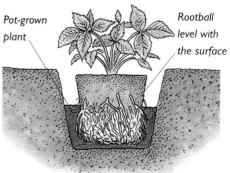

Pot-grown plant

Rootball level with the surface

# vegetables for small gardens

*Some vegetables, such as asparagus and globe artichokes, are perennials, and once established continue producing crops for several years. Others are sown each year and are rotated around a vegetable plot to insure that they produce the best possible crops.*

## Salad crops

These are popular and easily grown; there are many interesting and colorful varieties to choose from.

⊛ Outdoor cucumbers—also known as ridge cucumbers, are easily grown in fertile, moisture-retentive soil. They are best grown in a warm, sunny position sheltered from cold wind.

In mid-spring dig a hole 12in/30cm deep and wide. Fill it with a mixture of

◀ *Vegetables can be grown in even the smallest garden and often close together. Where possible, choose moderately vigorous varieties.*

equal parts of topsoil and well-decayed garden compost or manure, and make a mound of soil on the surface. In late spring or early summer, sow three seeds ¾in/18mm deep and 2in/5cm apart. Water and cover them with a large jelly-jar. Water regularly and after germination remove the cover. Later, pull up the two weakest seedlings. When sideshoots have five or six leaves, pinch out their tips to just beyond a leaf joint. Water plants regularly, and feed them when the first fruits start to swell.

⊛ Lettuces—these are popular, with a wide range of types. They include Butterheads (cabbage-type, with large, soft, smooth-edged leaves); Crispheads (another cabbage-type, with rounded heads and curled and crisp leaves; Romaine lettuces (upright growth and oblong heads); Loose-leaf lettuces (masses of loose, wavy-edged leaves that are picked individually).

By sowing seeds at various times, lettuces can be harvested throughout most of the year, though summer-sown lettuces are the easiest to grow. From mid-spring to the early part of late summer, sow seeds thinly and evenly in ½in/12mm-deep drills 10in/25cm apart. Keep the area moist. When seedlings are about 1in/2.5cm high, thin them first to 4in/10cm apart and later to 12in/30cm. Thin small varieties to 10in/25cm apart. From the latter part of early summer to fall harvest the lettuces.

⊛ Radishes—from mid-spring to late summer, sow seeds evenly and thinly every two weeks. Form drills ½in/12mm deep and 6in/15cm apart. Germination takes five to seven days and when the seedlings are large enough to handle, thin them to 1in/2.5cm apart. Re-firm the soil around them and water it. Harvest the radishes when they are young. If left, they become woody.

⊛ Scallions—in addition to bulbing types, there are scallions, also known as salad onions and bunching onions, which are delicious in salads.

## TOMATOES ON A PATIO

To grow tomatoes successfully choose a sheltered, sunny position, preferably in front of a south-facing wall. On a patio tomatoes can be grown in large pots or in a growing bag. When they are grown in pots the tall stems will need to be supported with bamboo canes, but for plants in a growing bag, a proprietary supporting framework is better. Plant two tomato plants in a standard-size bag. There are two types of tomato plant: cordon and bush. Cordon types produce sideshoots which must be snapped off when the plants are young, while bush tomatoes do not require this treatment. When cordon tomatoes have produced four trusses of fruits, pinch out the shoot at two leaves above the top truss. Water and feed plants regularly throughout the summer and pick the fruit as it ripens.

### Growing bag

*Keep the soil moist*

*Water the rootball before planting*

▲ *Varieties with globular roots are quick and easy to grow. Sow seeds evenly and thinly.*

▼ *Vegetable gardens can be decorative and with plenty of eye appeal. Vegetables can also be grown alongside flowers in cottage gardens.*

# picking and storing tree fruits

*The range of tree fruits is wide and includes apples, pears, nectarines, peaches, and plums. They all have a different nature, both with their picking and storage qualities. The times when they are picked are also variable.*

### Tree fruits

Careful picking is essential. Fruit that has been roughly handled becomes bruised and damaged, and does not last long when stored. It might start to decay and, worse, make others rot.

⚜ Apples—these vary in their picking time from midsummer to mid-fall. Their storage period is also variable, with some varieties needing to be eaten a few weeks after being picked while others last into next spring.

⚜ Pick apples when the stalk readily parts from the tree. Test each fruit by cupping it in the palm of your hand and gently raising and turning it. If the stalk parts from the tree it is ready for picking.

---

**HARVESTING SWEET CHERRIES**

---

These are left on the tree until they are ripe. Regularly test the fruits to check their sweetness. However, if their skins start to crack, pick them immediately. The stalks should be left attached to the fruits. Cherries are best eaten as soon as they are picked.

---

Store the apples by placing them slightly apart in slatted trays in a cool, airy, vermin- and frost-proof shed. If the air is dry, wrap them in oiled paper and place the folded side down. Also, regularly check the apples to make sure they are not starting to decay.

Another way to store apples is to place 4lb/1.8kg of the same variety in a polyethylene bag punctured with holes. Fold over the top and place it upside down in a similar shed.

⚜ Pears—these have a shorter storage life than apples and the picking time is more difficult to judge. Some varieties are ready in late summer, others in mid-fall. Judging when a fruit is ready to be picked is the same as for apples. Because early varieties, if left on a tree, become mealy and soft, pick them before they are completely ready by using scissors to sever the stalks. Store in a cool, dry, airy, dark, vermin-proof shed. Place pears individually in slatted trays, leaving space between them. Alternatively, you can wrap them but this prevents the onset of decay being seen.

⚜ Peaches and nectarines—pick the fruit when the skin reveals a reddish flush and the flesh around the stalk softens. This happens from the latter part of midsummer to early fall.

Pick by holding a fruit in the palm of your hand and gently lifting and twisting; it is ready when the stalk separates easily. The fruit is best eaten fresh, but can be stored in a cool place and unwrapped for about a week.

⚜ Plums—pick fruit from the latter part of midsummer to late fall, when it parts readily from the tree leaving the stalk behind. The exact time depends on the variety, but those used for preserving and cooking can be picked before they are ripe, whereas dessert types need to ripen on the tree. Store plums in slatted boxes lined with tissue paper. Check them daily for decay. When gages and damsons are picked the stalk also remains attached to the tree.

▶ *Do not squeeze apples or they will bruise. Cup the fruit in the palm of your hand and twist. If it comes away easily it is ready.*

# storing pears

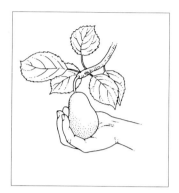
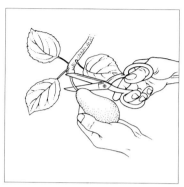
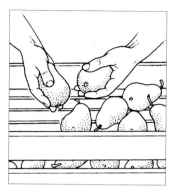
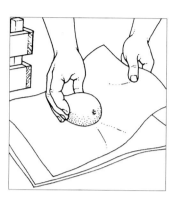

1 Supporting the pear in your palm, lift and twist the fruit very gently. If the stalk readily parts from the tree, the fruit is ready to be picked.

2 Early varieties can be picked before they are completely ready by using scissors. If left too long on the tree they become soft and mealy.

3 Store pears on slatted trays. Space the fruit apart, so that they do not touch. This reduces the risk of decaying fruit contaminating others.

4 Usually, pears can be left unwrapped, but in a dry atmosphere wrap them individually. However, this does cloak the early signs of decay.

# harvesting soft fruits

*These summer fruits are popular and best eaten as soon as possible after they are picked. Care is needed when picking them to prevent damage that will limit their life. Always put them into wide-based containers so that they cannot be knocked over.*

## Bush fruits

Blackcurrants—pick these from mid- to late summer. The fruit is ready for picking about one week after turning blue-black. Berries can be picked individually but they keep better when the entire cluster is removed. Place them in a cool, airy place. They can be stored in a refrigerator for about one week. Because not all the fruit will be ready for picking at the same time it is necessary to check it regularly.

Redcurrants and white currants—pick the fruit during midsummer when shiny and colored, picking entire clusters to avoid damage to individual berries. It is necessary to pick over the bush several times, on each occasion picking those

▲ *Gooseberries are a popular soft fruit with a distinctive flavor. Pick them individually when they are fully ripe and evenly colored.*

### SAFETY FIRST

❁ Apart from the risk of other people eating the fruit before you can get them safely into your house, care is needed when picking them. Systematically work down rows or around bushes, so that you do not miss ripe fruit. If you do, it will quickly be eaten by wasps.

❁ Place berries in small, wide-based flat containers that will not be knocked over. When half-full, transfer into a larger firm-based container. Do not put them where children or dogs can knock them over.

❁ Where several varieties are being picked, put them into separate containers so that their flavors can later be compared.

❁ As soon as possible, move the fruit into a cool room where they can quickly loose their "field" heat. And do not put them near strongly scented vegetables or herbs.

❁ Where freezing is appropriate, do this as soon as possible.

that are ripe. Currants are best eaten immediately, but can be stored in a refrigerator for about one week.

Gooseberries—pick the fruit from the end of early summer, through midsummer to the early part of late summer, depending on the variety. When fully ripe the berries are soft and fully colored. They can be stored in a refrigerator for a couple of weeks.

Strawberries—check the crop daily and pick fruit when it has reddened all over. Pull the fruit from the plant by holding the stalk, so that it remains attached to the fruit. They are best eaten within a few days.

### Cane fruits

Raspberries—pick summer-fruiting varieties from the early part of midsummer to the latter weeks of late summer, and fall-fruiting types from late summer to mid-fall. The berries can be picked when fully colored yet still firm. Hold the fruit gently and pull, leaving the stalk and plug attached to the plant. The fruit is best eaten immediately, but can be frozen. To do this, choose firm fruit and put it in the base of a shallow, plastic tray, keeping all the raspberries apart. Place the tray in a freezer and when frozen put the fruit into freezer bags or boxes.

Blackberries and hybrid berries— these are picked when soft and fully ripe. This is best done when the fruit is dry. Wet fruit, especially if slightly bruised, soon decays and becomes moldy. When picking, hold each fruit and pull gently. The plug usually comes away with the fruit. Best when eaten immediately, but can be frozen.

▲ *Redcurrants are an excellent culinary fruit. An established bush will provide about 10lb/4.5kg each year, in mid- or late summer.*

## picking and freezing raspberries

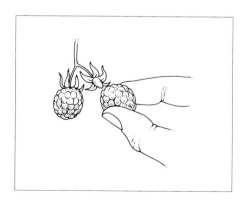

## picking gooseberries

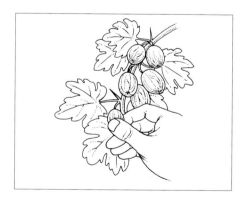

1 Pick the fruits individually, when fully colored yet still firm. The plug (the small stalk) should remain on the plant. It is necessary to pick over the plants several times. If left, the fruits soon decay.

2 Freeze raspberries as soon as possible after picking. Select small, under-ripe fruits and space them apart in a flat-based plastic container. Place in the freezer until frozen and then transfer to freezer bags.

Pick the fruits individually, when ripe and fully colored. This varies between varieties and some are early while others are late maturing and ripening. It is necessary to pick over each bush several times.

# growing herbs in small gardens

*Several herbs, such as the biennial angelica, are large and dominant—and best planted in herbaceous or large herb borders. Most herbs though, are suitable for small gardens, while prostrate types can be planted between paving slabs arranged in a chessboard pattern.*

## MAKING A HERB CARTWHEEL

Dig the soil, removing perennial weeds and, if necessary, mix in well-decayed garden compost to assist water retention. Firm the soil evenly, then rake level. Tie the ends of a 3ft/90cm-long piece of string to two canes and insert one in the center of the bed. Use the other end to describe a circle 6ft/1.8m in diameter. Place small pebbles in a 10–12in/25–30cm-wide circle in the center, and larger pebbles around the perimeter. Mark the positions of the spokes with more pebbles, creating triangles about 15in/38cm wide at the base. Water the plants in their containers the day before planting, then arrange them in their pots in the cartwheel in an attractive design. Plant them out, water the soil and, for more intense color, cover the soil with colored gravels.

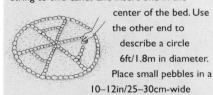

### Cartwheel herb gardens

These are ornamental and functional features that can be tailored to fit areas only 6ft/1.8m square. If possible, use an old cartwheel, but a simulated design is easily created by using large pebbles to mark out the circumference and spokes.

### Checkerboard designs

This is a novel way to grow low-growing herbs. Select an area, perhaps 7½ft/2.28m square, and prepare the soil as for a cartwheel garden. Then lay 18in/45cm-square paving slabs in a checkerboard arrangement leaving alternate squares uncovered. Plant the uncovered squares with a selection of low-growing herbs. Where herbs do not completely cover the soil, spread pea gravel or stone chippings over the soil. This will look attractive and has the added advantage of reducing moisture loss.

▼ *Herb wheels, closely planted with segments of contrasting thymes, create an attractive feature that is easy to manage.*

## Nine popular herbs

Caraway—biennial with fern-like leaves and umbrella-like heads of green flowers.
Chives—bulbous, with tubular leaves and rose-pink flowers.
Dill—hardy annual with feathery green leaves and umbrella-like heads of yellow flowers.
Fennel—herbaceous perennial with blue-green leaves and golden-yellow flowers in large, umbrella-like heads.

Lemon balm—herbaceous perennial with lemon-scented green leaves.
Mint—herbaceous perennial with invasive roots. Wide range, from spearmint to apple mint.
Parsley—biennial, with crinkled or flat (more strongly flavored) green leaves.
Sage—short-lived shrub, with gray-green leaves and spires of violet-blue flowers in early summer. There are forms with more ornamental leaves (purple, and

some variegated) but they are mainly used to create color in borders.
Thyme—low-growing, shrubby perennial. Garden thyme is a superb culinary herb, but there are varieties with colored leaves that may be used to add color to checkerboard designs.

▼ *Enhance herb gardens by positioning small and low-growing herbs in spaces left when paving slabs are laid in a checkerboard pattern.*

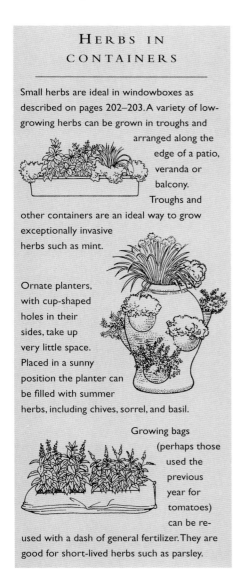

### HERBS IN CONTAINERS

Small herbs are ideal in windowboxes as described on pages 202–203. A variety of low-growing herbs can be grown in troughs and arranged along the edge of a patio, veranda or balcony. Troughs and other containers are an ideal way to grow exceptionally invasive herbs such as mint.

Ornate planters, with cup-shaped holes in their sides, take up very little space. Placed in a sunny position the planter can be filled with summer herbs, including chives, sorrel, and basil.

Growing bags (perhaps those used the previous year for tomatoes) can be re-used with a dash of general fertilizer. They are good for short-lived herbs such as parsley.

# using plants in small gardens

# colorful borders
## and beds

Borders bursting with color throughout summer are one of the goals of gardeners. In addition to rich and vibrant displays in a wide range of colors, it is possible to create borders with a distinctive single color theme, such as pink and red, blue and mauve, yellow and gold, and white and silver. Plants with variegated leaves also make attractive borders. They include evergreen and deciduous shrubs and herbaceous perennials.

# pink and red garden schemes

*Red is a dramatic, fiery, dominant color in a garden, especially when used en masse in full sun, while pink is a desaturated red with a warmer feel. The perception of red changes through the day. In strong light it is bright, but as evening approaches it assumes darker shades until it turns almost black.*

### Flower borders

There is a wide choice of red and pink flowers for herbaceous borders and flowering bedding displays that will carry the color scheme through from early spring into fall. In herbaceous borders the plants range from tuberous-rooted alstroemerias, through the red and pink forms of the late-flowering *Aster novi-belgii* (Michaelmass daisy) and *Aster novae-angliae* (New England aster), to the dramatic red flowers of *Schizostylis coccinea* 'Major', which is aptly called the crimson flag. Many dahlias, from the smaller ball varieties to giant decoratives with flowers 10in/25cm wide, have lovely red flowers and will provide strong accents of color in late summer.

Spring flowering displays using bulbs and biennials, planted in late summer or early fall, add plenty of color. For a red and blue display, perhaps at the top of a drystone wall, you could plant a blue-flowered form of *Aubrieta deltoidea* adding colorful 'Madame Lefeber' tulips below. Summer displays, mainly of seed-raised plants, also add red and pink flowers, but none so arresting as *Begonia semperflorens* 'Cocktail Series' and *Salvia splendens* (scarlet sage).

### BACKGROUND HARMONIES AND CONTRASTS

Many plants, from wall shrubs to ephemeral types in windowboxes, wall baskets, and hanging baskets, look even better against the right background.

Red and scarlet flowers are dramatically highlighted against white walls, while red and pink flowers harmonize with a gray stone wall.

◀ *Pink and red are romantic colors that give warm tones to a border. Pink flowers remain visible in the diminishing light of evening.*

## Trees and shrubs

These produce massed displays and distinctive individual flowers. The spring-flowering deciduous azaleas, often in demure shades of red and pink, are a sure sign that gardens are bursting into life. A wild garden, with a high and light canopy of leaves, provides the right setting. Many have the bonus of richly colored leaves in the fall.

Other shrubs with pink or red flowers include the magnificient *Hibiscus syriacus* and *Kolkwitzia amabilis*, aptly known as the beauty bush for its pink, foxglove-like flowers with yellow throats. More dramatic and distinctive are the flowers of the deciduous, spring and early summer flowering *Magnolia liliiflora* 'Nigra'. Its flowers are upright, 3in/7.5cm long and deep reddish-purple. Offering a totally different style, the deciduous shrub *Leycesteria formosa* (Himalayan honeysuckle) has pendulous flowers formed of small, white flowers surrounded by highly conspicuous dark-claret bracts. It has the bonus of purplish-red berries in the fall.

## Climbers and wall shrubs

This excellent range includes climbing and rambling roses, clematis and the rhizomatous-rooted *Tropaeolum speciosum* (Scottish flame flower) which dies down to soil level in the fall. From midsummer to fall it produces scarlet, trumpet-like flowers on long stems and loves to clamber through shrubs. Several large-flowered clematis have red or pink flowers including the popular 'Nelly Moser' in which each pale mauve-pink petal has a soft crimson stripe. 'Ville de Lyon' is bright carmine-red and 'Ernest Markham' is vivid magenta with a velvet sheen.

▲ *Many quite different plants create attractive combinations. Here a rose and a variety of slow-growing conifers form a pleasing group.*

▼ *Low beds, perhaps at the edge of a rock garden and mainly planted with pink and red plants, create a feature that radiates warmth.*

## Key to planting

1. *Myosotis* (forget-me-not)
2. *Primula* 'Wanda'
3. *Candelabra primulas*
4. *Anemone × fulgens*
5. *Magnolia liliiflora*
6. Rhododendrons
7. Azaleas
8. *Aubrieta deltoidea* (aubretia)

# blue and purple borders

*Blue is a calm color and when used in a garden will provide an atmosphere of tranquillity. Blue color schemes are thought to reduce blood pressure and slow up respiration and pulse rates. Enhance the color by adding patches of dull white and pale-lemon flowers, but not strong yellows.*

### Flower borders

Blue-flowered herbaceous borders usually come to life at the start of summer, when suddenly they abound in color. Perhaps no herbaceous perennial is more noticeable than *Delphinium elatum*.

▲ *Blue flowers create a contemplative and restful garden, while purple is more dramatic and looks best used in smaller groups.*

The large-flowered or elatum types have stiffly erect stems tightly packed with florets during early and midsummer, while the Belladonna forms are smaller, gracefully branched, and superb in cottage gardens. Within each type there is a wide range of colors.

Several perennial asters are blue, including *Aster amellus* (Italian aster) with large, daisy-like flowers with yellow centers. 'King George' is especially attractive, with soft blue-violet flowers. *Aster* × *frikartii* 'Mönch' is slightly less dramatic, with lavender-blue flowers. Again, the flowers have golden centers. Other blue-flowered herbaceous plants include *Echinacea purpurea* (purple coneflower) with purple-crimson, daisy-like flowers and distinctive large central cones, *Physostegia virginiana* (obedient plant) with spires of pink-mauve flowers, and *Tradescantia* × *andersoniana* 'Isis' which bears three-petaled, purple-blue flowers.

Several spring-flowering bulbs have blue flowers and include *Hyacinthus orientalis* (common hyacinth) and *Muscari armeniacum* (grape hyacinth), which is an

ideal companion for polyanthus. *Myosotis alpestris* (forget-me-not) is a hardy perennial invariably grown as a biennial for its small and fragrant, azure-blue flowers borne in large clusters. There are many varieties and most will happily increase by self-seeding.

Summer-flowering bedding plants include blue-flowered forms of *Ageratum houstonianum*, such as 'Blue Danube' with masses of lavender-blue flowers, and *Lobelia erinus* with varieties such as 'Blue Moon' and 'Cambridge Blue'. There are also several trailing forms that are ideal for planting in windowboxes and in hanging baskets.

### BACKGROUND HARMONIES AND CONTRASTS

Blue is a restful color that is at risk from being dominated by strong colors, but here are a few good combinations to try. Position plants with deep-blue or deep-purple flowers against gray stone walls. Soft blue flowers in large clusters harmonize with red brick walls.

## Key to planting

1. *Aster amellus*
2. *Delphiniums*
3. *Corylus maxima* 'Purpurea' (Purple-leaved filbert)
4. *Cotinus coggygria* 'Notcutt's Variety'
5. *Hydrangea macrophylla* (common hydrangea)
6. *Echinacea purpurea* (purple coneflower)
7. *Physostegia virginiana* (obedient plant)
8. *Ageratum houstonianum* (flossflower)

## Trees and shrubs

There are few blue-flowered trees and shrubs but close together they make a magnificient display. *Cercis siliquastrum* (Judas tree) has clusters of rich, rose-purple flowers on bare branches in early summer. Markedly different is *Ceanothus* × *delileanus* 'Gloire de Versailles', with long spires of fragrant, powder-blue flowers from midsummer to early fall. And most popular of all are the blue-flowered forms of *Hydrangea macrophylla* (common hydrangea).

Several shrubs and trees have richly colored leaves, including *Corylus maxima* 'Purpurea' (purple-leaved filbert), *Cotinus coggygria* 'Notcutt's Variety' with deep-purple leaves, and *Berberis thunbergii* 'Atropurpurea' which bears small, rich purple-red leaves.

## Climbers and wall shrubs

These provide superb displays and none more so than California lilacs. Look for *Ceanothus impressus* with clusters of deep

▲ *This partly cloistered water garden creates an oasis of peace and tranquillity.*

blue flowers in spring, and *C. thrysiflorus repens* with light-blue flowers. Clematis need support and few surpass *Clematis macropetala*, with double, light- and dark-blue flowers in late spring and early summer. Other blue-flowering climbers include *Solanum crispum* (Chilean potato vine), *Wisteria floribunda* 'Macrobotrys' and *Abutilon vitifolium* (flowering maple).

▶ *Pale-lemon and dull-white flowers will make the border more conspicuous in twilight.*

# yellow and gold gardens

*These are bright and dominant, especially when in strong sunlight. Plants with these radiant colors are readily seen in the gloom of early morning and in the diminishing light of evening. Yellow is therefore useful as an edging for summer-flowering bedding displays.*

### Flower borders

Herbaceous borders are sometimes themed as a single color, such as yellow, but this does not mean that the border only has one color. For example, in yellow and gold borders, yellow and green variegated shrubs can be added to create permanency, height, and contrasting color. Good yellow herbaceous perennials include *Achillea filipendulina* 'Gold Plate' (fern-leaf yarrow) with large, plate-like heads packed with deep-yellow flowers from mid- to late-summer. *Alchemilla mollis* (lady's mantle) is another superb plant, ideal for the edge of a border where it cloaks sharp, unsightly outlines.

The list of herbaceous plants for yellow borders is lengthy and includes *Coreopsis vertillata*, with bright yellow star-like flowers, dahlias, *Phlomis fruticosa* and *Verbascum bombyciferum* (mullein)—with tall flower stems and silver-haired oval leaves. Two others are *Rudbeckia fulgida* (coneflower); this has large, yellow flowers with purple-brown centers. It is superb with *Aster amellus* 'King George'. *Solidago* 'Goldenmosa' (goldenrod) bears fluffy heads of yellow flowers.

◀ *Plants with narrow, yellow-variegated leaves create a dramatic shape and color constrast in a garden. Grow tender plants in pots.*

### Trees and shrubs

Yellow-flowering winter and spring trees and shrubs include *Hamamelis* (witch-hazel), chimonanthus and mahonias in winter, and the glorious forsythias, *Berberis darwinii* and double-flowered gorse in spring. Many continue their display into summer, and later. Add accents of color by grouping plants in attractive duos. Around the spreading branches of *Hamamelis mollis* (Chinese witch-hazel) plant the winter-flowering *Rhododendron mucronulatum* with funnel-shaped, rose-purple flowers. For a summer leaf-color contrast, plant the deciduous shrub *Cotinus coggygria* 'Royal Purple', with dark plum-colored leaves.

### BACKGROUND HARMONIES AND CONTRASTS

Yellow is a dramatic color, especially when highlighted by a contrasting background. Yellow flowers look good against a white background, while lemon-colored flowers are better suited to a red brick wall.

## Climbers and wall shrubs

These range from annuals to shrubs and include the popular *Thunbergia alata*, (black-eyed Susan), a half-hardy annual raised in gentle warmth in spring before being planted in a border or against a trellis when all risk of frost has passed. Alternatively, it will scale a tripod of canes or poles. For winter color against a wall, plant *Jasminum nudiflorum*, the winter-flowering jasmine which produces bright yellow flowers on bare stems throughout winter.

Several slightly tender shrubs benefit from being planted on the sunny side of a wall and include *Cytisus battandieri*, (Pineapple broom). In midsummer it has pineapple-scented, cone-shaped, golden-yellow heads of flowers amid large, grayleaves like the laburnum. *Piptanthus nepalensis*, still better known as *Piptanthus laburnifolius* (evergreen laburnum), is also slightly tender and bears pea-shaped, bright yellow flowers like those of the laburnum.

in late spring and early summer. The deciduous and vigorous *Lonicera tragophylla* (Chinese woodbine) is ideal for covering archways, pergolas, and walls. It produces bright golden-yellow flowers from early to midsummer.

▶ *Yellow and gold borders introduce vitality into a garden, with plants ranging from yellow-leaved border plants to glorious sunflowers.*

### Key to planting

1. *Rudbeckia fulgida* (coneflower)
2. *Euonymus fortunei* 'Emerald 'n' Gold'
3. *Helianthus annuus* (sunflower)
4. *Thunbergia alata* (black-eyed Susan)
5. *Verbascum bombyciferum* (mullein)
6. *Achillea filipenndulina* 'Gold Plate' (fern-leaf yarrow)
7. *Solidago* 'Goldenmosa' (golden rod)
8. *Tagetes erecta* (African marigolds)

▲ *Gardens packed with yellow flowers and foliage are full of vitality. Hoop-like arches add interest and help to create height in a garden.*

# white and silver schemes

*With their brightness and purity, white flowers have a dramatic impact in strong sunlight. Silver is less dominant and is often described as grayish-white. It is less apparent because silver reflects light at many angles, whereas smooth-surfaced white petals are better reflectors of light.*

### Flower borders

There are many plants for gray, silver, and white herbaceous borders. Those with gray and silver foliage include *Anaphalis triplinervis* (pearly everlasting) with narrow, silver-gray, lance-shaped leaves that reveal white, wooly undersides. It also bears bunched heads of white flowers during late summer. Its near relative, *Anaphalis margaritacea yedoensis,*

◀ *Borders with white flowers and silver foliage sparkle in even the smallest amount of light, bringing unexpected vibrancy to a garden.*

has gray leaves and heads of white flowers from midsummer to fall.

Many artemisias have silver-colored leaves and none better than *Artemisia absinthium* 'Lambrook Silver', with its silvery gray, finely divided leaves and small, round, yellow flowers during mid- and late-summer. *Artemisia ludoviciana*, the white sage, has upright stems, deeply divided, wooly white leaves, and silver-white flowers during late summer and early fall. *Onopordum acanthium* (Scotch thistle) produces broad, jagged silver-gray leaves.

The range of silver-leaved plants continues with *Stachys byzantina* (lamb's ears), with oval leaves densely covered in white, silvery hairs that create a wooly appearance. The half-hardy perennial *Senecio cineraria*, usually grown as a half-hardy annual, clothes borders with deeply lobed leaves covered in white, wooly hairs. Herbaceous plants with

white flowers include the popular *Leucanthemum maximum*, still better known as *Chrysanthemum maximum* (Shasta daisy), with masses of large, white, daisy-like flowers with yellow centers from mid- to late-summer. *Gypsophila paniculata* (baby's breath) creates clouds of white flowers amid gray-green leaves. With fewer but larger white flowers, *Romneya coulteri* (California tree poppy) blooms from midsummer to fall.

The half-hardy annual *Lobularia maritima*, better known as *Alyssum maritimum* (sweet alyssum), is ideal as an edging to summer-flowering bedding arrangements.

## BACKGROUND HARMONIES AND CONTRASTS

Backgrounds suitable for white flowers are limited, and they usually look their best against a red brick wall. This color also suits silver-colored foliage.

## Key to planting

1. *Onopordum acanthium* (Scotch thistle)
2. *Anaphalis margaritacea yedoensis*
3. *Artemisia ludoviciana* (white sage)
4. *Carpenteria californica*
5. *Wisteria sinensis* 'Alba' (white Chinese wisteria)
6. *Romneya coulteri* (California tree poppy)
7. *Leucanthemum maximum* (Shasta daisy)
8. *Stachys byzantina* (lamb's ears)

## Trees and shrubs

The excellent range includes *Amelanchier lamarckii* (Juneberry) with a mass of white flowers in spring, while *Eucryphia × nymansensis* produces 2⅜in/6.5cm-wide, white or cream flowers in late summer and early fall. Other fine shrubs to consider are *Hydrangea arborescens* 'Grandiflora' with pure white flowers in slightly rounded heads from midsummer to early fall. Its relative *H. paniculata* 'Grandiflora' develops large, pyramidal, terminal heads of white flowers during late summer and fall.

Few small-garden shrubs with white flowers are as attractive as *Magnolia stellata* (star magnolia), with 4in/10cm-wide flowers during spring. The narrow, silver-gray, willow-like leaves of *Pyrus salicifolia* 'Pendula' are also attractive, and during spring, pure white flowers appear in terminal clusters. It is best set off by blue spring-flowering bulbs. *Spiraea × 'Arguta'* (bridal wreath) and *Viburnum opulus* 'Sterile', sometimes known as *V. o.* 'Roseum', are other superb shrubs for planting in white borders.

▲ A garden seat creates an ideal pivot for this white and silver garden, and is an ideal theme for a small garden where vibrancy is desired.

▲ Plants in pots, placed on a well-drained surface, create an attractive feature and are ideal as a focal point in small gardens.

# variegated foliage

*Foliage with several colors never fails to attract attention, and these qualities are found in a wide range of plants from herbaceous perennials to trees, shrubs, and climbers. Many have subdued colors, while others are bright and make a garden look vibrant.*

### Flower borders

There are more variegated herbaceous perennials than might, at first thought, be considered possible. Well-known variegated hostas include *Hosta* 'Fortunei Albopicta', *H.* 'Crispula' and *H.* 'Gold Standard'. There are many other hostas but perhaps one of the most unlikely variegated plants is *Aegopodium podagraria* 'Variegatum' (variegated goutweed or bishopsweed). It is not highly invasive, invasive, but is best grown in large tubs where it brightens patios with light-green leaves edged with white. The perennial grass *Hakonechloa macra* 'Aureola' is also superb in a large tub or at the corner of a raised bed. Its arching, ribbon-like leaves are variegated buff and gold, with touches of bronze.

Also ideal for borders with their vertical growth are *Iris pallida,* with sword-like, green and yellow striped leaves, and *I. p.* 'Argentea Variegata', with white stripes. The variegated phloxes 'Norah Leigh' and 'Harlequin' are both excellent in herbaceous borders, while *Yucca filamentosa* 'Variegata', with its sword-like leaves, always attracts attention. Give it a prominent position.

### Trees and shrubs

These often create dominant displays, especially *Euonymus fortunei* 'Emerald 'n' Gold', a dense, bushy evergreen with variegated bright gold leaves; in winter they are tinged bronze-pink. 'Emerald Gaiety' and 'Silver Queen' also have variegated leaves. *Aucuba japonica* 'Variegata' is also an old garden favorite with its yellow spotted green leaves creating a dominant display. It looks good in spring when surrounded by daffodils. *Elaeagnus pungens* 'Maculata' is another evergreen favorite, with stiff, leathery green leaves splashed gold.

*Salvia officinalis* 'Icterina' grows about 12in/30cm high and is ideal for planting beside a path, where it cloaks unsightly edges. With its green and gold leaves it

◀ *This small, decorative, rail-type fence harmonizes with ornamental grasses and low-growing plants to create an attractive feature.*

makes an eye-catching feature. An equally striking variety is 'Tricolor', with gray-green leaves splashed creamy white, suffused with pink.

The deciduous *Cornus alba* 'Spaethii' (dogwood) has light-green leaves with irregular gold-splashed edges, with the bonus of bright red stems in winter. A near relative, *C. alternifolia* 'Argentea', is a small tree or a large shrub with horizontally spreading branches bearing small green leaves with creamy white edges. Do not hide its attractive shape.

Variegated hollies have a permanent role in gardens, adding brightness throughout the year. *Ilex × altaclarensis* 'Lawsoniana' has green leaves, usually spineless, each with a central yellow splash. It bears orange-red berries in winter. *Ilex aquifolium* has many varieties with variegated, spine-edged leaves, notably 'Golden Queen' with cream-streaked green stems and large leaves broadly edged with gold.

## Climbers and wall shrubs

Perhaps the best-known variegated climbers are ivies. They range from the small-leaved *Hedera helix* 'Goldheart', now known as 'Oro di Bogliasco', with dark green leaves splashed yellow, to large-leaved types. They include the variegated *H. canariensis* 'Gloire de Marengo' (Canary Island ivy), with deep green leaves and silver-gray and white variegations. There are several variegated forms of the Persian ivy; *H. colchica* 'Dentata Variegata' has leaves conspicuously edged creamy yellow, and 'Sulphur Heart' has irregular yellow splashes. *Actinidia kolomikta*, a deciduous climber, has green leaves that develop pink-flushed white areas toward the tips.

▶ *Trailing and spreading plants help to clothe the edges of decking. Regular trimming may be necessary to prevent them becoming intrusive.*

▼ *Variegated plants soften this flight of steps and complement the distinctive tiered branches of Cornus controversa 'Variegata'.*

## Key to planting

1. *Hakonechloa macra* 'Aureola'
2. *Phlox* 'Norah Leigh'
3. *Yucca fillamentosa* 'Variegata'
4. *Cornus controversa* 'Variegata'
5. *Variegated phormium*
6. *Iris pallida* 'Argentea Variegata'
7. *Hosta sieboldiana* 'Frances Williams'
8. *Hosta fortunei albopicta*

# mixed colors

*There are two ways to consider "mixed" colors: one is a medley of colors within seed-raised plants such as summer-flowering bedding plants for beds and containers. The other is planning the arrangement of individual colors and this is most dramatically achieved in the larger theater of a garden.*

### Using mixed colors

Windowboxes, wall baskets, and hanging baskets look wonderful when planted with a single species or variety in a range of colors. For example, trailing lobelia comes in white, blue, lilac, crimson, and red varieties, and all are sold together as mixed seed. A practical advantage of devoting a hanging basket to one variety in a mix of colors is that all the plants will be equally vigorous, and none will grow to dominate its neighbor.

### Mixing colors

Mixing colors in a garden is as much a matter of personal preference as one of science. It is useful to use a color wheel formed of three main colors—yellow, blue, and red—and three secondaries—orange, green, and violet—to reveal those that complement or harmonize.

Complementary colors are those with no common pigments, while those that harmonize share some pigments. Yellow and violet, blue and orange, and red and green are complementary, while yellow harmonizes with green and orange, blue with green and violet, and red with orange and violet.

▲ *Plants with variegated leaves create color throughout summer and, if evergreen, the entire year. Many can be grown in pots and tubs.*

### SHINY AND MATT SURFACES

The surface of a leaf influences the way it reflects light. A smooth surface reflects light at the same angle at which it is struck by it, and makes the light appear bright. If the surface is matt, light is reflected at different angles and creates a dull surface. In nature, however, few plant surfaces are as smooth as glass, and the scattering of light occurs from most of them.

## Mixing and matching

Color planning a garden need not involve vast areas or be expensive. Consider planting a corner of a shrub border, or an area of a wall to start with.

Yellow and gold—many yellow-leaved trees and shrubs form ideal backdrops for purple-leaved plants. If the ratio of yellow to purple is about three to one they appear well-balanced. Plant the dark-leaved *Berberis thunbergii atropurpurea* with yellow-leaved shrubs like *Sambucus racemosa* 'Plumosa Aurea' (European red elder).

## Key to planting

1. *Calendula officinalis* (pot marigold)
2. *Coreopsis verticillata*
3. *Cotinus coggygria* 'Notcutt's Variety'
4. *Philadelphus coronarius* 'Aureus'
5. Lupins—in mixed colors
6. *Berberis thunbergii atropurpurea*
7. *Papaver orientale* (oriental poppy)
8. *Geranium* 'Johnson's Blue'

Blue and purple—to create a blue background display, plant *Ceanothus* 'Cascade' against a sheltered sunny wall. It grows about 10ft/3m high and wide, and bears small, rich blue flowers in late spring and early summer. For added interest, plant the slightly tender, evergreen shrub *Choisya ternata* (Mexican orange blossom) in front of it.

Red and pink—take care when using red because it is dominant, and can be overpowering. Against a mid-green background, bright-red flowers such as the hardy annual *Papaver rhoeas* (field poppy) have a three-dimensional effect. However, most red flowers are not totally color saturated and appear more as shades. Pink is a desaturated red and is easier to blend into a garden.

▲ Multicolored hanging baskets always capture attention and often suit more backgrounds than those of a single color.

▼ Packed borders with mixed colors are ideal features in small gardens. Remove dead flowers to encourage repeat flowering.

# seasonal displays

*Colorful displays of flowers and leaves are possible throughout the year. Summer is, of course, the main time when plants flower, and flowering plants range from hardy annuals to herbaceous perennials, shrubs, and trees. Fall is also colorful and is especially known for deciduous shrubs, trees, and climbers with leaves that turn rich colors before falling. Several trees flower during winter, and, in addition, small bulbs can be naturalized in short grass or around shrubs. Spring is eagerly anticipated for its glorious daffodils, flowering trees, and shrubs.*

# planting for spring color

*Bulbs are often thought to signal the start of spring, and several can be used in exciting combinations with shrubs. Spring is also the time of year when many ornamental cherry trees burst into flower and they may also be complemented when underplanted with bulbs, especially daffodils.*

### Spring-flowering shrubs

One of the most eye-catching shows of yellow is from the bell-shaped flowers of *Forsythia* 'Lynwood'. Like many other spring-flowering shrubs, the flowers appear on naked stems, but the leaves arrive soon after.

*Ulex europaeus* (gorse), is a yellow-flowered evergreen shrub. It is covered with masses of honey-scented, pea-shaped flowers during spring and early summer, and often continues bearing flowers sporadically until the following early spring.

*Amelanchier lamarckii* (Juneberry) is deciduous, with masses of pure-white, star-shaped flowers during midspring that never fail to attract attention. *Magnolia stellata* (star magnolia) is smaller, and another white-flowered deciduous shrub. Its individual, 4in/10cm-wide flowers are more dramatic if fewer in number. And *Kerria japonica* 'Pleniflora' is deciduous, with a lax habit and double, orange-yellow flowers about 2in/5cm wide on slender stems during late spring and early summer. Other spring-flowering shrubs include *Chaenomeles × superba* (flowering quince), *Cytisus × praecox* 'Warminster' (Warminster broom), *Berberis × stenophylla*, *Ribes sanguineum* (flowering currant), and *Viburnum × burkwoodii*.

> ### TREES FOR SPRING
>
> *Prunus padus* (bird cherry)—long tassels of almond-scented white flowers in late spring. 'Watereri' has longer tassels.
>
> *Prunus subhirtella* 'Pendula Rosea'—spreading and weeping tree with pinkish-white flowers.
>
> *Prunus* 'Accolade'—graceful and open tree with bluish-pink, semidouble flowers during early and midspring.

◀ *Colorful spring displays are essential for shedding winter gloom. Prepare for this by planting spring-flowering bulbs in early fall.*

## Spring-flowering bulbs

Some bulbs, such as *Crocus chrysanthus,* which often begin flowering in late winter, can be naturalized in large drifts in short grass, but a more reserved way is to plant groups of spring-flowering bulbs in rock gardens.

Some late winter-flowering bulbs continue their display into early spring and include the pale blue *Chionodoxa luciliae* (glory of the snow), yellow *Eranthis hyemalis* (winter aconite) and white *Galanthus nivalis* (common snowdrop). Others concentrate their flowering in spring and range from *Ipheion uniflorum* (spring starflower), with white to violet-blue, star-shaped flowers, to *Scilla siberica* (spring squill) with deep blue or white flowers. Two species of tulips for spring include *Tulipa tarda*, with clusters of white flowers that reveal large, bright yellow centers, and *Tulipa kaufmanniana* (waterlily tulip), which produces star-shaped white flowers flushed red and yellow on the outside.

### STAR PLANTS

*Amelanchier lamarckii*

*Clematis montana*

*Crocus chrysanthus*

*Eranthis hyemalis*

*Kerria japonica* 'Pleniflora'

*Magnolia stellata*

*Muscari armeniacum*

▶ Kerria japonica 'Pleniflora' *makes a lovely display of orange-yellow flowers in late spring and early summer.*

## Mixing and matching

As spring progresses there is increasing opportunity to arrange attractive combinations of plants in borders and against walls. For example, two flowers which pair well are *Rosa banksiae* 'Lutea', with double yellow flowers in spring, planted alongside the scented *Clematis montana* 'Elizabeth', a variety of the mountain clematis. The rose has fern-like leaves and lightly scented, clear yellow single flowers during late spring, while the clematis bears an abundance of pale pink flowers at the same time.

*Viburnum opulus* 'Roseum' (snowball bush), is a deciduous shrub with large, globular, creamy white flowerheads during late spring and early summer. The branches often bow under the weight of the magnificent flowers. For contrast, plant the herbaceous *Hosta sieboldiana* around its edges.

# planting for summer color

*The intensity of color in a summer garden is almost overwhelming. Herbaceous perennials, hardy and half-hardy annuals, and bulbs fill beds and borders, and climbers and wall shrubs cover walls, trellises, and pergolas. Variegated and colored foliage is a key ingredient.*

▲ *Bright-faced lilies, with their distinctive shapes, are beacons of brightness in informal borders, and are at home in cottage gardens.*

### Summer-flowering shrubs

A wide and varied choice includes early summer-flowering shrubs such as *Cistus × cyprius*, with 3in/7.5cm-wide white flowers blotched crimson, and *Cistus × purpureus* which has rose to purple flowers blotched dark maroon. *Potentilla fruticosa*, a deciduous shrub with many varieties in colors from yellow to bright vermilion, continues its display into late summer. The glorious philadelphus shrubs never fail to enrich gardens in early and midsummer. Many are richly scented, and there are varieties to suit small gardens.

With the onset of midsummer many hydrangeas burst into flower. *Hydrangea macrophylla* forms a rounded shrub with

### STAR PLANTS

*Hydrangea macrophylla*

*Hypericum* 'Hidcote'

*Laburnum × watereri* 'Vossii'

*Philadelphus coronarius* 'Aureus'

*Potentilla fruticosa*

*Senecio brachyglottis* 'Sunshine'

flowerheads up to 8in/20cm wide. These shrubs have the bonus of flowers into early fall. Late summer sees other hydrangeas bursting into color, none more spectacular than *Hydrangea paniculata* 'Grandiflora', with plume-like heads up to 18in/45cm long, packed with white flowers into early fall.

## Mixing and matching

Opportunities abound during summer to mix plants in colorful combinations. For an extra bright display, plant *Genista cinerea*, a large deciduous shrub with yellow, sweetly scented flowers during early and midsummer, with the evergreen shrub *Brachyglottis* 'Sunshine', still better known as *Senecio* 'Sunshine'. It has gray, white-felted leaves and yellow daisy-like flowers.

The deciduous tree *Laburnum* × *watereri* 'Vossii' (golden chain tree) is known for its long, pendulous clusters of yellow flowers and forms a background color contrast with purple lilac.

In wild gardens, the late spring and early summer flowering deciduous shrub *Rhododendron luteum* has sweet, honey-scented yellow flowers. It may be planted alongside a stream, with a dense planting of red variety of *Primula japonica* in front of it. Both plants thrive under a light canopy of deciduous trees. The evergreen shrub *Rosmarinus officinalis* (rosemary) has gray-green leaves and flowers that appear mainly in spring, and then sporadically through to the fall. It looks striking beside the yellow-leaved *Philadelphus coronarius* 'Aureus'.

▲ *Plants with all-green or variegated leaves add interest throughout summer, and they help to suppress the growth of weeds.*

## Lilies for summer color

Lilies are popular and are especially attractive when grouped with other plants. Look for *Lilium candidum* (madonna lily) with white, trumpet-shaped flowers during early and midsummer. Their centers have golden pollen. They are superb when highlighted against a background of the deciduous shrub *Cotinus coggygria* 'Royal Purple', with dark plum-purple leaves. For a less dramatic display, plant the lilies in combination with foxgloves (*Digitalis purpurea*) and a background of blue delphiniums. *Lilium regale* also has white flowers, with their exteriors shaded rose-purple. It creates a rustic and subtle combination with silver birches and ferns such as *Dryopteris filix–mas*.

### COLORFUL LEAVES

*Aucuba japonica* 'Variegata'—evergreen shrub with green leaves spotted yellow.

*Cotinus coggygria* 'Royal Purple'—deciduous shrub with dark plum-purple leaves.

*Elaeagnus pungens* 'Maculata'—evergreen shrub with green leaves splashed gold.

*Humulus lupulus* 'Aureus'—yellow-leaved hop, a herbaceous climber with rich yellow leaves.

*Philadelphus coronarius* 'Aureus'—deciduous shrub with yellow leaves.

*Prunus cerasifera* 'Pissardii'—deciduous tree with dark red young leaves that turn deep purple as they mature.

*Robinia pseudoacacia* 'Frisia'—deciduous tree with yellow leaves.

# planting for fall color

*Fall is thought to be a dull period in the garden, but it is full of colorful flowers, and leaves that turn yellow, orange, gold, and red before falling. And even where the flowers of herbaceous plants have turned brown, they look attractive when laced with dew-drenched spiders' webs.*

## Fall flowering shrubs and trees

Several shrubs that flower in late summer continue their display into the fall. They include the magnificent *Buddleja davidii* (butterfly bush) with long, tapering spires of lilac-purple, honey, and musk-scented flowers from midsummer to midfall. There are several varieties in white, deep violet, and lavender-blue. *Caryopteris* × *clandonensis* 'Kew blue' has aromatic gray-green leaves and dark blue flowers from late summer, while *Hibiscus syriacus* bears trumpet-shaped flowers from midsummer to early fall, in colors including violet-blue and rose-pink.

The popular *Hydrangea macrophylla* (common hydrangea) is bushy with large, mainly blue flowerheads that continue into fall. Another magnificent summer and fall-flowering shrub is *Lavatera* 'Rosea', (tree mallow), also known as *Lavatera olbia* 'Rosea'. The branching stems bear masses of rose-colored flowers.

## Glorious corms

Many people think that corms and bulbs are the same, but instead of having an onion-like structure, the stem bases of corms are greatly swollen. *Crocus longiflorus* has goblet-shaped, lilac and deep bluish-mauve flowers with prominent orange stigmas and orange feathering in the throat during mid- and late fall. And *C. sativus* (saffron crocus), has red-purple flowers, large red stigmas and orange stamens during midfall. A more popular and hardier corm is *Cyclamen hederifolium*, with flowers in a range of colors from white, through pale pink to mauve, from late summer to late fall.

## Lilies for fall color

Several summer-flowering lilies continue their display into fall and are welcome for the stately appearance of their

▲ *The leaves of the deciduous shrub* Rhus typhina *(staghorn sumac) turn brilliant shades of orange-red, yellow, and purple.*

flowers, but they need a sunny and wind-sheltered position. *Lilium auratum* (golden-rayed lily) has sweetly scented, funnel-shaped, brilliant white flowers during late summer and early fall. Each flower has a golden-yellow ray or band. *L. henryi* also has sweetly scented flowers, but they are pale apricot-yellow with red spots. They appear during late summer and early fall. A more popular variety is *L. speciosum*, a lily with white, partly crimson-shaded pendent flowers.

## STAR PLANTS

| | |
|---|---|
| *Buddlja davidii* | *Hydrangea macrophylla* |
| *Hibiscus syriacus* | *Lavatera* 'Rosea' |

## Mixing and matching

You can plant a late summer display that will, in part, continue to midfall or later by planting the 3ft/90cm-high, rose 'Ophelia' with blush-pink flowers among the sky blue, trumpet-like flowers of the early to late fall-flowering *Gentiana sino-ornata*. It grows about 6in/15cm high with a 12–15in/30–38cm spread. The rose continues flowering into early fall, especially in mild areas. For a richer color scheme plant a row of *Sedum* 'Autumn Joy', now known as *Sedum* 'Herbstfreude'. This colorful plant bears slightly domed heads packed with salmon-pink flowers that slowly change through orange-red to orange-brown in mid- and late fall.

▲ *Massed hydrangeas create dominant features from midsummer to early fall. The old flowerheads look very attractive when they are covered in frost.*

## SHRUBS AND TREES WITH FALL COLOR

*Hamamelis mollis* (Chinese witch-hazel)—sharp yellow

*Liquidambar styraciflua* (sweetgum)—rich orange and scarlet shades

*Koelreuteria paniculata* (golden-rain tree)—rich yellow

*Malus tschonoskii*—rich red and yellow

*Parrotia persica*—crimson, gold and amber tints

*Rhus typhina* (staghorn sumac)—rich orange-red, purple and yellow tints

# planting for winter interest

*Corners of gardens devoted to winter-flowering plants create oases of interest when the garden might otherwise be lacking color. Apart from winter flowers, many shrubs and trees have wonderfully colored stems or bark. Some make excellent focal points.*

## Winter-flowering shrubs and trees

These create a permanent framework around which other plants can be positioned. Many have scented flowers and they include *Hamamelis mollis* (Chinese witch-hazel) and *Hamamelis japonica* (Japanese witch-hazel), both with spider-like flowers borne on naked branches. *Viburnum × bodnantense* 'Dawn' has sweetly scented white flowers, flushed red, from early to late winter, and *V. farreri* bears white flowers over a similar period. Richly colored mahonias are also evident in winter, and few compare with the evergreen *Mahonia × media* 'Charity'. It has tapering spires of sweetly scented, yellow flowers from late fall to late winter.

## Glorious bulbs

Some winter-flowering bulbs are slightly variable in the exact time they flower, often blooming on the cusp of late winter and early spring, depending on the weather. The rich golden-yellow, goblet-like flowers of *Crocus chrysanthus* always get plenty of attention. They flower during late winter into early spring, and are superb in a rock garden or when naturalized around a silver birch. The slightly earlier flowering *Iris reticulata* creates a feast of violet-scented, deep blue-purple flowers each with an orange blaze during mid- and late winter. Its diminutive stature, about 4in/10cm high, makes it ideal for a rock garden or the edge of a path. *I. histrioides* 'Major' bears rich blue flowers at about the same time and looks good in a medley of golden crocuses and especially white *Galanthus nivalis* (snowdrops) which are an essential part of the winter garden. During mid- and late winter it bears white nodding flowers, some slightly scented.

▲ *The diminutive and bulbous-rooted* Iris reticulata *produces a wealth of flowers. It is ideal for planting in a rock garden.*

## Mixing and matching

Here are a couple of plants that pair well, with the added benefit of scented flowers. First, try *Helleborus niger* (Christmas rose) around the early to late winter-flowering shrub *Chimonanthus praecox* 'Grandiflorus' (wintersweet). The hellebore has saucer-shaped white flowers, while the wintersweet reveals spicily scented, claw-like flowers formed of yellow outer petals and red centers. The second plant association is *Hamamelis mollis* (Chinese witch hazel), with rich golden-yellow, spider-like flowers in midwinter, and an underplanting of the yellow-green evergreen shrub *Euonymus fortunei* (wintercreeper). A few plants of the low-growing evergreen shrub *Sarcococca confusa* (Christmas box), with white, sweetly scented flowers, add further color contrasts.

### ATTRACTIVE BARK

Many trees have distinctive colored bark that is especially welcome in winter.

*Acer griseum* (paperbark maple)—Buff-colored bark that peels to reveal orange-brown under bark.

*Acer pensylvanicum* maple 'Erythrocladum'—trunk and branches with jagged white lines.

*Arbutus × andrachnoides*—cinnamon-red bark.

*Betula utilis jacquemontii*—peeling bark, usually white but light pinkish-brown and ocher-cream forms are available.

▶ *Shrubs with colored stems in winter always attract attention. Here is the thicket-forming Cornus alba 'Sibirica', with bright crimson stems. It is ideal for planting alongside streams.*

### STAR PLANTS

*Hamamelis mollis*

*Mahonia × media* 'Charity'

*Crocus chrysanthus*

*Chimonanthus praecox*

*Jasminum nudiflorum*

*Sarcococca confusa*

### COLORED STEMS

If these suckering shrubs are radically pruned to near soil level in the spring, they develop attractive young stems during summer that color up for winter.

*Cornus alba* (red-barked dogwood)—rich red stems.

*Cornus alba* 'Sibirica' (Westonbirt dogwood)—brilliant crimson stems.

*Cornus stolonifera* (red osier dogwood)—dull red stems.

*Cornus stolonifera* 'Flaviramea' (dogwood)—bright yellow to olive-green stems.

◀ *The hardy, evergreen shrub Mahonia × media 'Charity' never fails to give a dominant display of yellow flowers in winter.*

# ornamental features

*Opportunities to create decorative features are wide in small gardens. These range from hanging baskets and windowboxes, to tubs and pots on a patio or a terrace, bamboo walks, and collections of ornamental grasses. Roses are popular; climbing and rambling roses are useful for draping trellises and pillars with color, while some can be encouraged to clamber up large trees. Scented flowers are always popular and drench gardens in fragrances from almond to vanilla.*

# windowbox color

*By using a combination of spring, summer, and winter displays it is possible to have a colorful garden throughout the year. Spring displays are mainly formed of bulbs and biennials, while summer arrangements rely on bedding plants. Winter displays usually depend on foliage plants.*

## Creating a year-round display

An attractive windowbox may be positioned on a window ledge or on brackets attached to the wall, about 8in/20cm below the ledge of a casement window. Fit three smaller boxes inside the box, and plant them with seasonal displays. In this way, the windowbox can be given new plantings three times a year.

▲ *Decorative, plaque-like plant containers create distinctive features when mounted on a wall. Eventually they become drenched in color.*

❀ Spring displays—plant these in the fall using spring-flowering bulbs such as hyacinths, tulips and *Narcissus* (daffodils), and biennials like *Erysimum* (wallflowers), *Myosotis* (forget-me-not) and double daisies. When planted, put the container in a cool, well-drained sheltered part of the garden. In spring, when the bulbs are breaking into bud and the biennials are starting to flower, remove the winter display and replace with the spring arrangement.

❀ Summer displays—plant in late spring and initially keep them in a sheltered, frost-free position outdoors or in a well-ventilated conservatory. In early summer, when the spring display is fading, replace with the summer display.

❀ Winter displays—in fall, as soon as the summer display has been dulled by frost, remove it and replace it with the winter arrangement. This should be mainly formed of hardy foliage plants, such as small pots of *Aucuba japonica* 'Variegata', small-leaved *Hedera* (ivy), miniature and slow-growing conifers, winter-flowering *Erica* (heath), and *Calluna* (heather),

variegated forms of *Euonymus japonicus*, and *Hebe × andersoniana* 'Variegata'.

## Wall baskets and mangers

These resemble hanging baskets cut in half and secured to a wall, but they are large and able to hold plenty of soil. They look good in any position and are especially useful for securing to walls abutting pavements or around patio interiors. Wall basket and manger displays are more limited than windowboxes and can have only spring and summer arrangements. Spring displays are planted directly into the container in fall and left until they flower in spring. When over, all the plants are removed, fresh soil put in its place, and a summer display planted. This lasts until fall, when the spring display is planted.

---

### STAR PLANTS

*Aucuba japonica* 'Variegata'

*Lobularia maritima*

*Muscari armeniacum*

---

### Three seasonal medleys

The range of possible plants is wide but the following suggestions are a fail-safe, attractive design for each season.

✿ Spring—this can be a combination of plants, using biennials such as *Erysimum* (wallflower), double daisies and *Myosotis* (forget-me-not), and bulbs like *Muscari armeniacum* (grape hyacinth), *Tulipa greigii* and *T. fosteriana*.

✿ Summer—For a colorful display plant a combination of trailing lobelia, zonal pelargoniums, *Lobularia maritima* (sweet alyssum), tuberous-rooted begonias and summer-flowering *Viola* (pansy). Position trailing plants at one end or along the front, with the begonia in the center. Container-grown plants will need some feeding and regular thorough watering throughout any dry weather.

▶ *Use upright and bushy plants to achieve a display at the top of a windowbox, and trailing foliage plants to drape the front in color.*

▼ *Instead of planting summer-flowering plants directly into soil in a windowbox, they can be left in their pots and replaced as they fade.*

✿ Winter—this can be a grouping of foliage plants such as small-leaved *Hedera helix* 'Glacier' (ivy), variegated *Euonymus japonicus* and dwarf varieties of the conifer *Chamaecyparis lawsoniana* will look attractive. The winter-flowering *Erica* (heath) adds color.

---

## HERBS IN WINDOWBOXES

A windowbox outside a kitchen window may be planted with a wide range of readily available herbs. Choose a medley of low-growing plants, such as mint, thyme, chives, parsley, marjoram, and French tarragon. The range of mints is wide and includes spearmint and apple mint. Leave individual plants in their pots and place them on a layer of gravel in the windowbox, so that their rims are slightly below the top. Pack moist peat around the pots to keep the soil moist and cool.

# hanging baskets

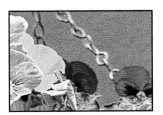

*Hanging baskets can bring summer color and winter greenery to featureless spots. They can enliven dull walls with decorative flowers and foliage, and brighten windows, doorways, and porches. They also look eyecatching in small paved areas, such as patios and courtyards.*

### Displaying hanging baskets

A planted basket should be hung in an eye-catching position—perhaps on either side of a window, about 15in/38cm from the frame. The edge of a balcony or a veranda may be decorated by hanging planted baskets along it to introduce

◀ *Brick columns are a useful site for fixing a hanging basket from a bracket. Position the basket where it cannot be knocked.*

round and cascading shapes to an area that is dominated by vertical and horizontal lines.

A featureless wall or a carport may be enlivened by hanging planted baskets along it, but do not hang them near corners or where they might be knocked. To prevent people knocking baskets hanging from a wall, range planted tubs along the base of the wall, but do not stand them directly below the baskets where water will drip onto them. A few white or pale-colored flowers in the baskets will make them noticeable in twilight. If you hang baskets in a lobby or a porch, they will need to have inbuilt drip trays, or water will spill onto the floor below.

### Choosing plants

A hanging basket will be successful only if it is well planted. That means resisting the temptation to cram it with plants.

Once the plants are established, weed out weak ones. A few large, healthy blooms look better than many stunted plants fighting for survival. One rule for achieving an eye-catching display is not to plant too many species. Mixed displays can look good, but four or five well-chosen plants look better than a dozen species in a basket.

Choose plants with contrasting growing habits for a mixed basket—trailing, bushy, and upright. Set a showy plant, such as a fuchsia or an upright geranium, in the center and put trailing plants around the edges and cascading from the sides of the basket. If you buy plants from a nursery or a garden center, your choice of varieties may be limited. Instead, try growing your own, choosing compact plants recommended for hanging baskets. Mix summer-flowering plants with hardy perennials and foliage plants, such as variegated small-leaved *Hedera* (ivy) and small forms of *Euonymus fortunei* with attractive leaves. If you do not want to spray your hanging baskets regularly with insecticides, avoid plants that are prone to pests, such as nasturtiums, which attract blackflies.

## Strawberries and tomatoes

Some varieties of these fruiting plants look attractive in hanging baskets. *Fragaria vesca*, the alpine strawberry or *fraise du bois*, is a decorative perennial. 'Alexander' bears small fruits used to decorate pastries. 'Temptation' bears aromatic sweet fruits from midsummer to the fall frosts. A bushy tomato such as 'Tumbler', which produces small, sweet fruits, will look decorative cascading from a basket.

▶ *To create a spectacular hanging basket, use a combination of upright, cascading, and trailing plants. Additionally, daily watering is vital.*

### SINGLE-SUBJECT HANGING BASKETS

The following produce eyecatching displays:

*Calceolaria integrifolia* 'Sunshine'—creates a dominant display packed with yellow, pouch-like flowers.

*Fuchsias*—use bushy and trailing types. Plants are sometimes slow to create a display, so insure that they are well developed.

*Impatiens* (busy lizzie)—bright colors.

*Solenopsis axillaris* —a mass of five-petalled, 1in/2.5cm-wide flowers in a range of colors including blue, white, and pink.

*Lobelia* (in mixed colors)—trailing plants make a dazzling display.

*Petunia grandiflora* supercascade series—very free-flowering over a long period, producing large flower heads in a wide variety of colors.

# pots and tubs

*These popular, versatile containers can accommodate plants of many sizes and types. The agapanthus, with tall stems bearing umbrella-like flower heads, looks good in square, Versailles-type planters, while rounded, evergreen shrubs look better in large, round tubs.*

### Displaying pots and tubs

There are plants to suit every container, and pots to suit any position in the garden. A small paved area, such as a courtyard, needs at least one dominant plant in an impressive container, around which other planted pots may be grouped. *Fatsia japonica* (false castor oil plant) planted in a very large clay pot is one suggestion. It needs a sheltered position in sun or shade. This evergreen shrub grows well in a container, and in gardens that are located in urban areas.

The top of a flight of steps looks better with several planted pots clustered on it. In a formal garden the stairs look best with just one plant on either side, while a group of small planted pots is better in an informal setting. On a patio, a large trough makes a focal point if placed beneath a window, with attractive planted pots either side.

Make containers for rural gardens from three or four tires stacked and wired together. Wedge a plastic bucket in the top and plant it with spring flowers, such as polyanthus. Paint the tires white to blend them in. In town gardens, small tubs planted with clipped, half-standard *Laurus nobilis* (bay trees) may stand either side of a front door. An ornate urn on a high pedestal makes a magnificent focal point at the junction of wide gravel paths in a large garden. Range planted troughs, available in plastic, glass-fiber,

◄ *Position pots alongside paths as well as on patios. Half-burying pots keeps the soil cool and reduces the need to water them.*

reconstituted stone, and other materials, along the top of a plain wall, the sides of a patio, or the edges of a veranda. Where there is vertical space to fill, choose upright plants like daffodils, but summer-flowering trailing plants look spectacular cascading down a wall or from a balcony.

## Foliage plants for tubs and pots

Plants with decorative leaves lend permanency to a patio or a terrace, and unify groupings of flowers, especially

annuals. There is a wide range of these. Evergreen shrubs with variegated leaves include *Aucuba japonica* 'Variegata' with green leaves splashed with yellow, *Hebe ×️ franciscana* 'Variegata' with glossy green leaves edged with cream, *Hebe ×️ andersonii* 'Variegata' with cream and green leaves, *Choisya ternata* 'Sundance' with radiant golden leaves, and *Yucca filamentosa* 'Variegata' , which has dramatic sword-shaped leaves edged with a creamy stripe.

▶ *Brighten walls by attaching brackets that support pots of many sizes. These can be used in combination with hanging baskets.*

▼ *Clean lines, formed by square containers planted with narrow-leaved, spiky plants, are right for a modern setting.*

---

### CLIMBERS IN CONTAINERS

Several climbers can be grown in containers, but regular watering is needed to make certain that the soil does not dry out. Some are perennials, others are annuals raised from seed each year.

Large-flowered clematis—choose a tub or a large pot. Flowers from early to late summer, depending on the variety, with a range of colors. Ornate metal railings look attractive when covered by the flowers.

*Clematis macropetala*—choose a large terracotta or wooden tub, fill its base with clean rubble, then add well-drained soil. Put several plants with light and dark blue flowers around the top to encourage cascading.

*Humulus lupulus* 'Aureus' (yellow-leaved hop)—select a large tub for this herbaceous climber and form a wigwam of 5–6ft/1.5–1.8m-long canes. They become smothered in yellow leaves.

*Ipomoea purpurea* (morning glory—grown as a half-hardy annual, with large, bell-like flowers in several colors.

*Tropaeolum majus* (nasturtium)—grown as a half-hardy annual, with flowers in several colors throughout summer.

# stone sinks on patios

*Where there is no space for a rock garden or even a scree bed, a stone sink on a patio or a terrace is an ideal home for small rock garden plants, dwarf bulbs, and miniature conifers. By selecting the combination of plants you can have an attractive feature throughout the year.*

▲ *A stone sink is a perfect place for a miniature rock garden. Standing the sink on bricks helps to reduce the ravages of snails and slugs.*

## Selecting and preparing a sink

Ideally, an old stone sink is best for planting. However, a deep, white-glazed sink can easily be modified to give an attractive, well-worn appearance. This is done by scratching the surface, coating it with PVA, and covering with a slightly moist mixture of equal parts of cement powder, horticultural sand, and peat.

Place the sink on four strong bricks; it should have a slight slope toward the drainage hole. Place a piece of fine-mesh wire net over the drainage hole so it cannot get blocked, then a layer of broken clay pots or pebbles over the entire base to facilitate drainage.

### POSITIONING A SINK GARDEN

Sink gardens need full sun or partial shade, and a position where they cannot be tripped over. Therefore, unless the patio or terrace is large with a rarely used corner, position a couple of columnar conifers in pots close to the sink to mark it out clearly. Light-colored conifers are better than dark green ones, because they are easily visible in the twilight.

Spread a 1in/2.5cm-thick layer of horticultural sand over the bottom of the sink and half-fill it with a mixture of equal parts of potting soil, moist peat, and grit. If the sink is deep, increase the amount of drainage material. The soil must not contain chalk if lime-hating plants are being used.

At this stage, a few large rocks can be pushed into the soil, inclined at a shallow angle. Add more soil to within 1in/2.5cm of the rim. Position the plants, then add a ½in/12mm-thick layer of rock chippings or pea gravel. The soil will settle, so be prepared to add more surface material later.

## Plants for stone sinks

The range of plants is wide and while some, such as dwarf conifers, create height, other rock garden plants are small. Spring-flowering dwarf bulbs create bright, diminutive, dainty features.

▲ *A miniature hedge makes an attractive background for a patio, especially when combined with flowering plants.*

Spring-flowering bulbs—include *Crocus chrysanthus* with golden-yellow, goblet-shaped flowers in late winter and early spring, also available in white, blue and purple; *Cyclamen coum* with pink and carmine flowers from midwinter to early spring; *Eranthis hyemalis* with lemon-yellow flowers backed by light green ruffs during late winter and spring; *Iris danfordiae* with honey-scented, lemon-yellow flowers during mid- and late winter; *Iris reticulata* with bluish-purple flowers with orange blazes in late winter and early spring; *Narcissus bulbocodium* with yellow, hoop-like flowers during late winter and early spring; and *Narcissus cyclamineus* with yellow, narrow trumpets with swept-back petals in late winter and early spring.

Rock garden perennials—*Antennaria rosea* has deep pink flowers during spring and early summer; *Campanula cochleariifolia* has blue bells from midsummer to fall; *Edraianthus pumilio*

▲ *A stone sink makes a home for hardy, succulent plants such as houseleeks. By leaving plants in their pots the display can be quickly and easily changed.*

has lavender-blue flowers from late spring to midsummer; *Erinus alpinus* has bright pink flowers from early spring to late summer; *Lewisia cotyledon* has pink flowers with white veins during late spring and early summer; and *Saxifraga burseriana* has white flowers during late winter and early spring.

Miniature and slow-growing conifers—plant these while they are still small and be prepared to remove them when they grow too large. Position tall ones at one end of the sink, and sprawling types at the other, because they help to create height and shape.

| STAR PLANTS | |
| --- | --- |
| Crocus chrysanthus | Eranthis hyemalis |

# scented gardens

*Scented flowers and aromatic leaves can enrich the air with many different fragrances. The range of scents is amazingly wide, and even in temperate regions there is a choice of over a hundred fragrances. They include scents from chocolate and pineapple to banana and lemon.*

## Siting fragrant plants

The perfect site for a perfumed garden is sheltered from strong winds, which disperse scents, free from frosts, which limit the growing period of tender plants, and slopes gently toward the sun, to capture the warmth that encourages plants to emit their fragrances. Few gardens have all these qualities, but garden areas suitable for perfumed plants can be made by planting hedges, erecting freestanding trellis, and introducing tender plants in frost-free areas.

## Flower borders

Many herbaceous perennials emit delicious scents, notably the short-lived, hardy *Hesperis matronalis* (sweet rocket). Its white, mauve, or purple flowers appear in early to midsummer to drench borders with their sweet fragrance, especially in the evening. *Saponaria officinalis* (soapwort) also emits a sweet scent from its single, pink, salver-shaped flowers which appear in mid- to late summer. *Phlox paniculata* has strongly perfumed flowers from mid- to late summer, and is perhaps better known. There are many varieties in colors from white to pink and red.

Establish summer color with rich fragrance in your garden quickly by planting a mix of *Matthiola bicornis* (night-scented stock), which bears pink to mauve flowers during mid- and late summer, and *Malcolmia maritima* (Virginia stock). Sow the seeds in friable soil beneath windows, and in successive sowings from spring to midsummer.

Once a favorite of the French Empress Josephine Bonaparte, *Reseda odorata* (mignonette) is a cottage-garden hardy annual with clusters of small, white and yellow richly scented flowers through the summer. It can be grown in windowboxes and in pots on balconies. It

◀ *This pairing of English lavender (*Lavandula angustifolia*) and rue (*Ruta graveolens*) brings scent and color to small gardens.*

### AROMATIC-LEAVED SHRUBS

*Caryopteris* × *clandonensis*—pungent

*Choisya ternata* (Mexican orange blossom)—orange

*Lavandula angustifolia* (lavender)—lavender

*Rosmarinus officinalis* (rosemary)—rosemary

*Ruta graveolens* (rue)—pungent and acrid

is said that success and good fortune will attend a lover who rolls in a bed of mignonette.

There are several diminutive bulbs which will bring color and perfume to a rock garden and along the edges of paths. *Galanthus nivalis* (common snowdrop) and *Iris reticulata* both have violet-scented flowers during late winter and early spring.

## Trees and shrubs

Many trees and shrubs are sweetly perfumed, and some have an unexpected fragrance. *Prunus padus* 'Watereri' (bird cherry) is a deciduous tree with a spreading habit. It bears drooping tassels of white flowers which are almond-scented in early summer. *Prunus* × *yedoensis* (Potomac cherry) is also almond-scented. For a cowslip fragrance plant the deciduous shrub *Corylopsis pauciflora*, with pale primrose yellow flowers in mid- and late spring. *Helichrysum serotinum* is known as the curry plant because it is redolent of curry spices.

For honey fragrance, plant the informal *Ulex europaeus* 'Flore Pleno' (double-flowered gorse). The deciduous philadelphus shrubs have flowers with an orange-blossom aroma that will pervade the garden in midsummer. *Cytisus battandieri* (pineapple broom) bears pineapple-scented, golden-yellow flowers if planted against a south-facing wall, and the deciduous tree *Malus* 'Brandywine' has abundant pink flowers.

### STAR PLANTS

*Galanthus nivalis*

*Helichrysum serotinum*

*Hesperis matronalis*

*Phlox paniculata*

*Ulex europaeus* 'Flore Pleno'

▼ *Few scented cottage garden plants are as attractive as* Hesperis matronalis *(sweet rocket), with a rich scent in the evening.*

# the flower arranger's garden

*Even a small garden can produce enough attractive flowers and foliage for cutting and displaying indoors. They are usually provided by herbaceous perennials and hardy and half-hardy annuals, although the leaves of many evergreen shrubs and climbers can also be added to arrangements.*

## Herbaceous perennials

These are ideal for providing flowers and leaves for summer arrangements, when they are fresh and bright. Most flowers and leaves are taken from plants growing in borders, but where space allows, grow a few blooms in a spare corner.

Never cut flowers from wilting plants because they soon fade. Water the plants the day before and cut them early in the morning. Place them in a bucket of water and keep the bucket in a cool room for 24 hours. Cut each stem at a 45° angle and remove the lower leaves.

Among the many herbaceous plants you can grow are *Achillea filipendulina* (fern-leaf yarrow), *Alstroemeria* (Peruvian lily), *Aster amellus*, *A. novae-angliae*, *Aster novi-belgii*, *Catananche caerulea* (cupid's dart), *Coreopsis verticillata*, *Leucanthemum ×superbum*, *Limonium latifolium*, *Lysimachia vulgaris* (yellow loosestrife), *Phlox paniculata*, *Rudbeckia laciniata*, *Solidago* (goldenrod) and *Tanacetum* (pyrethrum).

## Hardy and half-hardy annuals

These enable flower-arranging enthusiasts to have a different range of fresh, bright-faced flowers each year and

▲ *A border packed with a medley of plants creates a reservoir of colorful flowers and differently shaped leaves for cutting.*

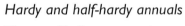

### STAR PLANTS

*Alchemilla mollis*

*Achillea filipendulina*

*Calendula officinalis*

*Coreopsis verticillata*

*Elaeagnus pungens 'Maculata'*

*Leucanthemum × superbum*

*Lysimachia vulgaris*

*Phlox paniculata*

they are cut and prepared for display just like herbaceous perennials. They include *Calendula officinalis* (pot marigold), *Cosmos bipinnatus* (cosmea), *consolida ajacis* (larkspur), *Gaillardia* (blanket flower), *Gypsophila elegans* (baby's breath), *Iberis umbellata* (globe candytuft), *Lathyrus odoratus* (sweet pea), *Nigella damascena* (love-in-a-mist), and *Reseda odorata* (mignonette).

Besides providing fresh flowers, a few hardy and half-hardy annuals can be grown to provide flowers for drying. They include *Celosia* (cockscomb), helichrysum, *Limonium sinuatum* and *Moluccella laevis* (bells of Ireland). Cut them with long stems, just as the flowers are opening. Tie them into small bunches and hang them upside-down in a dry, well-ventilated room.

## Attractive foliage

Many types of plants, including herbaceous perennials and evergreen shrubs and climbers, have foliage that can be added to flower arrangements. Those from herbaceous perennials include hostas with variegated and single-colored leaves. The large, leathery, rounded leaves of bergenias are ideal as a background display. Those of *Alchemilla mollis* (lady's mantle) are daintier and their lime-green color is not so dramatic.

Evergreen shrubs such as *Elaeagnus pungens* 'Maculata' are dramatic, with shiny green leaves splashed gold, while those of *Elaeagnus × ebbingei* are leathery and silver-gray. During early summer the stems of the *Lonicera nitida* 'Baggeson's

Gold' (boxleaf honeysuckle) look good, while the leaves of *Brachyglottis* 'Sunshine', better known as *Senecio* 'Sunshine', add a soft gray quality. Some displays have stems of evergreen shrubs meandering at the edges. They include variegated vincas and small and large-leaved *Hedera* (ivy).

▲ *Sweet peas introduce a feast of color to gardens, as well as providing flowers in many colors for decoration indoors.*

▲ *The stiffly erect flower heads of* Acanthus mollis *(bear's breeches) look dramatic in gardens and in flower displays.*

### SEED HEADS FOR DRYING

Dried seed heads taken from herbaceous perennials are especially useful for winter flower arrangements. There are many plants to choose from, including:

*Acanthus mollis* (bear's breeches)

*Dictamnus albus* (burning bush)

*Echinops ritro* (globe thistle)

*Iris foetidissima* (stinking iris)

*Limonium platyphyllum* (sea lavender)

*Onopordum acanthium* (Scotch thistle)

*Physalis alkekengi* (Chinese lantern)

# cottage gardens

*Few gardening styles have such a relaxed and informal atmosphere as a cottage garden. It is rich in nostalgia, and packed with flowers, fruits, vegetables, and herbs. Such informality can easily be created in small gardens, with arbors and trellises providing secluded areas.*

## Screening plants

Few climbers compare with the scrambling *Clematis vitalba* (old man's beard), widely seen in English hedgerows. It is usually remembered for its glistening, silky seed heads in fall, which often continue into winter. Elizabethans praised it for covering hedges, but in a small cottage garden it is too vigorous and there are other clematis with more attractive and delicate flowers. They include *Clematis macropetala, C. flammula*, and *C. orientalis. C. montana* is also attractive but often too rampant for small areas. Honeysuckle is also an excellent cottage garden climber, best given rustic supports. And as well as being grown for food, pole beans can be used as screening plants; try them clambering up a 6ft/1.8m-high tripod.

Cordon and espalier apples also make useful screens. Where possible, plant some of the older varieties with superb flavors and textures. Try 'Rome', a cooking apple, and for eating, 'Esopus Spuitzenberg', 'Gravenstein', 'Arkansas Black' and 'Northern spy' to bring back flavors that were common in the past.

## Flower borders

Aim for a medley of shrubs, trees, herbaceous perennials, bulbs, and annuals planted or sown in attractive groups, each plant complementing its neighbors. From spring to fall memorable plant associations can be created.

✽ Spring—tulips offer a wide range of colors. For a mixture of yellow, orange-red, and blue try a deep-blue forget-me-not and a combination of orange-red and yellow tulips. If you prefer a medley of blue, scarlet, and gold flowers, plant pale blue forget-me-nots and the scarlet and gold single early tulip 'Keizerskroon'. Alternatively, for a white and blue display, plant a carpet of the biennial *Bellis perennis* (common daisy) with violet-blue Parrot tulips. These arrangements are ideal for beds and under windows. For a larger spring display in a prominent border plant the yellow-flowered deciduous shrub *Forsythia* 'Lynwood' with small groups of red-flowered Kaufmanniana tulips.

▲ *The large, brilliantly colored flowers of* Papaver orientale *(oriental poppy) make a dramatic display during early summer.*

| STAR PLANTS | |
|---|---|
| *Clematis montana* | *Hydrangea macrophylla* |
| *Geranium endressii* | *Sedum* 'Herbstfreude' |

✿ Summer—*Lilium candidum* (madonna lily) has pure white flowers, and is a suitable companion for foxgloves, which have tall stems bearing bell-shaped flowers in a color range from purple, to pink to red. Plant the scrambling *Clematis flammula*, with small, sweetly-scented flowers, and *Aconitum napellus* (monkshood) with its deep blue, helmet-shaped flowers, for an unusual combination of climbers with perennials.

Roses are also superb in summer displays. 'Buff Beauty' bears warm, apricot-yellow flowers that form a pleasing partnership with the lavender-blue *Nepeta × faassenii* (catmint) and *Papaver orientale* 'Perry's White' (oriental poppy). Another good combination involves the damask rose 'Mme Hardy', with white flowers, and pink varieties of *Geranium endressii*. The bourbon rose 'Mme Isaac Pereire' is bushy and shrubby, with crimson flowers that harmonize with tulips, lilies, peonies, and lilacs.

✿ Fall—for a large display, plant blue varieties of the hardy, deciduous dome-shaped shrub *Hydrangea macrophylla* in front of the evergreen shrubby *Eucryphia × nymansensis*, with cream flowers.

Another attractive duo for the fall is the evergreen border plant *Sedum* 'Herbstfreude' and the bulbous *Colchicum* 'Waterlily'. The *Sedum* is well known for the display created by its richly colored fall flowers, which eventually become orange-brown.

▲ *A combination of tulips and fragrant forget-me-nots (myosotis) never fails to capture attention in spring and early summer.*

▼ *Border geraniums produce magnificant displays throughout summer. There are many varieties and colors.*

# ground-cover plants

*Plants that smother soil with foliage prevent the growth of weeds and are welcome in any garden. The choice is wide and includes herbaceous perennials, shrubs, and a few climbers such as large-leaved ivies like Hedera colchica 'Sulphur Heart'.*

## Border perennials

Most border perennials are herbaceous but some do retain their foliage through winter. Most prefer full sun or light shade, but others will grow out of the sun.

❋ Sun or shade—although some plants can grow in either light or shade, do not expect the same display in both. Most plants when given plenty of light and moisture will flower better than those in shade with little moisture. The range of plants you need includes *Alchemilla mollis* (lady's mantle) with lime-green, hairy leaves and yellow-green, star-shaped flowers. Bergenias, with their large, elephant-like leaves, also flower in spring. Epimediums are daintier and cover the ground with heart-shaped leaves that assume attractive tints in the fall and through much of winter. *Geranium grandiflorum* is herbaceous, with a spreading habit and blue-purple flowers in early and midsummer. And *Hemerocallis* (daylily) forms large clumps, with arching, strap-like leaves and lily-like flowers. Avoid heavy shade because this reduces its ability to flower.

*Persicaria affinis* forms mats of lance-shaped leaves and poker-like flower heads during mid- and late summer. *Saxifraga urbium* (London pride) has a more diminutive nature, with rosettes of leaves that carpet the soil and masses of pink, star-shaped flowers during late spring and early summer. *Lamium galeobdolon* 'Florentinum' (better known as *Lamium galeobdolon* 'Variegatum') is vigorous and spreading, with silver-flushed evergreen leaves that display bronze tints in winter. These plants will not thrive in dark shade.

◄ *Smothering the ground with plants looks attractive as well as making gardening easier by eliminating the need to pull up weeds.*

*Lysimachia nummularia* (creeping jenny) has sprawling stems of rounded leaves and bright yellow, cup-shaped flowers during early and midsummer.

⚙ Partial shade—the popular *Ajuga reptans* 'Multicolor' (bugleweed) has purple leaves, while *Brunnera macrophylla* has heart-shaped foliage and sprays of blue flowers in late spring and early summer; it dislikes dry soil. The range of hostas is wide and, with their often large leaves, they soon cloak the soil. *Pulmonaria angustifolia* (with the evocative name blue cowslip) has lance-shaped leaves and funnel-shaped, blue flowers in spring. *Pulmonaria saccharata* has leaves spotted silver-white. *Symphytum ibericum* spreads rapidly, with tubular, white flowers during spring, while *Tiarella cordifolia* (foam flower) is less dominant, with maple-like, light green leaves.

⚙ Full sun—in strong sun, plant *Nepeta × faassenii* (catmint). It covers the soil with gray-green leaves and lavender-blue flowers from spring to fall. The wooly leaved *Stachys byzantina* (lamb's ears) never fails to attract attention.

## Ground-covering shrubs

Many evergreen shrubs with a sprawling or bushy habit are ideal for covering soil with leaves and, sometimes, flowers.

### STAR PLANTS

*Alchemilla mollis*

*Hedera colchica* 'Sulphur Heart'

*Stachys byzantina*

*Hypericum calycinum* (rose of Sharon) is a robust, ground-smothering plant that establishes itself quickly and even covers large banks. Throughout summer it bears golden-yellow flowers. Vincas also smother soil, but are best kept out of mixed lower beds because they are invasive. However, variegated forms are less invasive than all-green types. *Calluna* (heather) and *Erica* (heath) soon cover the ground with attractive leaves and flowers. Like *Gaultheria procumbens* (checkerberry), heathers and ericas need an acid soil. There are many others, including *Pachysandra terminalis*, with deep green leaves.

▼ *Where a large, flat area is planted with ground-covering plants, position large stepping stones to make access and maintenance easier.*

# grasses and bamboos

*Grasses and bamboos can be used in all kinds of ways, from edging borders to creating screens. And some are ideal for adding to fresh flower arrangements and for drying for winter displays. There are both annual and perennial grasses, while bamboos are long-lived perennials.*

▲ *The ornamental grass* Miscanthus sinensis *has strap-shaped, arching stems. Do not constrict it or its natural shape will be spoiled.*

### Perennial grasses

Taller perennial grasses look spectacular when planted to fill entire beds, and smaller ones may be planted with annual grasses to make ornamental grass borders. Some are small enough to plant along the edge of a border. These include *Festuca glauca*, about 9in/23cm high with blue-gray leaves, and the dramatic *Melica altissima* 'Atropurpurea', which reaches

## BAMBOOS FOR CONTAINERS

A few bamboo varieties can be planted in large pots, tubs or wooden boxes, although eventually they will need to be planted in the garden or taken out and divided; this is best done in early summer. Because the roots of bamboos in containers can easily be damaged in cold winters, choose only the hardiest types such as:

*Fargesia murieliae* (umbrella bamboo)— 6–8ft/1.8–2.4m high.

*Pleioblastus auricomis* (golden-haired bamboo)—3–4ft/90cm–1.2m high.

*Pseudosasa japonica* (arrow bamboo)— 8–12ft/2.4–3.6m high.

about 5ft/1.5m high, with deep mauve spikelets that sweep downward. It is used fresh and dried in flower arrangements.

Perennial grasses come in a wide range of heights, colors, and decorative forms. Stipa tenuissima rises to about 2½ft/75cm and bears soft, wispy pony tails. *Miscanthus sacchariflorus* (silver banner grass) is probably the most dramatic of all perennial grasses. It grows rapidly each year to about 10ft/3m high, so it makes a useful screening plant. Space the plants about 18in/45cm apart. During the first year, as it becomes established, it may grow to only 6ft/1.8m, but will rise much higher during the following season. *Miscanthus sinensis purpurascens*, with purple-tinged stems, reaches a height of 5ft/1.5m.

## Annual grasses

These grasses can be sown where they are to flower. They are useful for filling gaps in herbaceous and mixed borders, and for achieving a different display in successive years. Many can be cut and dried for use in winter decorations. These include *Briza maxima* (big quaking grass), with graceful, pendent, nodding flowers, and *Hordeum jubatum* (squirrel-tail grass). *Lagurus ovatus* (hare's-tail) develops soft, silky flowerheads with a furry texture.

## Bamboos for all gardens

Most of these woody grasses are hardy. Their widely varying foliage and stems may be used to add color and interest to a garden. A few are semievergreen in cold winters, and some are deciduous. They are useful for masking unsightly features, and they make a pleasant rustling sound. A few bamboos, such as *Pleloblastus auricomis* (golden-haired bamboo), are about 5ft/1.5m high and can be grown in a 10in/25cm-wide pot on a patio, while others grow rapidly to 10ft/3m or more.

Three popular bamboos are *Fargesia murieliae*, with graceful, arching, bright-green canes, *Fargesia nitida* with purple stems and narrow, bright-green leaves, and *Pseudosasa japonica* with lance-shaped, dark-green leaves.

▲ *Where slugs and snails are a problem, spread stone chippings or gravel over the area and stand pots of ornamental grasses and bamboos on it.*

◄ Pleioblastus auricomus *(golden-haired bamboo) is a dwarf variety, with golden variegated leaves, ideal for borders or containers.*

# ornamental hedges

*Creating hedges is more than just forming a boundary or screen. They can be gloriously rich in scents, have colorful berries, color contrasts within the same hedge, and harmonize or constrast with nearby plants. Even the ubiquitous privet can be attractive.*

### Hedge duos

To grow an unusual privet hedge, set two plants of *Ligustrum ovalifolium* 'Aureum' to one of *L. ovalifolium* along a row. This ratio produces a decorative, rather formal hedge, and will not allow the more vigorous all-green hedging to smother the yellow. The hedge should be clipped regularly in order to keep it in shape. Plant variegated holly and yew to produce an attractive evergreen hedge which will grow very slowly. Set the plants in the ground alternately, about 4ft/1.2m apart.

### Fragrant hedging

There is an astonishing range of hedging plants with fragrant flowers or leaves. The scents they emit include apple and raspberry. Several conifers used for hedging give off an unusual fragrance when their leaves are bruised.

For an apple-like scent plant *Thuja occidentalis* 'Smaragd'. Its dark-green foliage makes a dramatic backdrop for other plants. If a lemon fragrance delights you, choose *Cupressus macrocarpa* 'Goldcrest'. It has soft yellow foliage which, with age, becomes light green. The pineapple-scented *Thuja plicata* (western red cedar) has scaly, shiny, rich green foliage with white marks underneath. It is best reserved for a large boundary hedge. A fusion of resin and parsley is the smell given by *Chamaecyparis lawsoniana* 'Allumii', with soft blue-gray foliage, and *Chamaecyparis lawsoniana* 'Fletcheri' with feathery, blue-green leaves.

◄ *The evergreen shrub* Berberis darwinii *has masses of rich orange flowers in spring, followed by blue berries.*

Roses used for hedging offer more unusual scents, none better than 'Zephirine Drouhin' with raspberry-scented, vivid pink flowers. 'Penelope' has musk-scented, pale pink, semidouble flowers that fade slightly as they age. Several roses used for hedging have a sweet fragrance, including *Rosa rugosa* 'Roseraie de l'Hay' with crimson-purple flowers, 'Felicia' with salmon-pink flowers, and 'Prosperity' with creamy white blooms.

Two evergreen shrubs with memorable scents include *Lavandula angustifolia* 'Hidcote', with deep purple flowers 2in/5cm long and silver-green leaves. *Rosmarinus officinalis* (rosemary) also makes a lovely informal hedge.

## Harmonies and contrasts

Color-themed herbaceous borders were traditionally backed by hedges that harmonized or contrasted with them. For example, the dark green leaves of yew highlight white, orange, blue, and green borders, while golden-variegated holly harmonizes with golden borders. Tamarisk (*tamarix*) was frequently used as a backcloth for a gray border.

The deciduous *Fagus sylvatica* (beech), with young leaves that darken from bright green in spring to mid-green in summer, can be a striking backdrop for herbaceous plants. In the fall the hedge has the bonus of leaves that take on yellow and russet tints, competing for attention with end of season flower colors and seed heads.

▼ *Many roses can be used to form floriferous screens. They bring the atmosphere of a cottage garden to an urban plot.*

---

### BERRIED DELIGHTS

Several shrubs used to make informal hedges also have attractive berries. These include:

*Berberis darwinii*—evergreen, holly-like leaves and clusters of rich orange flowers in spring, followed by blue berries.

*Berberis* × *stenophylla*—evergreen, with golden-yellow flowers in spring, followed by a peppering of globular, purple berries with a white bloom.

*Hippophae rhamnoides* (sea buckthorn)—deciduous, with thick clusters of orange berries during fall and early winter.

*Rosa rugosa* 'Roseraie de l'Hay'—deciduous, with crimson-purple flowers, followed by large, round, orange-red hips in early fall.

# bush and shrub roses

*The range of large-flowered bush roses (hybrid teas) and cluster-flowered bush roses (floribundas) is wide, and each year more are introduced. The many species roses with a dramatic and subtle range of colors extend the range, and the more recent New English Roses make the choice still harder.*

## Using roses

It was once thought that the only way to grow bush roses was in formal beds flanked by paths or lawns. Today, they are used in many other situations. Prostrate roses cover the soil, patio roses in pots decorate patios, species roses adorn shrub borders, and weeping standards rise from beds and lawns. Small rose bushes can be planted in rock gardens and also in windowboxes. These include 'Baby Masquerade' (yellow to pink and red), 'Cinderella' (white, tinged with pink), 'Darling Flame' (orange-red, with yellow anthers), 'Black Jade' (deep red, almost black) and 'Popcorn' (white, honey-scented).

Weeping standards are well known for their beautiful, cascading outlines. They are produced by nurserymen budding a variety on a rootstock about 51in/130cm high. When mature, the head is 5–6ft/1.5–1.8m high, with stems cascading from the top. Rambler varieties are mainly used and include 'Albéric Barbier' (cream), 'Crimson Shower' (red), 'François Juranville' (salmon-pink), and 'Goldfinch' (yellow, fading to white).

## Companion planting bush roses

Bush roses can be attractively grouped with other plants. Plant the buttercup-yellow floribunda 'Chinatown' in front of *Clematis* 'Countess of Lovelace', a large-flowered variety that will flourish sprawling over a fence or a garden wall. The clematis flowers through summer into the fall (double-flowered forms bloom during summer, and single forms in late summer and fall). Its deep lavender flowers look handsome beside those of the yellow rose. Underplant white-flowering bush roses with the evergreen perennial *Tiarella cordifolia* (foam flower), which has a low mound of maple-shaped leaves and creamy white flowers in late spring and early summer.

▲ Rosa gallica officinalis *(apothecary's rose or red rose of Lancaster) bears large, loosely-formed, semidouble, rose-crimson flowers.*

The popular floribunda 'Queen Elizabeth' has cyclamen-pink flowers that look superb highlighted against yew. Plant the large-flowered yellow 'Grandpa Dickson' against the dark purple leaves of the deciduous shrub *Berberis thunbergii* 'Atropurpurea'. And, for additional color, plant the half-hardy annual *Nicotiana* 'Lime Green' in front of them.

## Companion planting shrub roses

The range of shrub roses is wide and many are old roses. They range from Albas to Moss roses, and form attractive combinations with other plants. The Alba 'Königin von Danemark' has deep pink flowers that look striking against the silvery leaved, weeping tree *Pyrus salicifolia* 'Pendula'. A splendid

collaboration is the modern shrub rose 'Nevada' with creamy white flowers, and blue delphiniums and campanulas. The 'New' English Rose 'Constance Spry' has pink flowers best highlighted by a cluster of silver-leaved plants.

## PATIO ROSES

This is a relatively new group of roses, coming between miniature roses and small floribundas. They are sometimes called dwarf cluster-flowered bush roses and are ideal on a patio. Even when you are sitting down they do not obstruct the view. Most are between 1½ft/45cm and 2ft/60cm high, and include 'Anna Ford' (vivid orange-red), 'Living Easy' (apricot-orange blend), 'Betty Boop' (yellow ivory, edged red) 'Robin Redbreast' (red, with a pale center) and 'Top Marks' (bright, vivid orange-vermilion).

▲ *Roses make distinctive backgrounds for low border plants and often enrich the air around garden benches with rich fragrance.*

▼ *Many shrub roses have an informal habit and can be allowed to cascade and spread across paths and over lawn edges.*

# climbing and rambler roses

*Climbers and ramblers look dramatic in any garden and are still more spectacular when the color complements its background. A white wall makes a perfect backcloth for roses with yellow or scarlet flowers, whereas a gray stone wall is better for those with pink or red flowers.*

### Climber or rambler?

As mentioned on pages 146–147, climbing and rambling roses produce attractive flowers, but each is distinctive in several ways. Climbers have a more permanent framework than ramblers and their flowers, when compared with those of ramblers, are larger and borne singly or in small clusters. Rambling roses have long, flexible stems that sometimes grow 3–3.6m/10–12ft in length in one season and bear flowers in large trusses, usually only once a year.

### Covering trees

Old, perhaps slightly unsightly trees can be transformed by training climbers to scramble up through their branches. Plant them several feet to one side of the trunk, and replace the soil with a mixture of topsoil and well-rotted garden compost or manure. Firm the soil, plant the rose, water the soil, and use a stout stake to guide the stems to the tree trunk.

Suitable varieties range in vigor, and can be selected to suit the tree that needs brightening. Roses to consider include 'Rambling Rector' (9ft/2.7m, rambler, creamy white), 'Emily Gray' (15ft/4.5m, rambler, butter-yellow); 'Mme Grégoire Staechelin' (climber, 20ft/6m, rosy carmine-pink), 'Paul's Himalayan Musk' (rambler, 30ft/9m, blush-pink), 'Sympathie' (climber, 15ft/4.5m, blood-red) and 'Wedding Day' (rambler, 25ft/7.5m, creamy white to blush).

### Pillar roses

These contribute interest in small gardens. All you need is a rustic pole 8–10ft/2.4–3m high or a tripod made of rough-cut lumber. In quite a small area, several pillars can be inexpensively

◀ *Pergolas and free-standing trellis provide support for many roses. They can be positioned alongside paths and the edges of lawns.*

### GROUND-COVER ROSES

Ground-smothering roses do not form a weed-suppressing blanket of stems, leaves and flowers, but a low mass of color. Choices include 'Baby Blanket' (pink), 'Nozomi' (pearly-pink to white), 'Pheasant' (pink), 'Rosy Cushion' (pink), and 'Snow Carpet' (white). The County Series includes 'Avon' (pearly white), 'Essex' (rich reddish-pink), 'Hertfordshire' (carmine-pink), and 'Wiltshire' (pink).

constructed. Climbers with moderate vigor are best for clothing such structures and include 'Bantry Bay' (semidouble, deep pink), 'Compassion' (salmon-pink, tinted apricot-orange), 'Handel' (creamy, edged pink-red), 'Pink Perpetue' (bright rose-pink), and 'Reine Victoria' (shell-pink).

### Climbers for cold walls

A cold wall is not the best place for roses, but a few sturdy ramblers and climbers survive such conditions and produce acceptable displays. Hardy and vigorous varieties to consider include

'Albéric Barbier' (rambler, cream), 'Félicité et Perpétue' (rambler, white), 'Morning Jewel' (climber, bright pink), 'New Dawn' (climber, pink blush), and 'Zéphirine Drouhin' (climber, deep pink).

### Companion planting climbers and ramblers

In the same way that bush roses can be planted in attractive arrangements with other plants, so can climbers and ramblers. For example, the rambler 'Bobbie James', which is often grown over pergolas and clambering up trees, has large clusters of

semidouble, creamy white flowers that look attractive combined with the lavender-blue flowers of *Nepeta* × *faassenii* (catmint), a bushy perennial growing about 18in/45cm high. It flowers throughout summer. Another good combination is the modern climber 'New Dawn', with semidouble, blush-pink flowers with the vigorous hybrid *Clematis* 'Perle d'Azure' with light pink flowers. It flowers from early to late summer.

▼ *Rose 'Helen Knight', a distinctive climber, creates a mass of small, buttercup-yellow flowers in late spring and early summer.*

# ornamental plants

# annuals and biennials

## A

### Agrostemma githago 'Milas'
CORN COCKLE
Hardy annual with slender, light green leaves and masses of lilac-pink flowers at the tops of upright stems from midsummer to fall.
Height: 3–4ft/90cm–1.2m
Spread: 15–18in/38–45cm
Soil and position: Well-drained but moisture-retentive soil and full sun. Grows well in poor soil.

### Amaranthus caudatus
LOVE-LIES-BLEEDING/TASSEL FLOWER
Hardy annual with light-green leaves

and drooping tassels up to 18in/45cm long, packed with crimson flowers during mid- to late summer. 'Viridus' has pale green flowers.
Height: 3–4ft/90cm–1.2m
Spread: 15–18in/38–45cm
Soil and position: Deeply prepared, fertile, well-drained but moisture-retentive soil in full sun.

## B

### Begonia semperflorens
FIBROUS BEGONIA/WAX BEGONIA
Tender perennial invariably grown as a half-hardy annual for planting into beds and containers in early summer. The glossy green or purple leaves are surmounted from early to late summer by red, pink, or white flowers.
Height: 6–9in/15–23cm/

Spread: 20–25cm/8–10in
Soil and position: Fertile, moisture-retentive but well-drained soil, and a position in full sun or partial shade.

### Bellis perennis
ENGLISH DAISY
Hardy perennial, invariably grown as a biennial, for flowering from early spring to fall although it is mainly used in spring and early summer displays. The flowers are daisy-like, bright-faced and white tinged pink, with a central yellow disc. There are several varieties in colors including white, carmine, pink, salmon, and cherry red.
Height: 1–4in/2.5–10cm
Spread: 3–4in/7.5–10cm
Soil and position: Moderately fertile, moisture-retentive but well-drained soil in full sun or light shade.

## C

### Calendula officinalis
ENGLISH MARIGOLD/POT MARIGOLD
Hardy annual with light green leaves and bright-faced, daisy-like, yellow or orange flowers about 2in/5cm wide from early summer to fall. There are several varieties, some double and a few dwarf.
Height: 1½–2ft/45–60cm
Spread: 10–12in/25–30cm
Soil and position: Well drained, even grows in poor soil and full sun.

### Campanula medium
CANTERBURY BELL
Hardy biennial with tall, upright stems that bear blue, white, purple, or pink, bell-shaped flowers up to 1½in/36mm long from late spring to midsummer. The 15in/38cm-high variety 'Bells of Holland' is ideal for small gardens.
Height: 15–36in/38–90cm
Spread: 9–12in/23–30cm
Soil and position: Moderately fertile, well drained soil and full sun. Support plants with small, twiggy sticks.

### Cleome spinosa
SPIDER FLOWER
Half-hardy tall annual with lax, rounded heads, up to 4in/10cm wide, of white, pink-flushed flowers

◀ Digitalis purpurea *(common foxglove) is traditional in cottage gardens. With its tall habit it is an attractive background plant.*

from midsummer to late fall. 'Color Fountain Mixed' has flowers in pink, rose, lilac, purple, and white; 'Rose Queen' is rose-pink and 'Helen Campbell' is white.
Height: 3–3½ft/90cm–1m
Spread: 18–20in/45–50cm
Soil and position: Fertile, well-drained but moisture-retentive soil and full sun.

### Consolida ajacis
LARKSPUR
Hardy annual with finely cut leaves and sparsely branched, upright stems bearing spires of blue, purple, red, pink, or white flowers from early to late summer. There are several varieties and strains.
Height: 3–4ft/90cm–1.2m
Spread: 12–15in/30–38cm
Soil and position: Fertile, well-drained but moisture-retentive soil in full sun or light shade. Support plants with twiggy sticks.

## D

### Dianthus barbatus
SWEET WILLIAM
Short-lived perennial invariably grown as a biennial for flowering during early and midsummer. Some varieties are better grown as hardy annuals. It develops flattened heads 3–6in/7.5–15cm wide, densely packed with sweetly scented, single or double flowers in a wide color range including crimson, scarlet, salmon-pink, and cerise-pink.
Height: 12–24in/30–60cm—range
Spread: 8–15in/20–38cm—range
Soil and position: Well-drained soil and full sun.

### Digitalis purpurea
COMMON FOXGLOVE
Hardy biennial with upright stems bearing bell-shaped flowers during early and midsummer. The flower color is wide, ranging from purple, through pink, to red.
Height: 3–5ft/90cm–1.5m
Spread: 1½–2ft/45–60cm
Soil and position: Moderately fertile, moisture-retentive but well-drained soil, and partial shade.

## E

### Erysimum × allionii
SIBERIAN WALLFLOWER
Hardy, bushy perennial invariably grown as a biennial for flowering from midspring to early summer. It produces a mass of scented, orange

flowers in terminal clusters.
Height: 12–15in/30–38cm
Spread: 10–12in/25–30cm
Soil and position: Fertile, slightly
alkaline, well-drained soil, full sun.

### Eschscholzia californica
CALIFORNIA POPPY
Hardy annual with delicate, finely
dissected, blue-green leaves and
masses of saucer-shaped, bright
orange-yellow flowers up to
3in/7.5cm wide from early to late
summer. These are followed by blue-
green seed pods. Varieties in scarlet,
crimson, rose, orange, yellow,
white, and red.
Height: 12–15in/30–38cm
Spread: 6–9in/15–23cm
Soil and position: Light, poor, well-
drained soil and a position in full
sun. Fertile soil and a position in
shade reduces the color intensity
of flowers radically.

### Helianthus annuus
SUNFLOWER
Hardy annual with large, daisy-like
flower heads up to 12in/30cm wide
during mid- and late summer. There
is a wide range of varieties, some
dwarf, in colors from pale primrose
to copper-bronze. The central discs
are purple or brown.
Height: 3–10ft/90cm–3m
Spread: 1–1½ft/30–45cm
Soil and position: Fertile, well-
drained but moisture-retentive soil
in a sunny, sheltered position.

### Heliotropium arborescens
CHERRY PIE/HELIOTROPE
Half-hardy perennial, grown as a
half-hardy annual, with wrinkled,
dark green leaves and fragrant,
flowers like the forget-me-not in
slightly domed heads 3–4in/
7.5–10cm wide from early summer
to fall. Color range from dark violet
through lavender, to white.
Height: 15–18in/38–45cm
Spread: 12–15in/30–38cm
Soil and position: Fertile, well-
drained but moisture-retentive soil
and full sun.

### Hesperis matronalis
SWEET ROCKET
Hardy but short-lived perennial
invariably grown as a biennial.
Vertical growth and long spires of
fragrant, cross-shaped, white, mauve,
or purple flowers in early summer.
Height: 2–3ft/60–90cm
Spread: 15–18in/38–45cm

Soil and position: Light, moisture-
retentive but well-drained soil, and
full sun or light shade.

### Lavatera trimestris
ANNUAL MALLOW/MALLOW
Hardy annual with an erect but
bushy nature and flat-faced, trumpet-
shaped flowers up to 4in/10cm wide
from mid- to late summer. There are
several varieties, including 'Silver
Cup', 2ft/60cm high.
Height: 2–3ft/60–90cm
Spread: 15–20in/38–50cm
Soil and position: Moderately fertile,
well-drained but moisture-retentive
soil and full sun or dappled light.
Avoid excessively rich soil, which
encourages leaf growth at the
expense of flowers.

### Limnanthes douglasii
MEADOW FOAM/POACHED-EGG FLOWER
Low-growing and ground-
smothering hardy annual with
deeply cut leaves and masses of
scented, funnel-shaped yellow
flowers with white edges from
early to late summer.
Height: 6in/15cm
Spread: 6–9in/15–23cm
Soil and position: Well-drained soil
and full sun. Produces self-sown
seedlings the following year.

### Limonium sinuatum
STATICE/SEA LAVENDER
Hardy perennial, invariably grown as
a half-hardy annual, with 3in/7.5cm-
long clusters of blue and cream
flowers from midsummer to fall.
There are several varieties, extending
the colors to orange-yellow, salmon,
rose-pink, red, carmine, and lavender.
Height: 15–18in/38–45cm
Spread: 10–12in/25–30cm
Soil and position: Well-drained but
moisture-retentive soil and an open,
sunny position.

### Lobelia erinus
EDGING LOBELIA/TRAILING LOBELIA
Half-hardy perennial invariably
grown as a half-hardy annual. Masses
of blue, white, or red flowers from
late spring to fall. There are bushy
and compact varieties, often used
along the edges of borders, and
trailing types for planting in hanging
baskets.
Height: 4–9in/10–23cm
Spread: 4–6in/10–15cm
Soil and position: Moderately fertile,
moisture-retentive but well-drained
soil, and light shade.

▲ *The sunflower (Helianthus
annuus), a hardy annual, bears a
mass of large, daisy-like flowers up
to 12in/30cm wide.*

### Lobularia maritima
(formerly and still better known
as ALYSSUM MARITIMUM)
SWEET ALYSSUM
A popular hardy annual usually
grown as a half-hardy annual.
Densely branched stems bear
rounded clusters of white, violet-
purple, rose-carmine, or deep
purple flowers from early to late
summer. Ideal for forming an
edging to a border.
Height: 3–6in/7.5–15cm
Spread: 8–12in/20–30cm
Soil and position: Moderately fertile,
well-drained soil, and full sun.

### Myosotis sylvatica
FORGET-ME-NOT
Hardy biennial or short-lived
perennial with fragrant, pale blue
flowers in lax sprays during late
spring and early summer. There are
several varieties in mixed and single
colors.
Height: 8–12in/20–30cm
Spread: 6–8in/15–20cm
Soil and position: Moderately fertile,
moisture retentive but well-drained
soil and partial shade. Avoid heavy,
waterlogged soil because it
encourages the plants to die
during winter.

### Nicotiana × sanderae
TOBACCO PLANT
Half-hardy annual with erect stems
bearing loose clusters of heavily
scented, white, tubular flowers,
7.5cm/3in-long, from early to late
summer. There are many varieties,
in a color range including white,
cream, pink, crimson, yellow, and
lime-green. Some varieties are night-
scented.
Height: 15–24in/38–60cm
Spread: 10–12in/25–30cm
Soil and position: Fertile moisture-
retentive but well-drained soil in
full sun or light shade.

### Nigella damascena
LOVE-IN-A-MIST
Hardy annual with bright-green,
fern-like leaves and cornflower-
like blue or white flowers from
early to midsummer. Some varieties
have pale yellow flowers. There are
many varieties, with double and
semidouble flowers. Self-seeding
in full sun.
Height: 1½–2ft/45–60cm
Spread: 6–9in/15–23cm
Soil and position: Light, well-drained
moisture-retentive soil and best in
full sun.

▲ Flowering tobacco plants
(Nicotiana) fill the garden with a
sweet fragrance through summer,
especially at nightfall.

### Papaver rhoeas
FIELD POPPY/SHIRLEY POPPY
Hardy annual with deeply lobed
green leaves and upright stems
bearing 3in/7.5cm-wide red flowers
with black centers during early to
midsummer. Varieties extend the
color range to pink, rose, salmon, and
crimson.
Height: 1½–2ft/45–60cm
Spread: 10–12in/25–30cm
Soil and position: Ordinary, poor to
moderately fertile, well-drained soil
and full sun.

### Papaver somniferum
OPIUM POPPY
Hardy annual with deeply lobed,
gray-green leaves and white, pink,
scarlet or purple flowers up to
4in/10cm wide during early and
midsummer. Some flowers are
double.
Height: 2½–3ft/75–90cm
Spread: 12–15in/30–38cm
Soil and position: Well-drained soil
and full sun.

### Petunia × hybrida
PETUNIA
Half-hardy perennial usually grown
as a half-hardy annual, with trumpet-
shaped flowers, 2–4in/5–10cm wide,
from early summer to the fall frosts.
Color range includes white, cream,
pink, red, mauve, and blue, and
bicolored forms.
Height: 6–12in/15–30cm
Spread: 6–12in/15–30cm
Soil and position: Moderately fertile
soil and full sun. Dislikes cold, wet
and shady positions.

### Rudbeckia hirta
BLACK-EYED SUSAN
Short-lived perennial invariably
grown as a hardy annual, with
bright-faced, daisy-like flowers,
3in/7.5cm-wide, with golden-
yellow petals and brown-purple
cones at their centers from
midsummer to early fall. Wide
range of varieties.
Height: 1½–2ft/45–60cm
Spread: 1–1½ft/30–45cm
Soil and position: Fertile, moisture-
retentive but well-drained soil and
full sun.

### Salvia splendens
SCARLET SAGE
Half-hardy perennial invariably
grown as a half-hardy annual with
upright spires of scarlet flowers from
midsummer to fall. There are several
superb varieties, in single colors and
mixed colors, including rose, pink,
salmon, purple, and white.
Height: 12–15in/30–38cm
Spread: 8–10in/20–25cm
Soil and position: Fertile, moisture-
retentive but well-drained soil and
full sun.

### Scabiosa atropurpurea
PINCUSHION FLOWER/SCABIOUS
Erect, branching, wiry-stemmed
annual with mid-green leaves and
single flowers, 2in/5cm wide during
mid- to late summer. There are many
varieties in the color range, from
white through blue to purple.
Height: 1½–2ft/45–60cm
Spread: 6–9in/15–23cm
Soil and position: Moderately fertile,
well-drained neutral to slightly
alkaline soil in full sun.

### Tagetes patula
FRENCH MARIGOLD
Half-hardy annual with a bushy habit
and dark-green, deeply divided leaves
and yellow or mahogany red flowers,
up to 2in/5cm wide, from early
summer to fall. Wide range of
varieties, with both single and
double-flowered types. Some are
dwarf. Widely grown in summer
bedding displays, where it always
creates a feast of color.
Height: 12in/30cm
Spread: 10–12in/25–30cm
Soil and position: Moderately fertile
soil and full sun.

### Zinnia elegans
Half-hardy annual with upright
stems bearing bright purple flowers,
up to 2⅓in/6cm wide, from mid- to
late summer. There are many
varieties, in colors including white,
purple, yellow, orange, red, pink, and
even pale green. Some varieties
have double flowers.
Height: 6–30in/15–75cm
Spread: 6–15in/15–38cm
Soil and position: Fertile, well-
drained but moisture-retentive soil
and full sun.

◀ Tradescantia x andersoniana
(spiderwort or trinity flower) is a
distinctive and popular herbaceous
perennial.

Height: 2–2½ft/60–75cm
Spread: 15–20in/38–50cm
Soil and position: Fertile, moisture-
retentive soil and full sun or light
shade.

## C

### Camassia quamash
QUAMASH
Slightly tender, bulbous, herbaceous
perennial with broad, spire-like
clusters of star-shaped flowers during
early and midsummer. Flower colors
range from white to blue
and purple.
Height: 1½–2½ft/45–75cm
Spread: 12–15in/30–38cm
Soil and position: Fertile, moisture-
retentive soil and full sun or light
shade. Grows well in moderately
heavy soil.

### Campanula lactiflora
BELLFLOWER
Hardy herbaceous perennial with a
wealth of bell-shaped, light lavender-
blue flowers during early and
midsummer. There are several
varieties, extending the color range
to soft pink and deep lavender-blue.
Height: 3–5ft/90cm–1.5m
Spread: 18–20in/45–50cm
Soil and position: Light, fertile,
moisture-retentive but well-drained
soil and full sun or partial shade.

### Coreopsis verticillata
TICKSEED
Hardy herbaceous perennial with
finely divided, fern-like leaves and
masses of clear yellow flowers from
early summer to fall. For a small
garden there are compact and dwarf
varieties.
Height: 1½–2ft/45–60cm
Spread: 1–1½ft/30–45cm
Soil and position: Moderately fertile,
well-drained but moisture-retentive
soil and full sun.

## D

### Delphinium elatum
There are two distinct forms of this
popular, hardy, herbaceous perennial.
Elatum types have stiffly erect spires,
tightly packed with large florets,

# herbaceous perennials and other border plants

## A

### Acanthus spinosus
BEAR'S BREECHES
Hardy herbaceous perennial with
distinctive, deeply cut spiny leaves
and tall, upright spires of white and
purple flowers during mid- and late
summer.
Height: 3–3½ft/90cm–1m
Spread: 2–2½ft/60–75cm
Soil and position: Moderately fertile,
light, well-drained but moisture-
retentive soil, and full sun or light
shade.

### Achillea filipendulina
FERN-LEAF YARROW
Hardy herbaceous perennial with
deeply dissected fern-like leaves and
plate-like heads, 4–6in/10–15cm

wide packed with lemon-yellow
flowers from midsummer to fall.
Many excellent varieties.
Height: 3–4ft/90cm–1.2m
Spread: 3ft/90cm
Soil and position: Fertile, moisture-
retentive but well-drained soil and
full sun.

### Agapanthus praecox
AFRICAN LILY/LILY OF THE NILE
Half-hardy evergreen perennial with
fleshy roots and large, umbrella-like
heads of bright to pale blue flowers
from mid- to late summer. There is
also a white-flowered form.
Height: 2–2½ft/60–75cm
Spread: 18in/45cm
Soil and position: Fertile, well-
drained soil and shelter from cold
wind, in full sun.

### Alchemilla mollis
LADY'S MANTLE
Hardy herbaceous perennial with
hairy, light-green leaves with
rounded lobes and serrated edges.
From early summer to fall it bears
masses of tiny, sulfur-yellow flowers
in sprays above the leaves.
Height: 1–1½ft/30–45cm
Spread: 15–20in/38–50cm
Soil and position: Moderately fertile,
moisture-retentive but well-drained
soil, and full sun or light shade.

### Allium moly
GOLDEN GARLIC/LILY LEEK
Bulbous plant with gray-green,
strap-like leaves and bright yellow,
star-shaped flowers borne in
umbrella-like heads during early and
midsummer.
Height: 10–12in/25–30cm
Spread: 8–10in/20–25cm
Soil and position: Light, well-drained
soil and full sun. Eventually forms a
large, spreading clump.

### Aster sedifolius
RHONE ASTER
Hardy herbaceous perennial with
masses of clear lavender-blue flowers
with golden centers during late
summer into fall. 'Nanus' is shorter, at
30cm/1ft high.
Height: 2–2½ft/60–75cm
Spread: 15–18in/38–45cm
Soil and position: Fertile, moisture-
retentive but well-drained soil and
full sun.

### Astilbe × arendsii
Hardy herbaceous perennial with
fern-like, deep-green leaves and
masses of feather-like flowers
borne in lax, pyramidal heads from
early to late summer. There are many
varieties in colors including lilac-
rose, pink, rose-red, dark-red, and
white.

mainly in shades of blue but also in lavender, mauve, and white. Wide range of varieties and heights. Belladonna forms have branching spikes of cupped florets.
Height: 3–5ft/90cm–1.5m
Spread: 1½–2ft/45–60cm
Soil and position: Fertile, deeply prepared, moisture-retentive soil and full sun.

### Dictamnus albus
BURNING BUSH/DITTANY/GAS PLANT
Hardy herbaceous perennial with spire-like heads of fragrant, white, spider-like flowers during early and midsummer. 'Purpureus' has pink flowers with red stripes.
Height: 1½–2ft/45–60cm
Spread: 15–18in/38–45cm
Soil and position: Slightly alkaline, deeply prepared, well-drained soil and full sun.

### Echinacea purpurea
PURPLE CONEFLOWER
Hardy herbaceous perennial with 4in/10cm-wide purple-crimson

flowers from midsummer to fall. Each flower has a distinctive cone-shaped orange center. Varieties in white and purple-rose.
Height: 3–4ft/90cm–1.2m
Spread: 1½–2ft/45–60cm
Soil and position: Fertile, moisture-retentive but well-drained, deeply prepared soil, and full sun.

### Erigeron speciosus
FLEABANE
Hardy herbaceous perennial with masses of daisy-like, purple flowers from early to late summer. There are several superb varieties, in light pink, lavender-blue, violet-blue, and lavender-violet.
Height: 18–24in/45–60cm
Spread: 12–15in/30–38cm
Soil and position: Fertile, moisture-retentive yet well-drained soil and full sun or light shade.

### Filipendula purpurea
JAPANESE MEADOWSWEET
Hardy herbaceous perennial with deeply cut leaves and large, fluffy

heads of carmine to pink flowers during midsummer. There are white and rosy red varieties.
Height: 3–3½ft/90cm–1m
Spread: 15–18in/38–45cm
Soil and position: Slightly alkaline, well-drained but moisture-retentive soil, and full sun or light shade.

### Geranium endressii
CRANESBILL
Hardy, herbaceous, ground-covering perennial with deeply lobed leaves and pale-pink flowers, lightly veined in red, from early summer to fall. There are several varieties.
Height: 12–18in/30–45cm
Spread: 12–18in/38–45cm
Soil and position: Well-drained soil in full sun or light shade.

### Gypsophila paniculata
BABY'S BREATH
Hardy herbaceous perennial with finely divided stems bearing a mass of small, usually white flowers from early to late summer. There are several varieties, including double or single forms, in white or pink. Also, compact varieties.
Height: 2–3ft/60–90cm
Spread: 2–2½ft/60–75cm
Soil and position: Deeply prepared, slightly alkaline, well-drained but moisture-retentive soil in full sun.

### Helenium autumnale
SNEEZEWEED
Hardy herbaceous perennial with a mass of daisy-like flowers, 1–1⅖in/25–36mm wide, from midsummer to early fall. There are many varieties, in yellow, orange, copper, bronze-red, and crimson-mahogany.
Height: 4–6ft/1.2–1.8m
Spread: 15–18in/38–45cm
Soil and position: Well-drained but moisture-retentive soil and full sun.

### Hemerocallis thunbergii
DAYLILY
Hardy herbaceous perennial with large, trumpet-shaped, sulfur-apricot flowers at the tops of stems during

◄ Achillea *is popular in herbaceous borders, where it creates distinctive flower heads from midsummer to early fall.*

early and midsummer. There are many hybrids, in colors from golden-yellow to pink, orange, and brick-red. Most hybrids have flowers 5–7in/13–18cm wide.
Height: 2½–3ft/75–90cm
Spread: 2–2½ft/60–75cm
Soil and position: Fertile, moisture-retentive but well-drained soil in full sun or light shade.

### Kniphofia
RED HOT POKER
Hardy herbaceous perennial, with many species and hybrids. All develop distinctive, poker-like flowerheads from early summer to early fall, in a color range from cream and yellow to fiery red.
Height: 3–5ft/60cm–1.5m
Spread: 15–24in/38–60cm
Soil and position: Deeply prepared, moderately fertile, well-drained but moisture-retentive soil and full sun. Avoid soils that are cold and wet.

### Leucanthemum superbum
SHASTA DAISY
Hardy herbaceous perennial with wide, bright-faced, daisy-like white flowers, 3in wide, with large, golden centers from early to late summer.
Height: 2½–3ft/75–90cm
Spread: 1–1½ft/30–45cm
Soil and position: Fertile, well-drained but moisture-retentive, slightly alkaline soil and full sun.

### Lychnis chalcedonica
JERUSALEM CROSS/MALTESE CROSS
Hardy herbaceous perennial with small, bright scarlet flowers borne in flattened heads about 5in/13cm wide during mid- and late summer
Height: 2½–3ft/75–90cm
Spread: 15–18in/38–45cm
Soil and position: Well-drained but moisture-retentive soil in full sun or light shade.

### Lysimachia punctata
WHORLED LOOSESTRIFE
Hardy, long-lived, vigorous herbaceous perennial with a spectacular display of bright yellow, cup-shaped flowers in whorls up to 8in/20cm long from early to late summer.
Height: 2–3ft/60–90cm
Spread: 15–18in/38–45cm
Soil and position: Fertile, moisture-retentive but well-drained soil, and

full sun or partial shade. It grows well in a heavy soil.

### Monarda didyma
BEE BALM/OSWEGO TEA/
SWEET BERGAMOT
Hardy herbaceous perennial with dense heads, up to 3in/7.5cm wide, of bright scarlet flowers from early to late summer. Range of varieties, in pink, lavender, violet-purple, and white.
Height: 2–3ft/60–90cm
Spread: 15–18in/38–45cm
Soil and position: Moisture-retentive but well-drained soil in full sun or partial shade.

**P**

### Perovskia atriplicifolia
RUSSIAN SAGE
A hardy, deciduous, shrubby perennial usually grown in a herbaceous or mixed border. Finely dissected, aromatic leaves and upright, branching stems with violet-blue flowers during late summer and early fall. 'Blue Spire' is a variety with lavender-blue flowers.
Height: 3–5ft/90cm–1.5m
Spread: 1½–2ft/45–60cm

Soil and position: Deeply prepared, fertile, well-drained soil and full sun or light shade.

### Phlox paniculata
GARDEN PHLOX
Hardy herbaceous perennial with terminal clusters of purple flowers from midsummer to fall. There are many varieties, in colors including pink, violet-purple, mauve, white, bright purple, claret-red and scarlet.
Height: 1½–3½ft/45cm–1m
Spread: 18–24in/45–60cm
Soil and position: Fertile, moisture-retentive but well-drained soil and full sun or partial shade.

### Rudbeckia fulgida
CONEFLOWER
Hardy, herbaceous perennial with large, yellow to orange flowers about 2½in/6cm wide from midsummer to the fall. Each flower has a dominant, purple-brown, cone-like center. Numerous varieties, including the spectacular 'Goldsturm' with flowers up to 13cm/5in wide.
Height: 2–3ft/60–90cm
Spread: 1½–2ft/45–60cm
Soil and position: Moderately fertile, well-drained but moisture-retentive soil and full sun.

### Sedum 'Herbstfreude'
(also known as 'AUTUMN JOY')
Herbaceous perennial with pale green, fleshy leaves. In late summer it develops large, slightly domed heads packed with salmon-pink flowers which change slowly from orange-red to orange-brown during mid- to late fall.
Height: 1½–2ft/45–60cm
Spread: 18–20in/45–50cm
Soil and position: Light, well-drained but moisture-retentive soil and full sun.

### Solidago hybrids
GOLDENROD
A group of hardy herbaceous perennials with distinctive, plume-like, slightly arching heads of tiny yellow or golden flowers from midsummer to fall. There are many varieties in a range of heights.
Height: 3–5ft/30cm–1.5m
Spread: 10–24in/25–60cm
Soil and position: Moderately fertile, deeply prepared, well-drained soil and full sun or light shade.

### Stachys byzantina
(still better known as
STACHYS LANATA)
LAMB'S EARS
Half-hardy herbaceous perennial that smothers the ground with leaves

▲ *Stachys byzantina (lamb's ears) fills a bed with a sea of leaves with a wooly and silvery appearance.*

densely covered in silvery hairs which create a wooly appearance. During midsummer it develops spikes of purple flowers. 'Silver Carpet' is a nonflowering form and creates a large net of leaves.
Height: 12–18in/30–45cm
Spread: 12–15in/30–38cm
Soil and position: Well-drained soil and full sun or light shade.

### Tradescantia × andersoniana 'Isis'
SPIDERWORT
Hardy herbaceous perennial with distinctive, royal-purple, three-petaled flowers up to 1½in/36mm wide from early to late summer. Wide range of other varieties, in colors including white and rich purple.
Height: 1½–2ft/45–60cm
Spread: 18–20in/45–50cm
Soil and position: Well-drained but moisture-retentive soil in full sun or light shade.

# bulbs, corms, and tubers

## C

### Chionodoxa sardensis
GLORY OF THE SNOW

Hardy, bulbous plant with two strap-like leaves and stems bearing nodding, star-shaped, sky-blue flowers, ⅔in/18mm wide. with white centers from early to late spring.
Height: 4–5in/10–15cm
Spread: 2–4in/5–10cm
Soil and position: Light, well-drained soil and full sun. Avoid heavy, constantly moist soil. Ideal for planting in rock gardens and along the fronts of informal borders.

### Crocus chrysanthus

Hardy cormous plant with cup-shaped, honey-scented, bright-yellow flowers during late winter and early spring. Mainly hybrids available in a color range including golden-yellow, mauve-blue, purple-blue, and dark bronze.

Height: 3–4in/7.5–10cm
Spread: 2–3in/5–7.5cm
Soil and position: Well-drained but moisture-retentive soil and full sun or dappled light.

## D

### Daffodils—Trumpet types

Hardy, clump-forming bulbous plants with yellow flowers bearing large trumpets during late winter and early spring. The range of varieties is wide and some are bicolored (white and yellow), others all white.
Height: 13–18in/32–45cm
Spread: 3–4in/7.5–10cm
Soil and position: Well-drained but moisture-retentive soil and full sun or light, dappled shade. Ideal for planting in large drifts, under deciduous trees or in the open.

## E

### Eranthis hyemalis
WINTER ACONITE

Hardy, tuberous-rooted perennial with lemon-yellow, buttercup-like flowers backed by a distinctive ruff of deeply cut, green leaves. They sometimes appear during midwinter, but usually late winter and early spring.
Height: 4in/10cm
Spread: 3in/7.5cm
Soil and position: Well-drained but moisture-retentive soil and full sun or partial shade. Grows well in heavy loam.

### Galanthus nivalis
COMMON SNOWDROP

Hardy, bulbous, clump-formed plant with flat, strap-like leaves and white flowers from midwinter to early spring. Each flower has six petals, three long outer ones and three short inner ones. 'Flore Pleno' has double flowers.
Height: 3–7in/7.5–18cm
Spread: 3–5in/7.5–13cm
Soil and position: Fertile, moisture-retentive but well-drained soil and light shade. Ideal for naturalizing in woodland gardens.

## H

### Hyacinthoides hispanica
BLUEBELL/SPANISH BLUEBELL

Hardy bulbous plant with strap-shaped, glossy green leaves and purple-blue, bell-shaped flowers during late spring and early summer. There is also a beautiful white-flowered form.
Height: 10–12in/25–30cm
Spread: 4–6in/10–15cm
Soil and position: Fertile, moisture-retentive but well-drained soil and light shade. Ideal for naturalizing in woodland gardens.

## I

### Ipheion uniflorum
SPRING STARFLOWER

Hardy, bulbous, clump-forming plant with pale-green, grass-like leaves and scented, white to violet-blue, six-petaled, star-shaped flowers during late spring.
Height: 6–8in/15–20cm
Spread: 2–3in/5–7.5cm
Soil and position: Moisture-retentive but well-drained soil and a sheltered position in full sun or light shade.

◀ *Tulips are among the most popular garden plants. They are resilient, and will swamp the borders with color each year.*

## L

### Leucojum vernum
SPRING SNOWFLAKE

Hardy, bulbous, clump-forming plant with strap-like, shiny green leaves and six-petaled, bell-like, white flowers during late winter and early spring. The petals are tipped in green.
Height: 8in/20cm
Spread: 4in/10cm
Soil and position: Moisture-retentive but well-drained soil and light shade or dappled sunlight.

## M

### Muscari armeniacum
GRAPE HYACINTH

Hardy, bulbous, clump-forming plant with narrow leaves and upright stems crowded at the top with scented, bright-blue flowers, each with a white rim, during spring and early summer. Several varieties, including the double 'Blue Spike'.
Height: 8–10in/20–25cm
Spread: 3–4in/7.5–10cm
Soil and position: Well-drained soil and full sun. Once established it spreads and can become invasive.

## N

### Narcissus cyclamineus

Hardy, miniature bulbous plant with narrow, bright-green leaves and small, deep-yellow trumpets up to 2in/5cm long and petals that are swept back in late winter and early spring. Parent of many hybrids, including 'February Gold', with larger flowers.
Height: 5–8in/15–20cm
Spread: 3–4in/7.5–10cm
Soil and position: Well-drained but moisture-retentive soil and full sun or light shade.

## T

### Tulipa

A range of hardy, bulbous plants with globular-like flower-heads at the tops of upright stems during mid- and late spring. The range of flowers and colors is wide; some single-flowers, others double. They are often planted with hardy perennials in spring-flowering bedding displays.
Height: 6in–2½ft/15–75cm
Spread: 6–8in/15–20cm/
Soil and position: Fertile, well-drained but moisture-retentive soil and full sun.

# rock garden plants

## A

### Aethionema 'Warley Rose'

Hardy herbaceous perennial with loosely branched stems and gray-green leaves. Domed heads smothered with deep rose-colored flowers appear during mid- and late spring.
Height: 4–6in/10–15cm
Spread: 12–15in/30–38cm
Soil and position: Light, well-drained soil, and full sun.

### Arabis caucasica

ROCK CRESS
Hardy, spreading perennial with gray-green leaves; usually evergreen except in cold wet winters. From late winter to early summer it bears white, cross-shaped flowers; also a double-flowered form.
Height: 9in/23cm
Spread: 18–24in/45–60cm
Soil and position: Well-drained soil

and full sun or light shade. Can be too invasive for a small rock garden and is best grown on a dry stone wall or a bank where it can trail freely.

### Armeria maritima

THRIFT/SEA PINK
Hardy evergreen hummock–forming perennial and grass-like leaves. From late spring to midsummer it displays 1in/2.5cm-wide heads of pink flowers. Also white, and rose-red varieties.
Height: 6–10in/15–25cm
Spread: 10–12in/25–30cm
Soil and position: Well-drained soil and full sun.

### Aubrieta deltoidea

AUBRETIA
Hardy, low-growing, spreading and, sometimes, trailing evergreen perennial with small, hoary green leaves and masses of rose-lilac to purple flowers from early spring to early summer. Many varieties, including a variegated form.
Height: 3–4in/7.5–10cm
Spread: 18–24in/45–60cm
Soil and position: Well-drained, preferably chalky, soil and a position in full sun.

### Aurinia saxatilis

(still better known as ALYSSUM SAXATILE)
Hardy, shrubby perennial with gray-green leaves and masses of golden-yellow flowers clustered on branching stems from midspring to early summer. Several varieties including 'Citrina' (bright lemon-gold, 'Compacta' (golden-yellow and 6in/15cm high), and 'Dudley Nevill' (biscuit yellow).
Height: 9–12in/23–30cm
Spread: 12–18in/30–45cm
Soil and position: Well-drained soil and full sun. Ideal for planting in a dry-stone wall.

## C

### Campanula carpatica

BELLFLOWER
Clump-forming, hardy perennial with tooth-edged leaves and masses of cup-shaped flowers, 1–1⅛in/25–36mm wide flowers in varying shades of blue to purple, and white, during mid- and late summer.
Height: 9–12in/23–30cm
Spread: 12–15in/30–38cm
Soil and position: Moderately fertile, well-drained soil and full sun or partial shade.

### Corydalis lutea

YELLOW FUMITORY
Hardy, bushy, evergreen perennial with fern-like leaves and tubular, spurred yellow flowers from mid- or late spring to late fall.
Height: 15–20cm/6–8in

◀ Phlox subulata *'Temiskaming'* is a popular rock garden plant, with brilliant magenta-red flowers during mid- and late spring.

▲ Saxifraga *'Southside Seedling'* bears masses of white flowers, each speckled with red spots, in long, arching sprays.

Spread: 10–12in/25–30cm
Soil and position: Well-drained soil and full sun or partial shade. Thrives on old walls but can become invasive through self-sown seedlings.

## G

### Gentiana acaulis

TRUMPET GENTIAN
Hardy, herbaceous perennial which forms mats of glossy, oval leaves and masses of trumpet-shaped, upright, stemless, brilliant blue flowers, about 3in/7.5cm long, during late spring and early summer.
Height: 3in/7.5cm
Spread: 15–18in/38–45cm
Soil and position: Well-drained but moisture–retentive soil, and full sun or light shade.

## H

### Helianthemum nummularium

ROCK ROSE/SUN ROSE
Hardy, low-growing, evergreen shrub with small, glossy green leaves and masses of saucer-shaped flowers during early and midsummer. Many varieties, in a color range including yellow, rose-pink, and red, as well as bicolored forms.
Height: 4–6in/10–15cm
Spread: 18–24in/45–60cm
Soil and position: Light, well-drained soil and full sun. Grows well in poor soil.

## I

### Iberis sempervirens
PERENNIAL CANDYTUFT
Hardy, evergreen, spreading bushy perennial with narrow, dark-green leaves and masses of white flower-heads during late spring and early summer. The form 'Little Gem' is shorter at 4in/10cm high, and spreading to 9in/23cm.
Height: 9in/23cm
Spread: 18–24in/45–60cm
Soil and position: Well-drained soil and full sun. Thrives in poor soil.

## P

### Phlox subulata
MOSS PHLOX
Hardy, spreading, and tufted sub-shrubby perennial that forms mats of purple or pink flowers during mid- and late spring. Many varieties, in colors including salmon-pink, pale-pink, lavender-blue, scarlet, bright red, and magenta-red.
Height: 2–4in/5–10cm
Spread: 12–18in/30–45cm
Soil and position: Moderately fertile, light, well-drained but moisture-retentive soil, and full sun or light shade.

## S

### Saxifraga 'Southside Seedling'
Hardy perennial with a mat-forming habit, dark-green leaves and long, arching sprays of white flowers peppered with red spots during early and midsummer.
Height: 12in/30cm
Spread: 12–15in/30–38cm
Soil and position: Well-drained, gritty, slightly chalky soil, shelter from cold wind and semishaded area. Avoid direct sunlight. It is ideal for planting in crevices between rocks.

### Sedum acre
GOLDEN CARPET
Hardy, mat-forming and somewhat invasive, evergreen perennial with yellow-green overlapping leaves and yellow flowers borne in flattened heads during early and midsummer. The variety "Aureum' (formerly known as 'Variegatum') has bright yellow shoot tips from early spring to early summer.
Height: 2in/5cm
Spread: 18–24in/45–60cm—or more
Soil and position: Well-drained but moderately moisture-retentive soil and full sun.

# garden shrubs and trees

## A

### Amelanchier lamarckii
JUNEBERRY/SHADBUSH/SNOWY MESPILUS
Hardy, deciduous, large shrub with mid-green leaves that assume tints in the fall. Clouds of pure white, star-shaped flowers in midspring.
Height: 4.5–7.5m/15–25ft
Spread: 3.6–6m/12–20ft
Soil and position: Moisture-retentive but well-drained, lime-free soil, and full sun or light shade.

### Aucuba japonica 'Variegata'
GOLD-DUST TREE/SPOTTED LAUREL
Hardy, evergreen shrub with a rounded outline and oval, shiny, dark green-leaves spotted and splashed yellow.
Height: 1.8–3m/6–10ft
Spread: 1.8–2.4m/6–8ft
Soil and position: Well-drained but moisture-retentive soil and full sun or light shade.

## B

### Berberis darwinii
BARBERRY
Hardy, evergreen shrub with small, holly-like, glossy green leaves and masses of deep-yellow flowers in late spring followed by blue berries.
Height: 1.8–2.4m/6–8ft
Spread: 1.8–2.4m/6–8ft
Soil and position: Moderately fertile, well-drained soil, and full sun.

### Brachyglottis 'Sunshine'
(still better known as SENECIO 'Sunshine')
Hardy, mound-forming, evergreen shrub with silvery gray leaves, white-felted underneath. During early and midsummer it bears bright yellow, daisy-like flowers.
Height: 2–4ft/60cm–1.2m
Spread: 3–5ft/90cm–1.5m

▶ Ceanothus 'Concha', a Californian lilac, looks spectacular in shrub borders and in mixed borders.

Soil and position: Deeply prepared, moisture-retentive but well-drained soil and full sun.

### Buddleja alternifolia
Hardy, deciduous shrub with narrow, pale green leaves and sweetly scented, lavender-blue flowers borne along cascading stems during early and midsummer. Usually a shrub, but it can be grown as a standard tree.
Height: 10–15ft/3–4.5m
Spread: 10–15ft/3–4.5m
Soil and position: Deeply prepared, friable, moisture-retentive but well-drained soil and full sun.

### Buddleja davidii
BUTTERFLY BUSH/SUMMER LILAC
Hardy, deciduous shrub famed for its long, arching stems and plume-like heads of fragrant, lilac-purple flowers during mid- and late summer, and often into the fall. There are many varieties, in colors including white, dark violet-purple, lilac, and rich red-purple.
Height: 6–8ft/1.8–2.4m
Spread: 6–8ft/1.8–2.4m
Soil and position: Fertile, moisture-retentive but well-drained soil, and full sun.

## C

### Calluna vulgaris
HEATHER/LING
Hardy, low-growing, bushy evergreen shrub with scale-like leaves throughout the year ranging from green to shades of orange and red.

From midsummer to early winter plants bear spires of single or double flowers, in colors including white, pink, and purple. Wide range of heights and spreads.
Height: 3–24in/7.5–60cm
Spread: 5–24in/13–60cm
Soil and position: Acid, peaty, moisture-retentive soil, and an open sunny position.

### Caryopteris × clandonensis
Hardy, bushy, deciduous shrub with aromatic gray-green leaves and clusters of blue flowers during late summer into the fall. Several superb varieties including 'Arthur Simmonds' (bright blue), 'Heavenly Blue' (deep blue), and 'Kew Blue' (rich blue).
Height: 2–4ft/60cm–1.2m
Spread: 2–3ft/60–90cm
Soil and position: Friable, well-drained soil, and full sun.

### Ceanothus × delileanus 'Gloire de Versailles'
CALIFORNIA LILAC
Hardy, deciduous shrub with an open habit and large heads, 6–8in/15–20cm long, clustered with fragrant, soft powder-blue flowers at the ends of long stems from midsummer to fall.
Height: 6–8ft/1.8–2.4m
Spread: 6–8ft/1.8–2.4m
Soil and position: Fertile, deeply prepared, moisture-retentive but well-drained soil; shelter from cold wind and full sun or light shade.

### Ceratostigma willmottianum
CHINESE PLUMBAGO
Half-hardy, twiggy, deciduous shrub with diamond-shaped, dark-green leaves that assume rich tints in the fall. Rich blue flowers are borne in terminal clusters up to 2in/5cm wide during mid- and late summer.
Height: 2–3ft/60–90cm
Spread: 2–3ft/60–90cm
Soil and position: Light, well-drained soil and full sun.

### Chimonanthus praecox
WINTERSWEET
Hardy, bushy, deciduous shrub, often grown as a wall shrub, with cup-shaped, scented flowers with pale-yellow petals and purple centers from mid- to late winter. 'Grandiflorus' has larger flowers, with red centers.
Height: 6–10ft/1.8–3m
Spread: 8–10ft/2.4–3m
Soil and position: Well-drained but moisture-retentive soil. Often grown

against a warm, south- or west-facing wall.

### Choisya ternata
MEXICAN ORANGE BLOSSOM
Slightly tender evergreen shrub with glossy green leaves that emit the fragrance of oranges when bruised. During mid- and late spring and often intermittently through to late summer, the plant bears clusters of sweetly scented, orange-blossom-like white flowers. 'Sundance' has golden-yellow leaves throughout the year.
Height: 5–6ft/1.5–1.8m
Spread: 5–7ft/1.5–2.1m
Soil and position: Deeply prepared, fertile, well-drained soil and shelter from cold wind.

### Cornus mas
CORNELIAN CHERRY
Hardy, deciduous, somewhat twiggy shrub with small clusters of golden-yellow flowers on bare branches from midwinter to spring. Sometimes bears red, semitranslucent berries. Leaves assume rich reddish-purple shades in the fall.
Height: 8–12ft/2.4–3.6m
Spread: 6–10ft/1.8–3m
Soil and position: Moisture-retentive but well-drained soil and full sun or light shade.

### Cytisus × praecox 'Warminster'
WARMINSTER BROOM
Hardy, bushy, deciduous shrub with arching stems bearing creamy white, pea-shaped flowers during spring and early summer. 'Allgold' has sulfur-yellow flowers.

 Berberis × darwinii (*Darwin's berberis*) *is a hardy evergreen shrub with yellow flowers in spring.*

Height: 5–6ft/1.5–1.8m
Spread: 5–6ft/1.5–1.8m
Soil and position: Well-drained soil and full sun. Avoid excessively fertile soil.

### E

### Elaeagnus pungens 'Maculata'
THORNY ELAEAGNUS
Hardy, evergreen, rounded shrub with leathery, oval, glossy green leaves splashed in gold. Silver-white, fragrant flowers in the fall.

Height: 6–12ft/1.8–3.6m
Spread: 6–12ft/1.8–3m
Soil and position: Fertile, deeply
prepared soil and full sun or light
shade. Tolerant of salt spray in
coastal areas.

### Erica carnea
ERICA/HEATHER
Hardy, prostrate or low-growing
evergreen shrub with terminal
clusters of flowers in white, pink, red
or purple from late fall to late spring.
Height: 2–12in/5–30cm
Spread: 6–24in/15–60cm
Soil and position: Peaty, acid,
moisture-retentive soil, and full sun.

### Euonymus fortunei 'Emerald 'n' Gold'
Hardy, bushy, evergreen, densely
leaved shrub with bright golden-
variegated leaves which turn
bronze-pink in winter. Many other

attractive varieties, including
'Emerald Gaiety' (creamy white and
green) and 'Golden Prince' (young
leaves tipped bright gold).
Height: 12–18in/30–45cm
Spread: 18–24in/45–60cm
Soil and position: Ordinary soil and
full sun.

### Forsythia × intermedia
Hardy, deciduous shrub which in
early and midspring creates a wealth
of golden-yellow, bell-like flowers.
There are several superb forms,
including 'Lynwood' (large, yellow
flowers) and 'Spectabilis' (yellow).
Height: 6–8ft/1.8–2.4m
Spread: 5–7ft/1.5–2.1m
Soil and position: Deeply prepared,
fertile, moisture-retentive soil in full
sun or light shade.

### Fuchsia magellanica
Slightly tender, deciduous and bushy
shrub with a spreading habit and
pendent, crimson and purple flowers
up to 2in/5cm long from
midsummer to fall.
Height: 4–5ft/1.2–1.5m/
Spread: 2–4ft/60cm–1.2m
Soil and position: Fertile, moisture-
retentive, light soil and full sun.
Provides shelter from cold wind.
Ideal for coastal areas.

### Genista aetnensis
MOUNT ETNA BROOM
Hardy, deciduous shrub with a lax
nature and rush-like branches that
bear terminal clusters of golden-
yellow flowers during mid- and late
summer.
Height: 15–20ft/4.5–6m

Spread: 15–18ft/4.5–5.4m
Soil and position: Light, well-
drained, rather poor soil and full sun.

### Hamamelis mollis
CHINESE WITCH HAZEL
Hardy, deciduous shrub or small tree
with sweetly scented, rich golden-
yellow, spider-like flowers borne in
clusters along naked branches during
early and midwinter. Leaves assume
rich shades in the fall.
Height: 6–10ft/1.8–3m
Spread: 7–10ft/2.1–3m
Soil and position: Neutral or
slightly acid, moisture-retentive but
well-drained soil, and full sun or
slight shade.

### Helichrysum serotinum
CURRY PLANT
Slightly tender, deciduous shrub with
needle-like leaves that when bruised
emit a curry-like scent. During early
and midsummer it bears clustered
heads of mustard-yellow flowers.
Height: 12–15in/30–38cm
Spread: 15–24in/38–50cm
Soil and position: Light, moderately
poor, well-drained soil, and full sun.
Avoid soils that are cold, heavy, and
poorly drained.

### Hibiscus syriacus
Hardy, deciduous shrub with a bushy
habit and trumpet-shaped flowers,
3in/7.5cm across, in a wide color
range from midsummer to early fall.
Varieties include violet-blue, white
with red centers, and rose-pink.
Height: 6–10ft/1.8–3m
Spread: 4–6ft/1.2–1.8m
Soil and position: Fertile, moisture-
retentive but well-drained soil, and
full sun or light shade.

### Hydrangea arborescens
HILLS OF SNOW
Hardy, deciduous shrub with dull
white flowers borne in flat heads up
to 6in/15cm wide during mid and
late summer. In mild areas they
continue into early fall. 'Grandiflora'
has larger flower-heads.
Height: 4–6ft/1.2–1.8m
Spread: 4–6ft/1.2–1.8m
Soil and position: Fertile, moisture-

◀ *Ornamental flowering cherry
trees never fail to attract attention
in spring. Golden daffodils may
be planted at the base.*

▶ *Forsythia bursts into flower in spring and is an ideal companion to large-trumpeted daffodils. It is one of the easiest shrubs to grow.*

retentive soil, and full sun or light shade.

### Hydrangea macrophylla
BIGLEAF HYDRANGEA/FLORISTS HYDRANGEA
Hardy, deciduous shrub with a rounded shape. There are two forms, Lacecaps have flat heads, 4–6in/ 10–15cm wide, while Hortensias have mop-like flower-heads 5–8in/13–20cm wide. Both flower from midsummer to early fall.
Height: 4–6ft/1.2–1.8m
Spread: 4–6ft/1.2–1.8m
Soil and position: Fertile, slightly acid, moisture-retentive soil, and dappled light. Acid soil insures that blue varieties remain blue. Aluminum sulfate reduces the influence of alkaline soils.

### Hypericum 'Hidcote'
ROSE OF SHARON/ST. JOHN'S WORT
Hardy, evergreen or semievergreen, bushy shrub with dark-green leaves and saucer-shaped, waxy, golden-yellow flowers up to 3in/7.5cm wide from midsummer to the fall.
Height: 3–5ft/90cm–1.5m
Spread: 5–7ft/1.5–2.1m
Soil and position: Fertile, well-drained but moisture-retentive soil and full sun. Avoid dry soil in total shade.

 **K**

### Kerria japonica 'Pleniflora'
Hardy, popular, deciduous shrub with long, slender stems and tooth-edged, bright-green leaves and double, orange-yellow flowers, 2in/5cm wide during late spring and early summer.
Height: 6–8ft/1.8–2.4m
Spread: 6–7ft/1.8–2.1m
Soil and position: Moderately fertile, friable, moisture-retentive but well-drained soil and full sun or partial shade.

### Kolkwitzia amabilis
BEAUTYBUSH
Hardy, somewhat twiggy deciduous shrub with arching branches bearing pink, foxglove-like flowers with yellow throats during early summer.

The variety 'Pink Cloud' has bright, deep pink flowers.
Height: 6–10ft/1.8–3m
Spread: 5–8ft/1.5–2.4m
Soil and position: Well-drained but moisture-retentive soil and full sun or light shade.

 **L**

### Laburnum × watereri 'Vossii'
GOLDEN CHAIN TREE/GOLDEN RAIN TREE
Hardy, deciduous tree with fragrant, golden-yellow flowers borne in slender, pendulous clusters up to 2ft/60cm long during early summer.
Height: 10–15ft/3–4.5m
Spread: 10–12ft/3–3.6m
Soil and position: Moisture-retentive but well-drained soil and full sun or light shade.

### Lavatera 'Rosea'
TREE MALLOW
Hardy, vigorous, soft-stemmed and branching shrub with lobed, gray-green leaves and masses of rose-colored flowers to about 3in/8cm wide from midsummer to the fall.
Height: 5–7ft/1.5–2.1m
Spread: 6–8ft/1.8–2.4m
Soil and position: Light, well-drained but moisture-retentive soil in full sun. Thrives in warm, sheltered position.

 **M**

### Magnolia stellata
STAR MAGNOLIA
Hardy, slow-growing, deciduous shrub with lance-shaped leaves and white, fragrant, star-shaped flowers up to 4in/10cm wide during early and midspring. 'Rosea' has pink flowers.
Height: 8–10ft/2.4–3m
Spread: 8–10ft/2.4–3m
Soil and position: Deeply prepared, moderately fertile, moisture-retentive but well-drained soil, full sun, and shelter from cold wind.

### Mahonia × media 'Charity'
Hardy, distinctive, evergreen shrub with leathery, spine-edged leaves and long, upright spires of fragrant, deep lemon-yellow flowers from early to late winter.
Height: 6–8ft/1.8–2.4m
Spread: 5–7ft/1.5–2.1m
Soil and position: Peaty, slightly acid and moisture-retentive but well-drained soil and light shade.

 **P**

### Philadelphus hybrids
MOCK ORANGE
A large range of hardy, deciduous

shrubs with a lax habit and single or double, sweetly fragrant flowers during early and midsummer. Hybrids include 'Avalanche' and 'Virginal'.
Height: 3–10ft/90cm–3m
Spread: 3–12ft/90cm–3.6m
Soil and position: Deeply prepared, moderately fertile, moisture-retentive but well-drained soil, and full sun or light shade.

### Potentilla fruticosa
SHRUBBY CINQUEFOIL
Hardy, deciduous, bushy but compact shrub with masses of buttercup-yellow flowers, each about 1in/2.5cm wide, from early to late summer and sometimes into the fall. There are several superb hybrids, including 'Red Ace' (glowing red), 'Elizabeth' (soft yellow), 'Sunset' (orange to brick-red), and 'Tangerine' (tangerine-red).
Height: 3½–4ft/1–1.2m
Spread: 3½–4ft/1–1.2m
Soil and position: Light, well-drained but moisture-retentive soil and full sun.

### Prunus 'Accolade'
Hardy, deciduous, ornamental cherry with an open spreading shape and masses of blush-pink, semidouble, deep rosy pink flowers in pendulous clusters during early and midspring.

◀ Weigela *is ideal for small gardens, where it creates a wealth of flowers in late spring and early summer. There are many hybrids.*

### Viburnum opulus 'Sterile'
SNOWBALL BUSH
Hardy, deciduous, bushy shrub with white flowers borne in large, round heads during early summer.
Height: 8–12ft/2.4–3.6m
Spread: 8–12ft/2.4–3.6m
Soil and position: Fertile, deeply prepared, moisture-retentive but well-drained soil and full sun.

### Viburnum tinus
LAURUSTINUS
Hardy, densely leaved evergreen shrub with dark-green leaves and white flowers, pink in bud, borne in 4in/10cm-wide clusters from early winter to late spring. Several superb varieties, including 'Eve Price' with carmine buds and pink-tinged white flowers.
Height: 7–9ft/2.1–2.7m
Spread: 5–7ft/1.5–2.1m
Soil and position: Fertile, deeply prepared, moisture-retentive but well-drained soil and full sun.

Height: 15–20ft/4.5–6m
Spread: 15–25ft/4.5–7.5m
Soil and position: Slightly chalky, well-drained but moisture-retentive soil and full sun.

### Prunus subhirtella 'Pendula'
WEEPING SPRING CHERRY
Hardy, deciduous, spreading and weeping tree with branches packed with pinkish-white flowers during spring. Looks superb when yellow, large-cupped daffodils are planted around it.
Height: 12–15ft/3.6–3.5m
Spread: 10–20ft/3.6–6m
Soil and position: Slightly chalky, well-drained but moisture-retentive soil and full sun.

### Rhododendron luteum
Hardy, deciduous, stiff-stemmed shrub with fragrant, rich-yellow flowers borne in rounded trusses on naked branches during mid- and late spring. The leaves assume rich shades of purple, crimson, and yellow in the fall.

Height: 6–10ft/1.8–3m
Spread: 5–7ft/1.5–2.1m
Soil and position: Fertile, slightly acid, moisture-retentive light soil and dappled light.

### Salvia officinalis 'Icterina'
GOLDEN VARIEGATED SAGE
Slightly tender and relatively short-lived evergreen shrub with gold and green leaves. In cold areas it often becomes semievergreen. There are several other superb varieties, including 'Purpurascens' (suffused purple) and 'Tricolor' (leaves suffused purple and pink, and splashed creamy white).
Height: 18–24in/45–60cm
Spread: 18in/45cm
Soil and position: Well-drained soil, warm and sheltered position and full sun.

### Spiraea × arguta
BRIDAL WREATH/FOAM OF MAY
Hardy, deciduous, twiggy shrub with masses of pure-white flowers borne

in clusters during mid- and late spring. The green leaves create an attractive foil for the flowers.
Height: 6–8ft/1.8–2.4m
Spread: 5–7ft/1.5–2.1m
Soil and position: Deeply prepared, fertile, moisture-retentive but well-drained soil and full sun.

### Ulex europaeus 'Flore Pleno'
DOUBLE-FLOWERED GORSE
Hardy, spiny, evergreen shrub with honey-scented, golden-yellow, pea-shaped flowers during spring into early summer. Often flowers sporadically until the following spring.
Height: 5–7ft/1.5–2.1m
Spread: 5–7ft/1.5–2.1m
Soil and position: Poor, well-drained soil, and full sun.

### Weigela hybrids
Hardy, deciduous shrub with arching branches bearing masses of flowers 2.5cm/1in long in late spring and early summer. Hybrids include 'Abel Carrière' (soft rose) 'Bristol Ruby' (ruby red), and 'Newport Red' (bright red).
Height: 5–6ft/1.5–1.8m
Spread: 5–8ft/1.5–2.4m
Soil and position: Fertile, well-drained but moisture-retentive soil in full sun or light shade.

# climbers and wall shrubs

## Ceanothus thrysiflorus repens
BLUEBLOSSOM/CALIFORNIA LILAC
Hardy, evergreen shrub, with masses of small, light-blue flowers in clusters 3in/7.5cm long clusters during late spring and early summer. One of the hardiest California lilacs.
Height: 4–5ft/1.2–1.5m
Spread: 5–6ft/1.5–1.8m
Soil and position: Neutral or slightly acid, well-drained, light soil, shelter from cold wind and a position in full sun. Suitable for growing under a window.

## Clematis montana
Hardy, vigorous, deciduous climber with pure-white flowers, 2in/5cm wide during late spring and early summer. Several superb varieties, including 'Elizabeth' (soft pink and slightly fragrant), 'Alexander' (creamy white and fragrant), and 'Rubens' (slightly fragrant, rose-pink flowers and bronze-purple leaves).
Height: 18–25ft/5.4–7.5m—or more
Spread: 18–25ft/5.4–7.5m—or more
Soil and position: Fertile, neutral to slightly alkaline, moisture-retentive but well-drained soil, and full sun. Requires a supporting framework; also climbs into trees.

## Clematis, large-flowered hybrids
Hardy climbers with characteristic large flowers, usually 5–6in/13–15cm wide. Flowers during summer, the flowering period varying with the variety, with a wide range of colors.
Height: 4–15ft/1.2–4.5m
Spread: 5–8ft/1.5–2.4m
Soil and position: Fertile, neutral to slightly alkaline, moisture-retentive but well-drained soil and full sun. Not self-supporting and needs wires or a trellis.

## Fremontodendron californicum
FLANNEL BUSH
Slightly tender, deciduous or semi-deciduous wall shrub with three-lobed, dull-green and downy leaves. Golden-yellow, cup-shaped flowers, 2in/5cm wide, appear through summer into early fall. 'California Glory' is a free-flowering form.
Height: 6–10ft/1.8–3m
Spread: 6–10ft/1.8–3m
Soil and position: Light, well-drained but moisture-retentive soil, a warm and sheltered position and full sun. Is not self-supporting and needs a trellis or supporting wires.

## Hedera colchica 'Dentata Variegata'
VARIEGATED PERSIAN IVY
Hardy, vigorous, evergreen climber with thick, leathery, bright-green leaves edged and blotched creamy white and pale green. Leaves are up to 8in/20cm long.
Height: 20–25ft/6–7.5m
Spread: 20–25ft/6–7.5m
Soil and position: Well-drained but moisture-retentive soil and full sun or dappled light. Has a self-clinging habit.

## Hedera colchica 'Sulphur Heart'
Hardy, vigorous, evergreen climber with thick, leathery, deep-green leaves splashed and irregularly streaked bright yellow. As leaves age, they broaden and the yellowing becomes less pronounced.
Height: 18–20ft/5.4–6m
Spread: 18–20ft/5.4–6m
Soil and position: Well-drained but moisture-retentive soil and full sun or dappled light. It has a self-clinging nature.

## Hedera helix 'Goldheart'
Hardy, evergreen climber with small, shiny green leaves conspicuously splashed with yellow.
Height: 12–20ft/3.6–5m
Spread: 12–20ft/3.6–5m
Soil and position: Well-drained but moisture-retentive soil and full sun or dappled light. Has a self-clinging habit.

## Humulus lupulus 'Aureus'
GOLDEN–LEAVED HOP/
YELLOW-LEAVED HOP
Hardy, fast-growing herbaceous climber with a scrambling habit and stems smothered with three- or five-lobed, coarsely tooth-edged, bright-yellow leaves. In the fall, the plant dies down to soil level and produces new shoots in spring.
Height: 6–10ft/1.8–3m
Spread: 6–8ft/1.8–2.4m
Soil and position: Fertile, moisture-retentive but well-drained soil and full sun. Needs a structure up which to clamber.

## Jasminum nudiflorum
WINTER-FLOWERING JASMINE
Hardy, deciduous, rather lax wall shrub with pliable stems that bear bright yellow flowers, about 1in/2.5cm wide, from late fall to late spring.
Height: 4–6ft/1.2–1.8m
Spread: 6–8ft/1.8–2.4m
Soil and position: Light, well-drained soil and a position against a north-facing wall. Requires a framework to which the stems can be secured loosely.

## Lonicera periclymenum
HONEYSUCKLE/WOODBINE
Hardy, widely grown, deciduous climber with a twining habit and tangled mass of stems. There are two main forms; 'Belgica' (early Dutch honeysuckle) bears purple-red and yellow flowers in early summer, while 'Serotina' (late Dutch honeysuckle) has red-purple and creamy white flowers in late summer and early fall.
Height: 15–18ft/4.5–5.4m
Spread: 15–18ft/4.5–5.4m
Soil and position: Moderately fertile, light, moisture-retentive but well-drained soil. Requires a support.

## Wisteria floribunda
JAPANESE WISTERIA
Hardy, vigorous, deciduous climber with leaves formed of 12–19 leaflets. During late spring and early summer it bears large, pendulous clusters of fragrant, violet-blue flowers. There is also a white form.
Height: 25–30ft/7.5–9m
Spread: 20–25ft/6–7.5m
Soil and position: Fertile, moisture-retentive but well-drained soil and full sun. May be planted to cover a large pergola or arbor.

▲ Lonicera periclymenun 'Serotina' (late Dutch honeysuckle) is an informal climber with a relaxed nature and wealth of flowers.

# pests and diseases

Soft and tender plants in gardens and greenhouses provide succulent meals for pests and are ideal places for diseases to get established. This applies especially to soft-leaved plants such as hardy and tender annuals and herbaceous perennials. Groups of similar vegetables, such as cabbages and beans, are also at risk. Insects have limited aspirations and their main aims are eating and reproduction, which they do with great zeal in the right conditions.

## Why kill insects?

If you do not, plants become unsightly and yields of vegetables and fruits soon decrease. Sucking insects such as aphids cause mottling on leaves and flowers. They also inject plants with saliva that may spread viruses from plant to plant. Even worse, aphids excrete a sticky

### COUNTRY TIP

❀ Small pieces of chopped *Ulex europaeus* gorse when placed in drills of newly sown garden peas help prevent mice eating the seeds.

❀ Moles cause a problem by making mole hills and by eating worms, but do not kill them because they eat soil pests such as wireworms, leatherjackets, and millipedes. Pushing pieces of slate across their tunnels and inserting a child's windmill into a mole hill helps to deter them. Moles also dislike certain plants. Insert sprigs of elder into mole hills, or plant *Helleborus foetidus* (stinking hellebore), garlic, or *Euphorbia lathyris* (caper spurge) nearby.

substance known as honeydew that attracts ants and sooty mold. Chewing pests like caterpillars eat leaves and then excrete on them.

Pests can be eradicated and further infestations prevented in several ways. Spraying with chemicals is an easy option and some chemicals, such as those classified as systemic, make a plant toxic to insects for a specified period; this is influenced by the specific crop and time of year. However, many gardeners prefer to use nonchemical methods.

## Garden-friendly ways to control insects and diseases

• Slugs and snails can be lured by a mixture of beer and sugar in shallow saucers. Remove and destroy them the following morning.

• Trap earwigs in inverted pots filled with straw and placed on top of a garden stake. Remove the earwigs each morning.

• Removing dead flowers decreases the risk of diseases spreading.

• Nipping out the young tips of broad beans protects against blackfly infestation.

• Hoe weeds growing between plants. If left to grow, they encourage the presence of pests and diseases. Weeds in neglected corners should also be eradicated. However, if you wish to entice butterflies and moths into your garden it is best to leave them because they provide food and homes for many insects.

• Dig bare soil thoroughly early in the winter and leave the surface rough. Frost and birds will kill grubs and many other soil pests.

• Feeding plants with a balanced diet keeps them healthy and able to resist diseases. Excessive nitrogen makes plants soft and susceptible to diseases.

• Thinning young seedlings when they are large enough to be handled reduces the spread of diseases. Place all thinnings on a compost pile.

• Use bands of burlap or corrugated card in the spring to trap codling moth and gypsy moth caterpillars as they travel down the trunks of fruit trees. Hand pluck and destroy caterpillars periodically.

• Use varieties of vegetables with a degree of resistance to diseases.

• Several insects which feed on pests should be encouraged into gardens. Ladybugs (adults and grubs) eat aphids, scale insects, mealybugs, and thrips voraciously. Lacewing larvae also feed on aphids. Ground beetles live in the soil and eat grubs and the eggs of pests, while rove beetles, which also live in the soil, eat cabbage worms.

## Safety first with chemicals

All garden chemicals must be treated carefully and with respect. If carelessly used they can cause harm to the user, to children, and to pets and wildlife. Here are a few ways to insure their safe use:

- Before using a chemical, read the label carefully and check that it is suitable.
- Do not use chemicals from bottles or containers that have lost their labels. Instead, dispose of them safely (see right). Never move chemicals from their original container into a different one.
- Read and follow the instructions on the container. Using excessively high concentrations of chemicals may damage plants. Weak solutions may be ineffective.
- Store garden chemicals in a locked cabinet away from children.
- Check that the chemical will not harm your plants. Ferns, palms, and cacti are easily damaged by some chemicals.
- Before spraying vegetables, check the recommended time between application and harvesting.
- Do not use chemical sprays indoors when caged birds, fish, and other pets are present.
- Do not allow pets to chew or lick sprayed plants. Many chemicals have a residual effect for several weeks.

- Do not use the same equipment for spraying pesticides and weedkillers.
- Clean all spraying equipment very thoroughly after use.
- Wash your hands after using chemicals and, when recommended, use protective clothing such as gloves and a face mask.
- If you have an accident with a garden chemical and have to visit a doctor or a hospital, take along the chemical so that it can be identified.

### Keeping pets and wildlife safe

Take all possible precautions when using chemicals in a garden to prevent pets and wildlife from being harmed. Always bear in mind that some chemicals have long-lasting effects.

- When chemicals are being mixed or used, keep pets indoors.
- Use sprays late in the day when few beneficial insects are flying and bees are inactive. Avoid spraying open flowers because they attract beneficial insects.
- Do not spray during windy weather.

- Do not allow plant-eating animals such as rabbits and guinea pigs to chew recently sprayed plants.
- Do not use chemicals near garden ponds, bird baths, streams, or ditches.
- Do not spray near wildlife ponds where you may poison frogs, toads, newts, etc.
- When using slug bait, place the bait under tiles where it will be inaccessible to other wildlife.

## DISPOSING OF UNWANTED GARDEN CHEMICALS

Eventually, everyone has a shelf in a garden shed full of unwanted garden chemicals. They need to be disposed of in a safe way. Do not pour them down a drain, bury them in the garden or give to a refuse collector, perhaps camouflaged in an outer wrapping. Instead, consult your local waste disposal authority for advice, especially when the packaging indicates the chemical is either harmful, oxidizing, or an irritant. If the packaging has been lost, assume that it is one of these three.

## picture parade of pests and diseases

**ANTHRACNOSE** can affect all beans, causing black, sunken spots on pods, leaves, and stems. Apply a fungicide spray and do not touch wet leaves.

**ANTS** are encouraged by aphids and sometimes become a pest in rock gardens, loosening soil around roots. Dust the soil with an ant killer.

**APHIDS** are widely seen on plants in summer. They suck sap, causing mottling and distortion of leaves, flowers, and stems. Use a proprietary insecticide regularly.

**ASPARAGUS BEETLES** (square orange marks on a black body) chew asparagus leaves. Spray with insecticide as soon as they are seen, and pick off and destroy the beetles.

**BIRDS** scratch up and eat newly sown seeds and peck flowers. Place

twigs along newly sown rows or stretch black thread over the surface.

**BLACK LEG** is a disease of cuttings, especially those of pelargoniums. Bases of stems become black and soggy. It is encouraged by cold, wet, compacted, and airless soil.

**BLACK SPOT** is a fungal disease that affects roses, causing black spots on their leaves. Spray with a fungicide several times. Also, remove and burn fallen infected leaves.

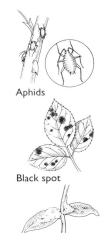

Aphids

Black spot

Botrytis

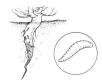

Cabbage maggots

Carrot fly

Carrot weevils

Clubroot

Japanese beetle grub

Cutworm

Flea beetle

Leatherjacket

Mealybug

**BOTRYTIS** (gray mold) is a gray, fluffy mold on flowers, stems, and leaves. It thrives in cool, damp, airless conditions. Reduce congestion among plantings, and spray.

**BRISTLY ROSESLUGS** disfigure leaves by eating soft tissue between veins. These hairy, slimy larvae usually feed at night, chewing on the undersides of leaves. Spray with an insecticide.

**CABBAGE MAGGOTS** tunnel into the roots and stems of newly transplanted brassicas, causing yellowing and stunted growth. Protect seedlings with floating row covers.

**CARROT FLIES** have small, cream-colored maggots that devastate carrots, parsnips, and celery. Rake an insecticide into the soil before sowing seeds.

**CARROT WEEVIL** larvae defoliate carrot and celery tops before tunneling into the crop. As soon as the symptoms are seen, spray with an insecticide. Pull off infested leaves.

**CATERPILLARS** are the larvae of moths and butterflies. Pick off and destroy, use insecticides and pull up and burn seriously infested plants.

**CATS** often scratch light, well-drained soil, disturbing newly sown seeds as well as established plants. Dust soil with pepper. A pea gravel mulch protects rock garden plants.

**CLUBROOT** attacks cabbages and related plants. Roots distort and plants die. When planting young plants, treat them with fungicide. Acid soil encourages this disease.

**CUCUMBER BEETLES** can spread disease rapidly through a vegetable garden. Cover seedlings with floating row covers to prevent beetles from feeding on young plants.

**CUTWORMS**, larvae of certain moths, live in the topsoil. They chew the bases of plant stems, causing them to collapse. Dust soil with an insecticide and remove weeds. Dig the soil in winter.

**DAMPING OFF** causes seedlings in greenhouses to collapse and die. It results from over-high temperatures, overcrowding, and excessively moist compost. Correct these conditions.

**DIEBACK** is a disease that causes shoots to die back and downward. Several causes include canker, frost, and waterlogging. Cut out and burn infected parts.

**EARWIGS** chew flowers, soft stems, and leaves, especially at night. Pick off and destroy, or trap in pots of straw inverted on garden stakes. Dust with an insecticide.

**FLEA BEETLES** eat holes in leaves of brassicas and related plants, and may kill young plants. They are generally worse in dry seasons. Keep plants watered, and dust with insecticide.

**JAPANESE BEETLE GRUBS** live in soil and graze upon roots. Later, they pupate and beetles appear. Pick up and destroy these grubs. Also, dig soil deeply in winter.

**LEAFHOPPERS** cause pale, mottled areas on leaves. They become distorted and may fall off if the

attack is severe. Spray plants with a systemic insecticide.

**LEAFROLLERS** cause leaves to roll lengthwise, enclosing a grayish-green grub. Pick off and burn small infestations, or prevent damage with an insecticide.

**MEALYBUGS** appear on stems, leaves, and branches in white, cottony masses. They suck sap and cause distortion. Wipe off small infestations with cotton swabs dipped in isopropryl alcohol.

**MICE** often dig down to bulbs in winter when searching for food. Cover bulbs with wire netting anchored to the soil. Mice may also infest stores of bulbs in summer.

**MINT RUST** attacks mint. Orange pustules appear on the undersides of leaves. It is difficult to eradicate. Spray plants regularly if it becomes a problem.

**MOLES** can be a problem, especially in rock gardens where plants cannot be moved out of the way of their tunnels, and on lawns when they make molehills. Use rocks to block tunnels. Do not use metal traps.

**ONION FLIES** have small, white maggots that burrow into bulbs. Leaves become yellow and wilt. Pull up and burn seriously infected bulbs. Use insecticides before sowing.

**POTATO SCAB** produces raised, scabby, distorted areas on skins of potatoes. Only the skin is affected and tubers can still be cooked and eaten. Do not add lime to the soil.

**POWDERY MILDEW** forms a white, powdery covering on leaves, flowers, and stems. It is encouraged by lack of air circulating around plants, and by dry soil. Keep soil moist and leaves dry, and use a fungicide.

**RED SPIDER MITES** suck leaves, causing mottling and spin webs. They are mainly a greenhouse pest. Spray plants with an insecticidal soap.

**ROOT APHIDS** are pests in warm areas where they graze on roots, causing discoloration and wilting. Drench the soil with insecticide.

**ROOT ROTS** are encouraged by cold, wet soils. Rock garden plants, which require well-drained soil, are especially susceptible. Mix in some builder's sand.

**ROSE SCALE**, usually seen on old and neglected rose bushes, promotes clusters of scales. Wipe off colonies with isopropryl alcohol and use a systemic insecticide.

**RUST** is especially a problem with Althaea (hollyhock). Rusts are difficult to control and the best preventive measure is to pull up and burn severely infected plants.

**SCALE INSECTS** form waxy brown discs under which young insects are born. They suck sap, causing speckling. Destroy seriously infected plants, or use a systemic insecticide.

**SLUGS** are a particular problem during warm, wet weather. They chew all parts of plants, usually feeding at night. Use slug bait.

**SNAILS**, like slugs, thrive in warm, wet weather, when they chew plants and rapidly cause damage. Look out for them and pick them off plants, and use snail bait.

**SOOTY MOULD** is a fungus that grows on honeydew excreted by aphids. It blackens leaves and stems. Spray plants regularly to kill aphids.

**TENT CATERPILLARS** build silken webs in branches of fruit and ornamental trees where they rest during the day, eating leaves voraciously at night. Although unsightly, they do little permanent damage. Remove the tents by hand, spray, or trap larvae with a sticky substance applied to tree trunks.

**THRIPS** are tiny flies that fly or jump from leaf to leaf, causing silvery streaks. Flowers become distorted. They are worse in dry conditions. Spray with an insecticide.

**VINE WEEVILS** are small white grubs that chew roots, so that plants wilt and die. Check the soil if a pot plant wilts unexpectedly. Treat with an insecticide.

**VIRUSES** attack many plants, causing reduced vigor and mottling of leaves and stems. They seldom kill plants. They are transmitted by sap-sucking insects.

**WEEVILS** are rather like beetles, often with long or divided snouts. They have legless larvae and, with the adults, chew the roots, stems, and leaves of fruit bushes and trees. Dust or spray with an insecticide.

**WHITEFLIES** are small insects rather like moths, which infest plants in greenhouses and conservatories. They suck sap, yellowing leaves and flowers. Use an insecticide.

**WIREWORMS** are the larvae of click beetles which inhabit soil. They chew roots and cause plants to die. Wireworms are especially troublesome in newly dug grassland. Use an insecticide.

Onion Fly

Pea Moth

Potato Scab

Rose Scale

Rust

Scale Insects

Thrip

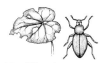

Vine Weevil

Whiteflies

Wireworms

Stinging Nettle

Chickweed

Pigweed

Groundsel

Shepherd's Purse

Lesser Celandine

Bindweed

Coltsfoot

# preventing and eradicating weeds

The prevention and eradication of weeds are inevitable garden tasks. There are few gardens without weeds in flower beds, vegetable plots, or at the base of a hedge. As well as being unsightly, they compete with garden plants for moisture, food, light, and space. They also encourage the presence of pests and diseases. Thistles are hosts for leafhoppers and weevils, while cutworms and other pests rely on weeds for winter protection.

Lawns do not escape weeds, and although a peppering of bright-faced daisies is acceptable, yarrow and plantains do not have the same appeal. Weeds in lawns soon cause unsightly patches of compacted soil.

## Controlling weeds

If weeds are not to become a problem you must regularly:
• Hand weed in the traditional way to remove weeds. This also enables plants to be closely examined, and pests and diseases to be seen at an early stage. Always place weeds in a box and put annual types on a compost pile; perennial weeds, especially ground elder and couch grass, are best destroyed.
• Hoe the surfaces of flower-beds and vegetables to chop off weeds at surface level. This is ideal for annual

weeds, but does not remove the perennial types. Use a Dutch or grubbing hoe to sever weeds. In seed beds and around small vegetables, a narrow grubbing hoe is useful. In vegetable gardens the yearly rotation of crops helps to discourage the growth of weeds.
• Mulch by spreading a layer of well-rotted manure, leafmold, shredded hardwood mulch or garden compost 3in/7.5cm deep over the soil. As well as depressing weeds, it reduces the loss of moisture from the soil, improves the soil's structure, and adds to its fertility. As an alternative to organic mulches, a layer of black plastic prevents the growth of weeds. A layer of pea gravel over soil in rock gardens also eliminates weed growth, while preventing heavy rain from washing away soil. Incidentally, the ancient Romans used stone mulches around vines and apricot trees.
• Use herbicides (chemical weedkillers) but not recklessly because pets and the environment may be at risk. There are three main types of these chemicals:
1. Pre-emergence weedkillers. These are sprayed on bare ground to kill weed seedlings as they emerge.
2. Total weedkillers. These destroy all plants. Some have long-lasting effects and are ideal for killing weeds on paths and driveways, while others are short-lived for use in beds.
3. Selective weedkillers. These kill weeds without harming the crop.

## Annual weeds

These grow each year from seed, then flower, and die. There are often several generations seeded each year. Most grow abundantly and need regular control.

**ANNUAL STINGING NETTLE**—Upright, nettle-like leaves and small green flowers through summer but does not have a creeping rootstock. Grows in light, cultivated soil and on waste land.

**CHICKWEED**—Low, sprawling, bushy plant with masses of small white flowers in lax clusters from early spring to late summer. It grows mainly in moist, cultivated, fertile soil.

**GROUNDSEL**—Upright, with weak and floppy stems, lobed leaves and clusters of small yellow flowers mainly during summer. Grows in waste and also on cultivated soil, especially where it is disturbed regularly.

**PIGWEED**—Also called goosefoot and lamb's quarters. Upright with diamond- to lance-shaped leaves and green or white flowers through summer into fall. Grows in waste areas, and on cultivated land.

**SHEPHERD'S PURSE**—An annual with a long, tapering root and upright stems bearing loose clusters of white flowers, mainly in summer. Grows on waste areas and also on cultivated ground.

## Perennial weeds

These weeds are long lived and with a strong root system. They are more difficult to eradicate than annual weeds, and soon grow again if any root is left in the ground.

**BINDWEED**—Pernicious, scrambling climbing perennial with roots that often penetrate the soil to 6ft/1.8m deep. Pink or white flowers appear from early summer to early fall. Widely seen except in woodland.

**COLTSFOOT**—Distinctive perennial with large, rounded but slightly heart-shaped basal leaves and upright stems bearing yellow, daisy-like flowers from late winter to mid-spring. Widely seen in slightly chalky, moist soils in gardens, and on waste areas.

**COMMON SORREL**—Also known as sheep's sorrel. Pear-shaped, stem-clasping leaves and reddish-green flowers during early and midsummer. Widely seen in gardens, fields, and on heathland, especially where the soil is acid.

**CREEPING BUTTERCUP**—Spreading plant with a creeping rootstock that frequently sends up shoots that bear toothed and lobed leaves. Stems bear yellow, buttercup-like flowers from late spring to late summer. Found on wasteland and in cultivated soil.

**DANDELION**—Also known as the common dandelion. Well-known plant with thick, penetrating roots long, deeply incised leaves, and stems bearing golden-yellow, daisy-like flowers through the year, especially during summer. Widely seen in most areas.

**FIREWEED**—Also known as hairy willow herb. Tall and patch-forming with upright stems that bear bright purple flowers from midsummer to early fall. Widely found on wasteland roadsides, and meadows.

**GOUTWEED**—Also known as bishopsweed. A pernicious perennial with a creeping rootstock of slender white roots. Bears small white flowers in terminal clusters from early to late summer. Common in gardens and on waste land.

**HORSETAIL**—A pernicious perennial with creeping roots that send up shoots. Widely seen in cultivated land, in fields, and on dunes.

**LESSER CELANDINE**—Also known as pilewort. Has creeping roots and stems and rather fleshy, heart-shaped leaves. Bright, golden-yellow flowers, fading to white, appear in spring. Widely seen on bare ground, in woodland, and alongside hedges.

**PLANTAIN**—Also known as the common plantain. Has a short, thick rootstock and broad, oval leaves. Spikes of insignificant flowers appear through summer into early fall. Widely seen in waste areas, lawns, and grassland.

**QUACKGRASS**—Pernicious, rampant plant with spreading, rhizomatous roots that frequently send up shoots. Found in waste places and also on cultivated soils.

**RAGWORT**—A biennial or perennial with a short, thick rootstock, upright, with much-divided stems and dense, flat-topped clusters of yellow, daisy-like flowers from early summer to fall. Widely found in wet meadows and swamps, and in moist woodlands.

**SOW THISTLE**—Also known as field sow thistle and common sow thistle. An upright, vigorous perennial with a creeping rootstock and stems bearing loose clusters of yellow, thistle-like flowers from midsummer to late fall. Found on cultivated land, on waste areas, an alongside roads.

**STINGING NETTLE**—Has creeping roots that send up vertical stems packed with nettlelike leaves and narrow, catkinlike flowers from midsummer to early fall. Widely found on wasteland and at roadsides.

**YARROW**—Also known as milfoil. Creeping roots develop erect stems with finely divided leaves and flat, umbrella-like heads of white or pink flowers through summer. Widely seen in waste areas, cultivated soil, meadows, and sometimes on lawns.

Creeping Buttercup

Dandelion

Plantain

Goutweed

Horsetail

Ragwort

Sow Thistle

Yarrow

# glossary

**Acid** refers to acid soil; a pH below 7.0 (see pH).

**Alkaline** refers to alkaline soil; a pH above 7.0 (see pH).

**Alpine** generally, a small plant suitable for a rock garden, alpine house or a stone sink, but correctly one that in its natural habitat grows on mountains, above the level at which trees thrive but below the permanent snow line.

**Annual** a plant that grows from seed, flowers, and dies within the same year. However, many plants that are not strictly annual are treated as such. For instance, *Lobelia erinus* is a half-hardy perennial usually grown as a half-hardy annual, *Mirabilis jalapa* (Marvel of Peru) is a perennial grown as a half-hardy annual, and *Impatiens walleriana* (busy Lizzie) is a greenhouse perennial invariably treated as a half-hardy annual.

**Anther** the pollen-bearing male part of a flower. A small stem called a filament supports each anther; anthers are collectively known as stamen.

**Aphid** (greenfly) a well-known and widely seen pest, which breed rapidly and sucks sap. Besides causing leaves, stems, and flowers to pale and pucker, this pest transmits viruses which cause further deterioration.

**Aquatic plant** generally, a plant that grows in garden ponds, partially or totally submerged.

**Axil** the junction between a stem and leaf, from where side-shoots or flowers may develop.

**Bedding plant** a plant raised and used as a temporary decoration in a bed or a border. Biennials, such as wallflowers, are planted in the fall to create a spring display, and half-hardy annuals that have been raised from seeds, sown in spring in gentle warmth in a greenhouse, are planted into beds as soon as all risk of frost has passed.

**Biennial** a plant that makes its initial growth one year and flowers the next, then dies. Many plants are treated as biennials. For example, *Bellis perennis* (common daisy) is a hardy perennial usually grown as a biennial. *Dianthus barbatus* (sweet William) is perennial frequently grown as a biennial, although some are now grown as annuals.

**Black spot** a fungal disease that attacks and disfigures roses.

**Blanching** the exclusion of light from the stems of some vegetables to whiten and improve their flavor. Leeks and celery are examples of vegetables that are blanched.

**Blind** a shoot with a growing point that has not developed properly.

**Bog garden plant** a plant that thrives in perpetually moist conditions. Such positions can be created around a garden pond or in a specially constructed bog garden.

**Bolting** the premature shooting up and flowering of vegetables. Lettuces, beetroot, spinach, and radishes are most susceptible.

**Bonsai** the growing of a mature plant in a miniature form in a small, shallow container. Bonsai began more than 1,000 years ago in China, and spread to Japan. Plants are kept dwarf by regular pruning of roots, leaves, and stems.

**Botrytis,** also known as gray mold, a fungal disease chiefly found in badly ventilated and damp greenhouses. Soft tissue plants such as lettuces and delicate flowering plants are particularly susceptible.

**Bract** a modified leaf, usually resembling a petal. The brightly colored flower-like heads on poinsettias, the white petal-like appendages around the flowers on *Davidia involucrata* (handkerchief tree), and the white or pink-flushed petal-like structures on *Cornus florida* (flowering dogwood) are all bracts.

**Budding** a method of increasing plants when a dormant bud of a desired variety is inserted into a T-shaped cut in the stem of a rootstock. Roses and fruit trees are often increased in this way.

**Bulb** a storage organ with a bud-like structure. It is formed of fleshy scales attached at their base to a flattened stem called a basal plate. Onions, tulips, and daffodils are examples. The term is used wrongly to include tubers, rhizomes, and corms, which have a different structure.

**Bulbil** an immature miniature bulb at the base of a mother bulb.

**Callus** corky tissue that forms over damaged or cut stems. Before rooting, the cut ends of cuttings produce a callus.

**Capillary** the passage of water upward through soil. The finer the soil, the higher the water rises. The same principle is used in self-watering systems for greenhouse plants in pots.

**Catch crop** a quick crop, usually of salad vegetables, that is sown, grown, and harvested between crops that take longer to develop.

**Chlorophyll** the green coloring materials found in all plants, except a few parasites and fungi. It absorbs energy from the sun and plays an important role in photosynthesis, the conversion of sunlight to energy.

**Chlorosis** a disorder, mainly of leaves, with parts showing as whitish areas. It can be caused by viruses, mutation, or mineral deficiencies.

**Cloche** the French word for bell-glass, meaning any tunnellike structure made of glass or plastic used to protect early crops, usually vegetables. Also used to extend the growing season of vegetables into the fall.

**Clone** a plant raised vegetatively from another and identical to its parent.

**Compost additives** materials such as vermiculite and perlite that are added to compost in hanging baskets to aid the retention of moisture.

**Container grown** a plant raised in a container for subsequent sale and transplanting to its permanent position in a garden, either in the ground or in a container. Such plants, including trees, shrubs, roses, and herbaceous perennials, can be planted at any time of the year when the soil is not too wet, dry, or frozen. Container-grown plants experience little root disturbance and soon become established.

**Cordon** a form of trained fruit tree. Cordoning is an ideal way to grow apples and pears in a small garden. Some cordons have a single stem, others two or three.

**Corm** an underground storage organ formed of a stem base greatly swollen laterally (eg a gladiolus). Young corms (cormlets) form around its base, and can be removed and grown in a nursery bed for several seasons before reaching flowering size.

**Courtyards** originally, open areas surrounded by buildings or walls, perhaps inside a castle. Nowadays, usually paved areas at the rear of a building and surrounded by a wall.

**Crocks** pieces of broken clay pots used to cover drainage holes in containers. They are placed concave side downward.

**Cultivar** a shortened term for "cultivated variety" and indicating a variety raised in cultivation. Strictly speaking, most modern varieties are cultivars, but the term variety is still widely used because it is familiar to most gardeners.

**Cutting** a vegetative method of propagation by which a severed piece of a parent plant is encouraged to develop roots.

**Deadheading** the removal of faded flowers to prevent the formation of seeds and to encourage the development of more flowers.

**Deciduous** a plant that loses its leaves at the beginning of its dormant season, which is usually in the fall or early winter. This usually applies to trees, shrubs, and some conifers, such as Ginkgo biloba (maidenhair tree).

**Disbudding** the removal of buds from around the sides of a main, central bud to encourage its development. Some chrysanthemums and roses are treated in this way.

**Division** a vegetative method of propagation or plant reproduction, by splitting a root clump. Herbaceous perennials with fibrous roots are usually propagated by division.

**Drawn** thin and spindly after being in crowded or dark conditions.

**Drill** a narrow depression made in the surface of soil, usually formed with a draw hoe or a pointed stick, in which seeds are sown. Most vegetables are sown in this way, but peas are sometimes sown in flat-bottomed trenches so that three rows can be sown close together.

**Dry-stone wall** a retaining wall of natural stone made without cement. Plants can be set between the stones so the wall becomes draped in plants.

**Earthing-up** the drawing up of soil around the base of a plant to exclude light or to give support against strong wind.

**Espalier** a method of training fruit trees in which lateral branches are trained horizontally along tensioned wires spaced 9-12in/23-30cm apart.

**Evergreen shrubs** trees and conifers that stay green through the year without shedding their leaves. In fact they drop some of their leaves all year round, while producing others.

**F1** the first filial generation, the result of a cross between two pure-bred parents. F1 hybrids are large and strong plants, but their seeds will not produce replicas of the parents.

**Fan-trained** a method of training fruit trees so their branches radiate outward like the spokes of a fan.

**Fascination** a freak condition in which stems or flowers are fused and flattened. The affected parts are best cut out.

**Fertilization** the sexual union of the male cell (pollen) and the female cell (ovule). Fertilization may be the result of pollination, when pollen falls upon the stigma. However, not all pollen germinates after falling on a stigma.

**Fertilize** to encourage the growth of plants by feeding them with manure or chemicals.

**Filament** the slender stalk that supports the anthers of a flower.

**Fillis** a type of soft string, usually green, used for tying up plants.

**Floret** a small flower that is part of an entire flower.

**Floribunda rose** a rose classification now termed cluster-flowered bush rose.

**Floriferous** flowering freely and bearing an abundance of flowers.

**Foam liner** used to help retain moisture in hanging baskets.

**Foliar feed** a fertilizer applied to foliage to encourage growth. Not all fertilizers are suitable.

**Friable** soil that is crumbly, light, and easily worked. The term applies especially to soil being prepared as a seed bed in the spring.

**Frost tender** plants that are killed or seriously damaged by frost.

**Fungicide** a chemical used to combat fungal diseases, such as black spot and mildew.

**Garden compost** vegetable waste from kitchens plus soft parts of garden plants, decomposed and subsequently dug into the soil or used to form a mulch around plants.

**Genus** a group of plants with similar botanical characteristics. Some genera contain many species, others just one.

**Germination** the process that occurs within a seed when given adequate moisture, air, and warmth. The coat of the seed ruptures and a seed leaf or leaves grow up toward the light. A root develops at the same time. However, to most gardeners germination is when seed leaves appear through the surface of the compost in pots or seed trays, or through the soil in a garden.

**Glaucous** grayish-green or bluish-green color, usually describing stems, leaves, or fruit of ornamental trees, shrubs, and herbaceous perennials.

**Graft** a method of propagation, when the tissue of a chosen variety is united with a rootstock of known vigor. It is used to increase fruit trees and, sometimes, roses.

**Green manuring** the growing of a crop such as mustard that can be subsequently dug into the soil to improve its physical structure and nutritional value.

**Groundcover** a low, ground-hugging plant that forms a mat of foliage. It is frequently used to discourage the growth of weeds.

**Growing bag** originally introduced to grow tomatoes on disease-infected soil, but now widely used to grow many flowering and food crops.

**Half-hardy** a plant that can withstand fairly low temperatures, but needs protection from frost.

**Half-hardy annual** an annual plant that is sown in gentle warmth in a greenhouse in spring. The seedlings are transferred to wider spacings in pots or seed trays and planted into the garden or a container when all risk of frost has passed.

**Half-standard** a tree with a stem (trunk) 2½-4ft/75cm-1.2m long between the ground and the lowest branches which form the head.

**Hardening off** the gradual acclimatization of protected plants to outside conditions. Garden frames are often used for this purpose.

**Hardwood cuttings** a vegetative method of reproducing woody plants, such as trees, shrubs, and soft fruits, by severing pieces of stem when ripe and inserting them in a rooting medium. The cuttings are usually inserted later into a nursery bed in a sheltered part of a garden.

**Hardy** a plant that is able to survive outdoors in winter.

**Haulm** the top growth on some vegetables, such as peas, beans, and potatoes.

**Heel** a hard, corky layer of bark and stem torn off when a side-shoot is pulled away from a main stem to form a cutting. Heel cuttings usually root more rapidly than normal cuttings. There is also less chance of the base of the cutting decaying.

**Heeling-in** the temporary planting of trees, shrubs, and conifers while awaiting transfer to their permanent

sites. It is often done because the final planting position has not been prepared, or the soil is too wet or frozen for planting to take place.

**Herbaceous** a plant that dies down to soil level in late summer or fall, after the completion of its growth. The following spring it develops fresh shoots.

**Herbicide** a chemical formulation that kills plants and is commonly known as a weed killer.

**Hermaphrodite** having male and female organs on the same flower.

**Hormone** a growth-regulating substance that occurs naturally in plants and animals. Additional and synthetic amounts are used to induce plants to root rapidly. Others are used to stimulate the growth of weeds so they burn themselves out.

**Humus** microscopic dark brown and decayed vegetable material.

**Hybrid** the progeny from parents of different species or genera.

**Hybridization** the crossing of one or more generations to improve a wide range of characteristics, such as flower size, time of flowering, sturdiness, fruit size and quality, and plant size.

**Hybrid tea rose** a rose classification now replaced by Large-flowered bush rose.

**Inflorescence** the part of a plant which bears the flowers.

**Insecticide** a chemical used to kill insects.

**Internode** the part of a stem or shoot between two leaf joints (also called nodes).

**John Innes compost** loam-based compost, formulated during the 1930s at the John Innes Horticultural Institute in the UK. Composts for sowing seeds and potting were standardized. They are made up of loam, horticultural sand, and peat, with fertilizers.

**Lateral** a side-shoot growing from a main stem of a tree or a shrub. The term is often used when discussing the fruiting and pruning of fruit trees.

**Layering** a vegetative method of propagation by lowering stems and burying a small part of them in the ground. By twisting, bending or slitting the stem at the point where it is buried, the flow of sap is restricted and roots develop. Rooting takes up to 18 months. Once rooting has taken place, the new plant can be severed from its parent.

**Leaching** the draining of nutrients from the soil. Leaching is most apparent in sandy soil since the fine particles in clay soils tend to retain nutrients.

**Leader** the terminal shoot or branch that will extend the growth of a plant.

**Leafmold** decayed leaves. Leafmold can be spread over the surface of soil as a mulch, or dug into the ground during winter.

**Lime** an alkaline substance used for countering acidity in the soil and improving clay soil.

**Loam** fertile, well-drained, good-quality top-soil.

**Loam-based compost** compost mainly formed of fertile topsoil with the addition of sand, peat, and general fertilizers.

**Maiden** the first year of a fruit tree after having been budded or grafted.

**Mangers** containers similar to wire-framed wall baskets, but with a wider metal framework.

**Marginal plants** plants that live in shallow water at the edges of ponds. Some marginals also thrive in boggy soil surrounding a pond.

**Mildew** a fungus disease that attacks soft-tissued plants. There are two main types of mildew. Downy mildew affects chiefly lettuce and onions, while powdery mildew affects mainly fruit trees, roses, and chrysanthemums.

**Mulching** the technique of covering the soil around plants with well-decayed organic material such as garden compost, peat or, in the case of rock garden plants, stone chippings or ¼in/6mm gravel.

**Mutation** A part of a plant, usually the flower, that differs from the plant's inherited characteristics.

**Neutral** soil that is neither acid nor alkaline (on the pH scale this would be 7.0). Most plants grow in a pH of about 6.5.

**Node** a leaf joint, or the point where another stem branches out from the main one.

**NPK** a formula for the percentages of nitrogen, phosphate, and potash in a compound fertilizer.

**'New English Roses'** a group of roses raised by David Austin Roses in the UK, in which modern rose varieties were hybridized with old roses. This created a new group that combines recurrent flowering with the colors and flowers characteristic of old varieties.

**Organic** the cultivation of plants without the use of chemical fertilizers or pesticides.

**Pan** a compacted and impervious layer in the soil that restricts the flow or water and air.

**Patio** originally the Spanish word for an inner court, open to the sky and surrounded by a building. The term was introduced into North America, where it came to mean any paved area around a dwelling.

**Peat** partly decayed plants. Peat is usually acid

**Peat-based compost** compost made mainly from peat, with the addition of fertilizers.

**Perennial** the popular term for a herbaceous perennial; also any long-lived plant, including trees, shrubs and, perennial climbers.

**Pesticide** a chemical compound for killing insects and other pests.

**pH** a scale used to define the acidity or alkalinity of a soil-water solution. The scale ranges from 0–14, with 7.0 as neutral. Figures above 7.0 indicate increasing alkalinity, and figures below 7.0 indicate increasing acidity. Most plants grow well in a pH of 6.5 and this is usually taken to be the neutral for plants, rather than the chemical and scientific neutral 7.0.

**Photosynthesis** the growth-building process in plants when chlorophyll in leaves and other green parts is activated by sunlight. It reacts with moisture absorbed by the roots and carbon dioxide from the atmosphere to create growth.

**Pinching out** the removal of the tip of a shoot or a terminal bud to encourage the development of side shoots.

**Pleaching** the technique of training and pruning a line of trees planted close together to form an aerial hedge. The base of each tree is free from branches, but from head height upward, their branches are interlaced. They are pruned to form a neat outline.

**Pollen** the male fertilizing agent from the anthers.

**Pollination** the transfer of pollen from the anthers onto the stigma.

**Potting compost** traditionally, a compost formed of loam, sand, peat, fertilizers, and chalk. The ratio of the ingredients is altered according to whether the compost is used for sowing seeds, potting-up or repotting plants into larger containers. However, the destruction of peat beds to acquire peat is not environmentally friendly and therefore many modern composts are formed of other materials.

**Potting-on** transferring an established plant into a larger pot.

**Potting-up** transferring young plants from a seed tray or a seed box into a pot.

**Pricking-out** removing seedlings from a seed tray or a seed box into another container with more space.

**Propagation** raising new plants.

**Pruning** the removal with a knife, shears or a pruning saw of parts of woody plants. Fruit trees are pruned to encourage better and more regular fruiting, and to ensure that they remain healthy for a long period. Shrubs are pruned mainly to encourage better flowering. Pruning some shrubs also encourages the yearly development of attractive stems.

**Reconstituted stone** a manufactured stone used to produce a wide range of plant containers and garden ornaments. Its surface mellows to a pleasing color.

**Rhizomatous** an underground or partly buried horizontal stem. Rhizomes can be slender or fleshy. Some irises have thick, fleshy rhizomes, while those of *Convallaria majalis* (lily-of-the-valley) are slender and creeping. They act as storage organs, and perpetuate plants from one season to another.

**Ridging** a method of winter digging that leaves a large surface area of soil exposed to the elements. Long ridges are left on the soil's surface.

**Ring culture** a method of growing tomatoes in bottomless pots on a gravel base.

**Rotation** the division of a vegetable plot into three, with no crop grown on the same plot in consecutive years.

**Runner** a shoot that grows along the ground, rooting into the soil at intervals (eg strawberry runners).

**Scion** a shoot or a bud that is grafted or budded onto a rootstock.

**Scree** a freely drained area of grit, gravel and small stones for growing alpine plants.

**Seed leaf** the first leaf (sometimes two) that appears after germination.

**Self-fertile** a plant with flowers that can be fertilized by its own pollen. This applies chiefly to fruit trees.

**Self-sterile** the opposite of self-fertile (see above).

**Shrub** a woody perennial with stems growing from soil level and no trunk. Some plants can be grown either as shrubs or trees.

**Sideshoot** a shoot growing out from the side of a main shoot.

**Sink garden** an old stone sink partly filled with drainage material, then with free-draining compost. Sink gardens are planted with miniature conifers, dwarf bulbs, and small rock garden plants. They are usually displayed on terraces and patios.

**Softwood cutting** a cutting of non-woody growth (ie a green shoot).

**Species** a group of plants that breed together and have the same characteristics.

**Species rose** a term popularly used to describe a wild rose or one of its near relatives.

**Sphagnum moss** a type of moss, once used widely to line wire-framed hanging baskets. It is moisture-retentive and creates an attractive feature. Now, it has been almost entirely replaced by black plastic.

**Spit** the depth of a spade's blade, usually 10–12in/25–30cm. The term is usually given to the depth at which soil is dug.

**Sport** an accidental change in shape, size or color of a flower or a plant.

**Spur** a short branch on a fruit tree, from which fruits are borne.

**Stamen** the male part of a flower, formed of the anthers and filaments.

**Standard** a tree with a stem (trunk) about 6ft/1.8m long between the ground and the lowest branch which forms the head.

**Stigma** the female part of a flower which receives pollen.

**Stock** the root part of a budded or a grafted plant.

**Stomata** a minute hole, usually on the underside of a leaf, that enables the exchange of gases to take place. During respiration plants absorb air, retaining and using oxygen, and giving off carbon dioxide. During photosynthesis plants absorb air, using the carbon dioxide and giving off oxygen.

**Stooling** the process of cutting down a tree or a shrub to or near soil level to encourage the development of young shoots. This may be done when budding or grafting fruit trees. The term is also used to describe the cutting down of some ornamental shrubs (eg dogwoods) to near ground level to produce attractively colored stems.

**Strain** seed-raised plants from a common ancestor.

**Stratify** a method of helping seeds with hard coats to germinate. The seeds are placed between layers of sand that are kept cold, usually for the duration of one winter.

**Style** part of the female reproductive organs of a flower; linked to the stigma and the ovary.

**Sub-shrub** a small, spreading shrub with a woody base. A sub-shrub differs from a normal shrub in that when grown in a temperate region its upper stems and shoots die back during winter.

**Subsoil** soil that lies below the depth at which soil is normally cultivated.

**Sucker** a basal shoot arising from the rootstock of a grafted or budded plant.

**Synonym** a previously used botanical name for a plant. It frequently happens that a plant is better known and sold under a name by which it was formerly known.

**Systemic** chemicals that enter a plant's tissue, so that when an insect sucks the plant's sap, it dies. The length of time systemic chemicals are active within a plant depend on the type of plant and the temperature.

**Tap root** a long, strong, primary root on some plants, going deep down into the soil.

**Tender** a plant that is damaged by low temperatures.

**Tendril** a thread-like growth which enables a climber to cling to a support.

**Terrace** an open, paved area lying immediately outside a house. Terraces on successive levels may be connected by flights of steps.

**Thinning** the removal of seedlings or shoots to allow others to develop more strongly.

**Tilth** friable topsoil in which seeds are sown. It also acts as a mulch on the surface of soil, helping to reduce moisture loss.

**Tine** a prong on a rake or a garden fork.

**Tip-bearing** usually a type of fruit tree which bears its flowers and fruit at the tips of shoots.

**Top-dressing** spreading and lightly forking fertilizer into the surface soil.

**Topiary** the clipping and shaping of densely leaved shrubs and hedging plants into patterns and shapes.

**Topsoil** the top layer of soil, often taken to mean the top-spit (q.v.), 10–12in/25–30cm deep. The soil at this level should not contain subsoil (q.v.), which is sticky, heavy, and often composed of clay.

**Transpiration** the loss of moisture from a plant.

**Tree** a woody plant with a single, clear stem between the roots and the lowest branches.

**Truss** a cluster of flowers or fruit. The term is usually used to describe clusters of tomatoes.

**Tuber** a swollen, thickened, fleshy stem or root. Some tubers are swollen roots (eg. dahlia), while others are swollen stems (eg. potato). Tubers are storage organs that perpetuate plants from season to season.

**Variegated** having two or more colors. The leaves of many plants are variegated.

**Variety** see Cultivar

**Veranda** a word derived from a Hindi word, meaning a gallery at ground level and on one side of a house (sometimes surrounding it). The sides of a veranda are partly or wholly open on the garden side.

**Versailles planter** a large, square-sided container originally from Versailles, France. Early Versailles planters were made of lead or slate, while modern ones are constructed from fiberglass or wood.

**Watershoot** a sappy, quick-growing shoot that arises from buds on trunks and branches, especially on old, neglected fruit trees.

**Wildlife pond** an informal pond, usually positioned toward the far end of a garden, inhabited by frogs, birds, insects, and small mammals.

**Windbreak** a shrub, tree or conifer used to create a screen to reduce the wind's speed.

# Index

# Acknowledgements

*With thanks to*

Roger Benjamin

Georgina Steeds

SMITH'S NURSERIES, NEW DENHAM, MIDDLESEX


PICTURE CREDITS

Liz Eddison/Designer: Artisan Landscape Company, Tatton Park 2000 111r/
Susanna Brown, Hampton Court 200 207b/David Brum, Hampton Court 2000 28b, 182b,
206b/Chelsea 2000 7b, 10-11, 51bl/Designer: Julian Dowle 41/Designer: Kevin Dunne,
Tatton Park 2000/Designer: Alison Evans, Tatton Park 2000 23t/Designer: Guy Farthing,
Hampton Court 2000 43, Tatton Park 2000 75br/Designer: Alan Gardner, Hampton Court
2000 27/Designer: Gavin Landscaping 101/Designer: Chris Gregory, Chelsea 1999
74b/Designer: Toby & Stephanie Hickish, Tatton Park 2000 194b/HMP Leyhill,
Chelsea 2000 120/Designer: Carol Klein 12b, 185b/Designer: Lindsay Knight, Chelsea 2000
29r, 47, 56-57/Designer: Land Art, Hampton Court 2000 20-21, 22-23b, 42b/Designer:
Karen Maskell, Hampton Court 2000/Designer: Natural & Oriental Water Garden 31b, 100b,
112-113, 114/Designer: Room in the Garden 51t/Designer: Alan Sargent, Chelsea 1999 39t,
45t Chelsea 2000 14, 26b, 115/Designer: Paul Stone 52b/Designer: Jane Sweetser,
Hampton Court 1999 39b/Designer: Michael Upward & Richard Mercer 217/Designer:
Pamela Woods, Hampton Court 1999 176-177, 183; The Garden Picture Library front cover,
170b; Neil Holmes 138, 139, 161, 164, 198b, 199t,b, 220b, 231, 235t,b, 237, 240, 241;
Peter McHoy 99tl,tr,bl,br; Harry Smith Collection 94b, 95, 97, 98, 111l, 136, 142, 143,
144, 146, 147t, 148-149, 150, 151t,b, 152, 153t,b, 162, 163; Spear & Jackson 88, 89;
David Squire 83tl,tc,tr,br, 91, 127br, 135bl,bcl,bcr,br, 154, 155, 208, 211, 225, 233.